D0548861

# THEMES

## An Introduction to Literature

Perfection Learning®

| | |
|---|---|
| EDITORIAL DIRECTOR | Julie A. Schumacher |
| WRITER | Rebecca Burke |
| DESIGNER | Tobi S. Cunningham |
| IMAGE RESEARCH | Anjanette Miner |
| | Lisa Leatherman |
| PERMISSIONS | Meghan Schumacher |
| | |
| COVER ART | *River Gathering* by Miles G. Batt |

Printed in the United States of America

3 4 5 6 7 8 RRD 15 14 13 12 11 10

RRD/Crawfordsville, Indiana, USA
09/10

Hardbound ISBN-13: 978-0-7569-7105-2
Hardbound ISBN-10: 0-7569-7105-5

# THEMES
## An Introduction to Literature

**Perfection Learning**®

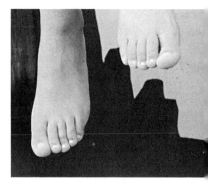

# Unit Three   Best of Friends?

# Unit Four   Decisions, Decisions

# Unit Five   To Be a Hero

# Unit Six   On the Edge

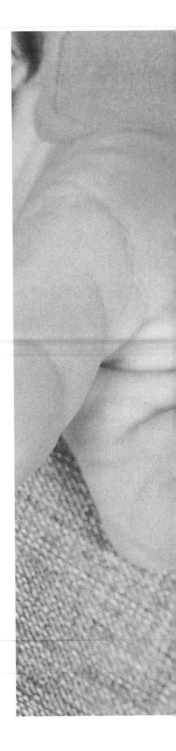

Unit One

# WHO AM I?

*Which can say more than this rich praise—*
*that you alone are you?*

William Shakespeare

The theme of the selections in Unit One is self-discovery, the search for answers to the question "Who am I?" So how do you go about examining your life? One sure source of self-knowledge lies in stories and poetry. The writings in Unit One share the idea that each of us is formed by relationships—with friends and family, acquaintances, places we live in, and nature itself. We are also shaped by what happens to us and how we react to it.

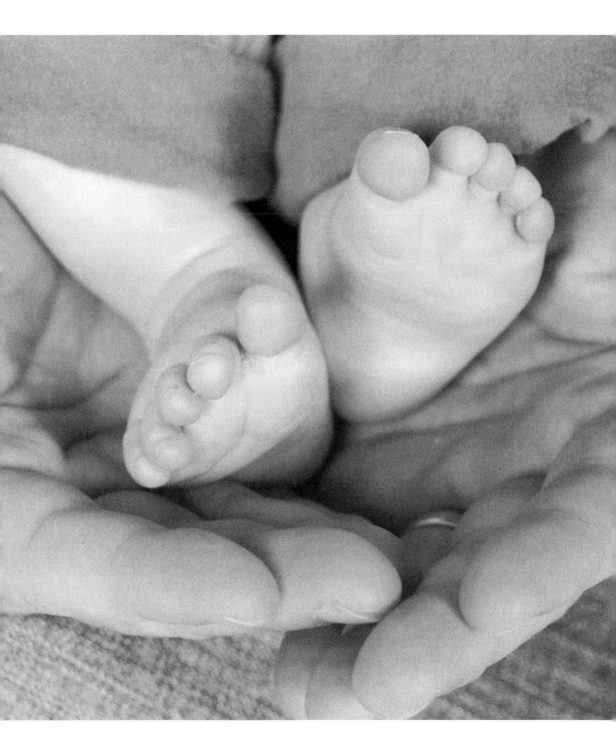

# Building Vocabulary

## Base Words and Roots

A word may have only one part, such as *help*, or it may have several parts, such as *unhelpfulness*. Every word, no matter how long, has a main part. This main part may be a "base word," or it may be a "root."

## Base Words

A **base word** is a complete word that can be used to build other words. The base word in *friendship*, *friendless*, *befriend*, and *unfriendly* is *friend*. Even though *end* can also be found in these words, it isn't the base word. That's because the words are not built from *end* and have nothing to do with *end*.

When a word part is added at the end of the base word, the spelling at the end may change a little. For example, *nap* is the base word in *napping*, *pollute* is the base word in *pollution*, and *mercy* is the base word in *merciful*.

The following words can be found in Unit One selections. Notice the slight changes in spellings to some base words.

| BASE WORDS | UNIT ONE WORDS |
|---|---|
| 1. stagger | staggered |
| 2. humiliate | humiliating |
| 3. imagine | imagination |
| 4. legend | legendary |
| 5. mystery | mysteriously |
| 6. prayer | prayerfully |
| 7. rehearse | rehearsals |
| 8. fortune | unfortunately |
| 9. institute | institution |
| 10. form | reformation |

The words on the next page also contain base words. Notice the many different word parts that can be added to both the beginnings and the ends of base words.

| BASE WORDS | ADDITIONAL WORDS |
|------------|------------------|
| 1. free | freedom |
| 2. know | knowledge |
| 3. worth | worthless |
| 4. explore | exploration |
| 5. glory | glorious |
| 6. stop | unstoppable |
| 7. fool | foolishness |
| 8. strength | strengthen |
| 9. courage | courageous |
| 10. happy | unhappiness |

## Root Words

A word **root** is the main part of some words. It has a special meaning, but it is not a complete word. For example, the root of *science* is *sci*, which means "to know." Roots are trickier than base words because they aren't whole words and they come from other languages. Many of the roots of English words come from Greek and Latin.

This table shows five common roots and their meanings.

| ROOT | MEANING | EXAMPLES |
|------|---------|----------|
| cycl | circle | bicycle, cycling |
| ject | throw | inject, reject |
| ped | foot | pedal, pedestrian |
| port | carry | portable, transport |
| vac | empty | vacant, vacuum |

If you learn the meaning of root words, you can figure out many English words without having to consult a dictionary. Your vocabulary will grow by leaps and bounds.

For example, if you know that *ped* means "foot," you can guess that a "*ped*ometer" measures steps, or footfalls. And knowing that *cycl* means "circle" leads you to believe that the winds in a *cycl*one go around and around.

Latin and Greek are not usually studied in schools these days. If you want a commanding vocabulary, you should master as many of these root words as possible on your own.

# Understanding Fiction

## Short Stories

The two main types of fiction are short stories and novels. How do they differ? Short stories can usually be read in one sitting, have fewer characters, and take place in a limited setting. They generally have just one theme, unlike a novel, which is multi-themed. Both types of fiction contain the following basic elements.

**Plot**  The plot is the action of a story—what happens in it. As one old saying has it, the writer gets the hero up a tree and then gets him back down again. A good plot shows how one event leads to another, which causes another, and so on until the story ends. A problem or **conflict** is needed to move the story forward. No "trouble" equals "no story"!

But fictional conflict doesn't necessarily mean things blowing up. In fiction, a conflict means that the main character wants something, and someone or something is in the way of getting it. The "opponent" can be anything from a raging hurricane to a picky math teacher. And some conflicts occur from within. Perhaps the main character wants to be popular, but his or her basic nature—shy and awkward—makes that goal difficult. Inner conflicts can be the worst kind.

In a well-made story, the conflict builds until there is a **climax**, or high point of the action. Here the bully is confronted, or the inner demon is conquered. In the story's **resolution**, the conflict sorts itself out.

**Character**  As a reader, you keep turning the pages of stories mainly because you are interested in what happens to the characters. Writers create believable characters by describing their actions, speech, thoughts, feelings, and interactions with others. There are **round characters**—characters who are drawn realistically and seem capable of change— and **flat characters**, who are undeveloped.

**Setting**  A story's setting includes the time period and location in which the events of the plot occur. A setting can actually influence the plot and characters, sometimes even becoming a character itself. When nature is given human characteristics—an angry sea, a forbidding forest—setting is being used as a character.

**Theme**  The theme is the underlying meaning or message of a story. A *story* is about a particular character and what happens to him or her. The *theme* of the story is how the reader interprets what the author is saying about the story. Usually, the theme is not directly stated. The reader must discover it through careful reading and analysis.

# Previewing

## What's the Worst That Could Happen?
by Bruce Coville

### Reading Connection
Bruce Coville's story was inspired by a real-life crush that he had on a girl in his junior high social studies class. As in the story, this girl invited him to be in a skit with her. And he was terrified. And a Hostess cupcake was involved. But what happens in the climax of the story didn't take place in actual fact until many years later. Coville cites it as proof that you never really outgrow being thirteen.

### Skill Focus: Humor
By reading this story's title alone, you can predict that it will be funny. True, humor is a matter of taste. What some people find funny, others will not find funny at all. But it's hard to resist this story about a thirteen-year-old boy who is so love struck that he agrees to do what he fears most. As you read, look for things that contribute to the story's humor. Focus on funny speech, witty or exaggerated language, and absurd images.

### Vocabulary Builder
You'll find these words and their definitions on the pages of this story.

| | | | |
|---|---|---|---|
| theory | eloquent | clenches | fiasco |
| bogus | barbarian | repulsed | delusion |
| baffled | staggers | improvisation | |

The Gifted Boy, Paul Klee

# What's the Worst That Could Happen?

Bruce Coville

If thirteen is supposed to be an unlucky number, what does it mean that we are forced to go through an entire year with that as our age? I mean, you would think a civilized society could just come up with a way for us to skip it.

Of course, good luck and I have rarely shared the same park bench. Sometimes I think Murphy's Law—you know, "If something can go wrong, it will"—was invented just for me. I suppose the fact that my name is Murphy Murphy might have something to do with that feeling.

Yeah, you read it right: Murphy Murphy. It's like a family curse. The last name I got from my father, of course. The first name came down from my mother's side, where it is a tradition for the firstborn son. You would think my mother might have considered that before she married Dad, but love makes fools of us all, I guess. Anyway, the fact that I got stuck with the same name coming and going, so to speak, shows that my parents are either spineless (my **theory**) or have no common sense (my sister's theory).

**theory**
idea; belief

I would like to note that no one has ever apologized to me for this name. "I think it's lovely," says my mother—which, when you consider it, would seem to support my sister's theory. Anyway, you can see that right from the beginning of my life, if something could go wrong, it did.

To begin with, I want to say here and now that Mikey Farnsworth should take at least part of the blame for this situation. This, by the way, is true for many of the bad things that have happened in my life, from the paste-eating incident in first grade through the **bogus** fire-drill situation last year, right up to yesterday afternoon, which was sort of the Olympics of Bad Luck as far as I'm concerned. What's amazing is that somehow Mikey ends up coming out of these things looking perfectly fine. He is, as my grandfather likes to say, the kind of guy who can fall in a manure pile and come out smelling like a rose.

**bogus**
false; not genuine

The one I am not going to blame is Tiffany Grimsley, though if I hadn't had this stupid crush on her, it never would have happened.

Okay, I want to stop and talk about this whole thing of having a crush. Let me say right up front that it is very confusing and not something I am used to. When it started, I was totally **baffled**. I mean, I don't even like girls, and all of a sudden I keep thinking about one of them? Give me a break!

**baffled**
puzzled; confused

In case it hasn't happened to you yet, let me warn you. Based on personal experience, I can say that while there are many bad things about having a crush, just about the worst of them is the stupid things you will do because of it.

Okay, let's back up here.

I probably wouldn't even have known I had a crush to begin with if Mikey hadn't informed me of this fact. "Man, you've got it bad for Tiffany," he says one day when we are poking around in the swamp behind his house.

"What are you talking about?" I ask. At the same time, my cheeks begin to burn as if they are on fire. Startled, I lift my foot to tie my shoe, which is a trick

I learned in an exercise magazine and that has become sort of a habit. At the moment, it is mostly an excuse to look down.

What the heck is going on here? I think.

Mikey laughs. "Look at you blush, Murphy! There's no point in trying to hide it. I watched you drooling over her in social studies class today. And you've only mentioned her, like, sixteen times since we got home this afternoon."

"Well, sure, but that's because she's a friend," I say, desperately trying to avoid the horrible truth. "We've known each other since kindergarten, for Pete's sake."

Mikey laughs again, and I can tell I'm not fooling him. "What am I going to do?" I groan.

He shrugs. "Either you suffer in silence, or you tell her you like her."

Is he nuts? If you tell a girl you like her, it puts you totally out in the open. I mean, you've got no place to hide. And there are really only two possible responses you're going to get from her: (a) She likes you, too, which the more you think about it, the more unlikely it seems; or (b) anything else, which is like, totally, utterly humiliating. I'm sure girls have problems of their own. But I don't think they have any idea of the sheer terror a guy has to go through before any boy-girl stuff can get started.

I sure hope this gets easier with time, because I personally really don't understand how the human race has managed to survive this long, given how horrifying it is to think about telling a girl you like her.

Despite Mikey's accusation, I do not think I have actually drooled over Tiffany during social studies class. But it is hard not to think about her then, because she sits right in front of me. It's the last class of the day, and the October sunlight comes in slantwise and catches in her golden hair in a way that makes it hard to breathe.

It does not help that eighth-grade social studies is taught by Herman Fessenden, who you will probably see on the front of the *National Enquirer* someday as a mass murderer for boring twenty-six kids to death in a single afternoon. It hasn't happened yet, but I'm sure it's just a matter of time.

> Mikey laughs again, and I can tell I'm not fooling him. "What am I going to do?" I groan.

I spend the entire weekend thinking about what Mikey has said, and I come up with a  bold plan, which is to pass Tiffany a note asking if she wants to grab a slice of pizza at Angelo's after school. I am just getting up my nerve to do it—there are only five minutes of class left—when Mr. F. says, "So, what do you think the queen should have done then, Murphy?"

How am I supposed to know? But I blush and don't hand the note to Tiffany after all, which wouldn't have been so bad, except that Butch Coulter saw I had it and grabs it on the way out of class, and I have to give him the rest of my week's lunch money to get it back.

Tuesday I try a new tactic. There's a little store on the way to school where you can pick up candy and gum and stuff, and I get some on the way to school and then kind of poke Tiff in the back during social studies class, which is about the only time I see her, to ask if she wants a piece of gum. Only before she can answer, Mr. Fessenden comes up from behind and snatches the whole pack out of my hand. So that was that.

Then on Wednesday, it's as if the gods are smiling on me, which is not something I am used to. Tiffany grabs my arm on the way out of social studies and says, "Can I talk to you for a second, Murphy?"

**eloquent**
expressive

"Sure," I say. This is not very **eloquent**, but it is better than the first thought that crosses my mind, which is, "Anytime, anywhere, any moment of the day." It is also better than, "Your words would be like nectar flowing into the hungry mouths of my ears," which was a line I had come up with for a poem I was writing about her.

She actually looks a little shy, though what this goddess-on-Earth has to be shy about is more than I can imagine.

She hands me a folded-over set of papers, and my heart skips a beat. Can this be a love letter? If so, it's a really long one.

"I wrote this skit for drama club, and I thought maybe you would do it with me next Friday. I think you'd be just right for the part."

**barbarian**
uncivilized

My heart starts pounding. While it seems unlikely that the part is that of a **barbarian** warrior prince, just doing it means I will have an excuse to spend time with Tiffany. I mean, we'll have to rehearse and. . . well, the imagination

**staggers**
moves
unsteadily

**staggers**.

"Yes!" I say, ignoring the facts that (a) I have not yet read the script and (b)

I have paralyzing stage fright.

She gives me one of those sunrise smiles of hers, grabs my arm and gives it a squeeze, and says, "Thanks. This is going to be fun." Then she's gone, leaving me with a memory of her fingers on my arm and a wish that I had started pumping iron when I was in first grade, so my biceps would have been ready for this moment.

Mikey moves in a second later. "Whoa," he says, nudging me with his elbow. "Progress! What did she say?"

"She wants me to do a skit with her."

He shakes his head. "Too bad. I thought maybe you had a chance. How'd she take it when you told her no?"

I look at him in surprise. "I didn't. I said I would do it."

Mikey looks even more surprised. "Murphy, you can't go onstage with her. You can't even move when you get onstage. Don't you remember what happened in fifth grade?"

As if I could forget. Not only was it one of the three most humiliating moments of my life, but according to my little brother, it has become legendary at Westcott Elementary. Here's the short version: Mrs. Carmichael had cast me as George Washington in our class play, and I was, I want to tell you, pretty good during rehearsals. But when they opened the curtain and I saw the audience. . . well, let's just say that when my mother saw the look on my face, she actually let out a scream. She told me later she thought I was having a heart attack. As for me, my mouth went drier than day-old toast, some mysterious object wedged itself in my throat, and the only reason I didn't bolt from the stage was that I couldn't move my arms or legs. Heck, I couldn't even move my fingers.

I couldn't even squeak!

Finally, they had to cancel the performance. Even after the curtains were closed, it took two teachers and a janitor to carry me back to the classroom.

"This time will be different," I say.

Mikey snorts.

> "Murphy, you can't go on stage with her . . . Don't you remember what happened in fifth grade?"

I know he is right. "Oh, man, what am I gonna do?" I wail.

"Come on, let's look at the script. Maybe all you have to do is sit there and she'll do all the acting."

No such luck. The script, which is called "Debbie and the Doofus," is very funny.

It also calls for me to say a lot of lines.

It also calls for me to act like a complete dork.

Immediately, I begin to wonder why Tiffany thinks I would be just right for this role.

"Maybe she imagines you're a brilliant actor," says Mikey.

He is trying to be helpful, but to tell the truth, I am not sure which idea is worse: that Tiffany thinks I am a dork or that she thinks I am a brilliant actor.

"What am I gonna do?" I wail again.

"Maybe your parents will move before next week," says Mikey, shaking his head. "Otherwise, you're a dead man walking."

I ask, but my parents are not planning on moving.

I study the script as if it is the final exam for life, which as far as I am concerned, it is. After two days I know not only my lines, but all of Tiffany's lines, too, as well as the lines for Laurel Gibbon, who is going to be playing the waitress at the little restaurant where we go for our bad date.

My new theory is that I will enjoy rehearsals and the excuse they give me to be with Tiffany, and then pray for a meteor to strike me before the day of the performance.

The first half of the theory actually seems to work. We have two rehearsals—one at school and one in Tiffany's rec room. At the first one she is very impressed by the fact that I know my lines already. "This is great, Murphy!" she says, which makes me feel as if I have won the lottery.

At the second rehearsal I actually make Laurel, who is perhaps the most solemn girl in the school, laugh. This is an amazing sound to me, and I find that I really enjoy it. Like Tiffany, Laurel has been in our class since kindergarten. Only I never noticed her much because, well, no one ever notices Laurel much, on account of she basically doesn't talk. I wondered at first why

Tiffany had cast her, but it turns out they are in the same church group and have been good friends for a long time.

Sometimes I think the girls in our class have a whole secret life I don't know about.

Time becomes very weird. Sometimes it seems as if the hours are rushing by in a blur, the moment of performance hurtling toward me. Other times the clock seems to poke along like a sloth with chronic fatigue syndrome.[1] Social studies class consists of almost nothing but staring at the sunshine in Tiffany's hair and flubbing the occasional question that Mr. Fessenden lobs at me. Some days I think he asks me questions out of pure meanness. Other days he leaves me alone, and I almost get the impression he feels sorry for me.

Mikey and I talk about the situation every night. "No meteor yet," he'll say, shaking his head.

"What am I gonna do?" I reply, repeating the question that haunts my days. I can't possibly tell Tiffany I can't do this.

"Maybe you could be sick that day?" says Mikey.

I shake my head. "If I let her down, I will hate myself forever."

Mikey rolls his eyes. "Maybe you should run away from home," he suggests, not very helpfully.

Finally, we do come up with a plan, which is that Mikey will stay in the wings[2] to prompt me in case the entire script falls out of my head. I don't know if this will really do much good, since if I freeze with terror, mere prompting will not be of any use. On the other hand, knowing Mikey will be there calms me down a little. It's like having a life jacket.

Ha! Little do I know what kind of life jacket he will turn out to be.

To my dismay, I have not been able to parlay[3] my time working on the

> Sometimes I think the girls in our class have a whole secret life I don't know about.

---

1 **chronic fatigue syndrome**: an illness of unknown origin that causes tiredness

2 **wings**: the areas on either side of the stage that are out of sight

3 **parlay**: to add value to

skit with Tiffany into anything bigger. This is partly because she is the busiest person in the eighth grade, with more clubs and committees and activities than any normal person could ever be involved with. It is also because I am stupid about this kind of thing and don't have the slightest clue how to do it. So I treasure my memory of the two rehearsals and, more than anything else, the sound of her laughing at some of what I have done.

I go through the day in a state of cold terror.

Despite my prayers, Friday arrives. I don't suppose I really expected God to cancel it, though I would have been deeply appreciative if He had. I go through the day in a state of cold terror. The drama club meeting is after school. Members of the club have invited their friends, their families, and some teachers to come see the skits. There are going to be four skits in all. Tiffany, Laurel, and I are scheduled to go last, which gives me more time to sweat and worry.

Mikey is backstage with us, but Tiffany does not know why. I tell her he came because he is my pal. Getting him aside, I check to make sure he has the script.

At 2:45 Mrs. Whitcomb, the drama club coach, comes back to wish us luck. She makes a little speech, which she ends with, "Okay kids—break a leg!"

This, of course is how people wish each other luck in the theater. According to my mother, the idea is that you're not going to get your wish anyway, so you wish for the thing you don't want and you may get the thing you do want instead.

I suddenly wonder if this is what I have been doing wrong all my life.

On the other hand, Tiffany is standing next to me, so that is one wish that is continuing to come true.

"Are you excited?" she asks.

"You have no idea," I answer, with complete honesty.

Laurel, who is standing on the other side of me, whispers, "I'm scared."

"Don't worry, you'll be fine," I reply.

I am fairly confident this is true, since I expect to make such an ass of myself that no one will notice anything else anyway. Inside me, a small voice is screaming, "What were you thinking of, you moron? You are going to humiliate yourself in front of all these people, including the girl you would cut out your heart for, who will be even more humiliated than you are because it's her skit that you are messing up! Run away! Run away!"

If I could get my hands on this small voice, I would gladly beat it to a bloody pulp. Instead, I keep taking deep breaths and reminding myself of how funny I was during the rehearsals.

> "**W**hat were you thinking of, you moron?"

The first skit goes up. I think it's funny, but at first no one laughs. This terrifies me all over again. Then someone snickers. A moment later someone else lets out a snort. Pretty soon everyone is laughing. Clearly it takes people a while to get warmed up when they are trying to have fun.

At first the sound of that laughter is soothing. But it takes only a few minutes for me to get terrified by it. What if they don't laugh at *our* skit? Even worse, what if they laugh for the wrong reasons? What if Tiffany is totally humiliated and it's all my fault?

I go back to wanting to die.

The second skit goes up and dies in my place. It just lies onstage, stinking the place up like a week-old fish. It's as boring as last month's newspaper. In fact, it's almost as boring as Mr. Fessenden, which I would not have thought possible. I feel a surge of hope. We can't look worse than this. In fact, next to it we'll seem like geniuses. Too bad we can't go on right away!

Unfortunately, we have to wait for the third skit, which turns out to be brilliant, which makes me want to kill the people who are in it. Now we'll be compared to them instead of the dead fish of that second skit.

The curtain closes.

"Our turn," whispers Tiffany. "Break a leg, Murphy."

"Break a leg," I murmur back. Then, so Laurel won't feel left out, I say the same thing to her as we pick up the table that is our main prop and move it onto the stage. Tiffany is right behind us with a pair of chairs. Once they're in place, we scurry to our positions, Tiffany and me stage right, Laurel stage left.

My stomach **clenches**. Cold sweat starts out on my brow.

"Murphy!" hisses Tiffany. "Your shoelace!"

I glance down. I have forgotten to untie it, which is the key to one of my first funny bits. Out of habit I lift my foot to take care of the lace. At that instant the curtain opens, which startles me so much that I lose my balance and fall over, landing onstage in full view of the audience.

There they are. The enemy. The people who are going to stare at me, judge me, whisper about me tomorrow. I am so frozen with terror I cannot move. I just lie there looking at them

And then the laugh begins. My temperature goes in two directions, my blood turning to ice at the same time that the heat rises in my face. I have a long moment of terror—well, it feels like a long moment; according to Mikey, it was less than two seconds—while I think that this is it, I will never stand up again, never come to school again, never leave my house again. I will ask whoever finally picks me up to carry me home and put me in the attic. My parents will have to shove my meals through a slot in the door because I will never be able to face another living human being.

Love saves the day. "Murphy, are you all right?" hisses Tiffany.

For the sound of that voice, I would do anything—even get back on my feet.

And then, the second miracle. Some brilliant portion of my brain realizes that this is a comedy and I have just started us off with a big laugh. I stand at the edge of the stage to do a fake knock. In rehearsal, I only mimed[4] it. Now, for some reason, I say loudly, "Knock-knock. Knockity-knock-knock."

To my surprise, the audience finds this funny. Another laugh.

Tiffany comes to the door, and we go through our opening business,[5] which establishes that she is prim and proper and I am a total idiot, which doesn't take much acting because it is pretty much real life anyway. But something is happening. I'm not making up lines, but I am making bigger gestures, broader moves, weirder voices than I did in rehearsal. People are howling. Tiffany's eyes are dancing, and

---

4 **mimed**: acted without using words

5 **business**: bits of onstage action

I can see that she is trying not to laugh. I am feeling like a genius.

We get to the imaginary restaurant. Laurel comes out to take our order, and I have the same effect on her.

I am starting to feel as if I'm having an out-of-body experience. Who is this funny person, making everyone laugh? How long can it go on? Can I keep it going, keep cranking up the jokes, hold on to this glorious lightning bolt I'm riding?

Laurel disappears to get our order. I fake blowing my nose on the cloth napkin, then inspecting it to see the results. I act as if I am fascinated by my imaginary boogers. Tiffany acts as if she is **repulsed**, but I can see she is hardly able to keep from bursting into laughter—especially when I hand the napkin across the table so she can examine it, too.

**repulsed**
disgusted

The audience is just about screaming. I am beginning to think that this kind of laughter is even better than the sound of Tiffany's voice.

Laurel comes back with our "order," which, because this is a skit and we are on a low budget, is a plate of Hostess cupcakes. Chocolate.

I am supposed to eat in a disgusting way. The script does not specify how. Still riding my wave of **improvisation** inspiration, I pick up a cupcake and stuff the entire thing into my mouth. Tiffany's eyes widen, and she turns her head to hide the laugh she can't hold in. Her shoulders are shaking. This is too good to be true.

**improvisation**
acting without a script or rehearsals

I deliver my next line—which is about how beautiful she is—with bits of chocolate spewing out. It's disgusting but hilarious. Tiffany has tears streaming down her cheeks from trying to hold in her laughter.

Desperate to keep the riff[6] going, I cram another entire cupcake into my mouth.

This is when disaster strikes. Suddenly, I discover that I can't breathe because there is a chocolate logjam in my throat. I only need a minute, I think, and I'll get this. I try to give my next line, but nothing comes out. Tiffany looks alarmed. The audience is still laughing, but the laughter is starting to die down, as if some of them realize I am in trouble.

Which is when Mikey comes barreling on stage from behind me, screaming, "He's choking! He's choking!" Then he grabs me around the waist and jabs his fists into my belly.

I've been Heimliched!

Those of you who know about the Heimlich maneuver will remember that basically it forces the air out of your lungs, blowing whatever is blocking your breathing out of your mouth.

Those of you who have been staging this in your mind as you read will remember who is directly across from me.

Those of you with even minimal powers of prediction will know what happens next. An unholy mix of partially chewed Hostess chocolate cupcakes spews out of my mouth and spatters all over Tiffany.

I am filled with deeper horror than any I have ever known. Wrenching my way out of Mikey's grasp, I bolt around the table to clean her off.

Unfortunately, the table is close to the edge of the stage. Too close. Tripping over my untied shoelace, I hurtle headfirst into the darkness.

My body makes some very unpleasant sounds as it lands.

Okay, I probably could have accepted the broken leg.

I might even have been able to live with the memory of the look on Tiffany's face.

But when the ambulance guys came and put me on a stretcher and everyone stood there watching as they rolled me out of the school, and Mikey followed after them to tell me that my fly had been open during the entire **fiasco**, I really thought that was too much.

**fiasco**
disaster

---

6 **riff**: a theatrical routine

Anyway, that's how I ended up in this hospital bed, staring at my right leg, which is up in traction.

Tiffany came to visit a while ago. That would have been wonderful, except she brought along her boyfriend, Chuck. He goes to another school and is old enough to drive.

Something inside me died when she introduced him.

To make things worse (and what doesn't?), it turns out that Chuck was in the audience yesterday.

"You were brilliant, man," he says. "At least, until the part where it all fell to pieces."

I want to shove a Hostess cupcake down his throat.

After they are gone, Mikey shows up.

"Tough luck, Murphy," he says, looking at my cast.

I try to remember that he is my best friend and really thought he was saving my life when he Heimliched me.

It is not easy.

"Cheer up," he says. "It couldn't get worse than this."

He's lucky my leg is in traction and I can't get out of bed. He is also lucky I don't have a cupcake on me.

After Mikey leaves, I make two decisions: (a) I am going to change my name and (b) I never want to be thirteen again as long as I live.

There is another knock on my door.

"Hello, Murphy," says a soft voice.

It's Laurel.

She smiles shyly. "Can I come in?"

I've never noticed how pretty she is when she smiles. For a brief moment I think life may not be so bad after all.

I am fairly certain, however, that this is a **delusion**.

After all, my name is still Murphy Murphy.

And I'm still thirteen years old.

I don't even want to think about what might happen next.

**delusion**
fantasy; illusion

# Reviewing

## What's the Worst That Could Happen?

### Discussing the Selection

1. What do you find funny in this story? List all the things that tickled you, such as fresh and funny language, character details, and dialogue. Be specific.

2. Explain why Murphy agrees to act in the play. Does the play unfold as you expected?

3. In the very last line, Murphy says, "I don't even want to think about what might happen next." Predict what might happen.

4. Why do you think people always remember their most embarrassing moments?

### Writing an Anecdote

An anecdote is a brief, often comical story describing a memorable incident. Write an anecdote on the theme of embarrassing moments. Feel free to give it a twist. For example: "The Most Embarrassing Moment I Can Imagine," or "My (Pet/School Bus Driver/Ancestor)'s Most Embarrassing Moment.'"

### About Bruce Coville (1950–)

New York writer Bruce Coville grew up in the fifties and early sixties, a self-described "bookaholic" who also enjoyed reading "zillions of comic books." In sixth grade, he found that he enjoyed writing fiction as much as reading it. Before he could support himself as a writer, however, he worked as a gravedigger, toymaker, and elementary school teacher. Now he's the best-selling author of over eighty books, including *My Teacher Is an Alien*. A lot of his books are science fiction and fantasy titles that display his unstoppable sense of humor. "I try . . . to make my stories the kinds of things that I would have enjoyed myself when I was young; to write the books I wanted to read, but never found."

# Previewing

## Eleven
by Sandra Cisneros

### Reading Connection
Sandra Cisneros says that she still feels like she's eleven years old inside. "When I was eleven years old in Chicago, teachers thought if you were poor and Mexican you didn't have anything to say. Now I think that what I was put on the planet for was to tell these stories. Because if I don't write them, they're not going to get the stories right." Cisneros was often the "new kid" at school because her struggling family moved so often. Her background and constant transfers made fitting in difficult. "I didn't like school because all they saw was the outside me."

### Skill Focus: Simile
A simile is a comparison between two things that are not alike. The comparison includes the word *like* or *as*. For example, "The kitten looked *like* a soft puddle of gold." Often writers use similes to draw images, or word-pictures, which give a fresh feel to familiar ideas, feelings, or things. As you read this story, note any similes that you find.

# Eleven

Sandra Cisneros

Russian Nesting Dolls

What they don't understand about birthdays and what they never tell you is that when you're eleven, you're also ten, and nine, and eight, and seven, and six, and five, and four, and three, and two, and one. And when you wake up on your eleventh birthday you expect to feel eleven, but you don't. You open your eyes and everything's just like yesterday, only it's today. And you don't feel eleven at all. You feel like you're still ten. And you are—underneath the year that makes you eleven.

Like some days you might say something stupid, and that's the part of you that's still ten. Or maybe some days you might need to sit on your mama's lap because you're scared, and that's the part of you that's five. And maybe one day when you're all grown up maybe you will need to cry like if you're three, and that's okay. That's what I tell Mama when she's sad and needs to cry. Maybe she's feeling three.

Because the way you grow old is kind of like an onion or like the rings inside a tree trunk or like my little wooden dolls that fit one inside the other, each year inside the next one. That's how being eleven years old is.

You don't feel eleven. Not right away. It takes a few days, weeks even, sometimes even months before you say Eleven when they ask you. And you don't feel smart eleven, not until you're almost twelve. That's the way it is.

Only today I wish I didn't have only eleven years rattling inside me like pennies in a tin Band-Aid box. Today I wish I was one hundred and two instead of eleven because if I was one hundred and two I'd have known what to say when Mrs. Price put the red sweater on my desk. I would've known how to tell her it wasn't mine instead of just sitting there with that look on my face and nothing coming out of my mouth.

"Whose is this?" Mrs. Price says, and she holds the red sweater up in the air for all the class to see. "Whose? It's been sitting in the coatroom for a month."

"Not mine," says everybody. "Not me."

"It has to belong to somebody," Mrs. Price keeps saying, but nobody can remember. It's an ugly sweater with red plastic buttons and a collar and sleeves all stretched out like you could use it for a jump rope. It's maybe a thousand years old, and even if it belonged to me, I wouldn't say so.

Maybe because I'm skinny, maybe because she doesn't like me, that stupid Sylvia Saldívar says, "I think it belongs to Rachel." An ugly sweater like that, all raggedy and old, but Mrs. Price believes her. Mrs. Price takes the sweater and puts it right on my desk, but when I open my mouth nothing comes out.

"That's not, I don't, you're not . . . Not mine," I finally say in a little voice that was maybe me when I was four.

"Of course it's yours," Mrs. Price says. "I remember you wearing it once." Because she's older and the teacher, she's right and I'm not.

Not mine, not mine, not mine, but Mrs. Price is already turning to page thirty-two, and math problem number four. I don't know why but all of a sudden I'm feeling sick inside, like the part of me that's three wants to come out of my eyes, only I squeeze them shut tight and bite down on my teeth real hard and try to remember today I am eleven, eleven. Mama is making a cake for me tonight, and when Papa comes home everybody will sing Happy birthday, happy birthday to you.

But when the sick feeling goes away and I open my eyes, the red sweater's still sitting there like a big red mountain. I move the red sweater to the corner of my desk with my ruler. I move my pencil and books and eraser as far from it as possible. I even move my chair a little to the right. Not mine, not mine, not mine.

In my head I'm thinking how long till lunchtime, how long till I can take the red sweater and throw it over the schoolyard fence, or leave it hanging on a parking meter, or bunch it up into a little ball and toss it in the alley. Except when math period ends, Mrs. Price says loud and in front of everybody, "Now Rachel, that's enough," because she sees I've shoved the red sweater to the tippy-tip corner of my desk and it's hanging all over the edge like a waterfall, but I don't care.

"Rachel," Mrs. Price says. She says it like she's getting mad. "You put that sweater on right now and no more nonsense."

"But it's not—"

"Now!" Mrs. Price says.

This is when I wish I wasn't eleven, because all the years inside of me—ten, nine, eight, seven, six, five, four, three, two, and one—are pushing at the back of my eyes when I put one arm through one sleeve of the sweater that smells like cottage cheese, and then the other arm through the other and stand there with my arms apart like if the sweater hurts me and it does, all itchy and full of germs that aren't even mine.

That's when everything I've been holding in since this morning, since when Mrs. Price put the sweater on my desk, finally lets go, and all of a sudden I'm crying in front of everybody. I wish I was invisible but I'm not. I'm eleven and it's my birthday today and I'm crying like I'm three in front of everybody. I put my head down on the desk and bury my face in my stupid clown-sweater arms. My face all hot and spit coming out of my mouth because I can't stop the little animal noises from coming out of me, until there aren't any more tears left in my eyes, and it's just my body shaking like when you have the hiccups, and my whole head hurts like when you drink milk too fast.

But the worst part is right before the bell rings for lunch. That stupid Phyllis Lopez, who is even dumber than Sylvia Saldívar, says she remembers the red sweater is hers! I take it off right away and give it to her, only Mrs. Price pretends like everything's okay.

Today I'm eleven. There's a cake Mama's making for tonight, and when Papa comes home from work we'll eat it. There'll be candles and presents, and everybody will sing Happy birthday, happy birthday to you, Rachel, only it's too late.

I'm eleven today. I'm eleven, ten, nine, eight, seven, six, five, four, three, two, and one, but I wish I was one hundred and two. I wish I was anything but eleven, because I want today to be far away already, far away like a runaway balloon, like a tiny *o* in the sky, so tiny-tiny you have to close your eyes to see it.

# Reviewing

## Eleven

### Discussing the Selection

1. According to Rachel, the narrator of this story, why is being eleven so hard?

2. Describe Rachel and Mrs. Price, her teacher. Use specific details that show what each character is like.

3. Why doesn't Rachel stand up for herself? Explain what you would do in her situation.

4. What similes are used to describe growing old? Do they sound like comparisons an eleven-year-old girl might make? Decide whether you think they are effective.

### Writing a Description

What do you remember about being eleven? Write a paragraph describing the "one person in the world who is you." What did you look like? What were some of your favorite things? What people, situations, or events from this year will stick in your mind for a long time?

### About Sandra Cisneros (1954–)

When Sandra Cisneros was growing up, her large Mexican-American family moved from one rundown Chicago neighborhood to another. They also went back and forth to Mexico to visit relatives. She coped with these painful moves by retreating inside herself and writing poetry, eventually editing the literary magazine for her high school. Cisneros's novel *The House on Mango Street* (1984) is a classic of American literature and a favorite on teachers' reading lists. In 1995, the author won the MacArthur Foundation Fellowship, one of the most prestigious and high-paying awards in the arts world. By writing honestly and poetically about growing up poor and Latina, Cisneros creates stories that appeal to readers everywhere.

# Previewing

## Charles
by Shirley Jackson

### Reading Connection

In the 1950s, the job of most American women was to create the "perfect" home for their families. Not Shirley Jackson, who didn't mind chaos if it meant her children were happy, and she could continue to read and write books. In an interview she once said, "Our house is old, noisy and full. When we moved into it we had two children and about five thousand books; when we finally overflow and move out again we will have perhaps twenty children and easily half a million books . . ." The story "Charles" was inspired by her oldest child's bumpy transition into kindergarten.

### Skill Focus: Inference

An inference is a reasonable judgment you can make based on what a writer presents in a story and what you already know. Using inferences, or educated guesses, you can fill in details about what you are reading. For example, if characters speak in stilted, formal language, you might infer that they come from a different social class or culture. Look for details in the story "Charles" that help you make inferences. Think about how the use of inference, in this story especially, adds to your enjoyment.

### Vocabulary Builder

This story contains many challenging vocabulary words, but don't let a word you don't know keep you from enjoying the story. If you come to an unfamiliar word, make a guess at the meaning and *keep on reading!* Be on the lookout for the words below. They are defined on the page where they occur.

| | | | |
|---|---|---|---|
| renounced | elaborately | simultaneously | maneuvered |
| raucous | deprived | scornfully | |
| insolently | unsettling | cynically | |

MY MOM'S HOUSE IS RIGHT AROUND THE CORNER, Maura Vazakas

# Charles

Shirley Jackson

The day my son Laurie started kindergarten he **renounced** corduroy overalls with bibs and began wearing blue jeans with a belt; I watched him go off the first morning with the older girl next door, seeing clearly that an era of my life was ended, my sweet-voiced nursery-school tot replaced by a long-trousered, swaggering character who forgot to stop at the corner and wave goodbye to me.

He came home the same way, the front door slamming open, his cap on the floor, and the voice suddenly become **raucous** shouting, "Isn't anybody *here*?"

At lunch he spoke **insolently** to his father, spilled his baby sister's milk, and remarked that his teacher said we were not to take the name of the Lord in vain.

"How *was* school today?" I asked, **elaborately** casual.

"All right," he said.

"Did you learn anything?" his father asked.

**renounced**
gave up; rejected

**raucous**
noisy

**insolently**
rudely; without respect

**elaborately**
taking pains to do something perfectly

Laurie regarded his father coldly. "I didn't learn nothing," he said.

"Anything," I said. "Didn't learn anything."

"The teacher spanked a boy, though," Laurie said, addressing[1] his bread and butter. "For being fresh,"[2] he added with his mouth full.

"What did he do?" I asked. "Who was it?"

Laurie thought. "It was Charles," he said. "He was fresh. The teacher spanked him and made him stand in a corner. He was awfully fresh."

"What did he do?" I asked again, but Laurie slid off his chair, took a cookie, and left, while his father was still saying, "See here young man."

The next day Laurie remarked at lunch, as soon as he sat down, "Well, Charles was bad again today." He grinned enormously and said, "Today Charles hit the teacher."

"Good heavens," I said, mindful of the Lord's name. "I suppose he got spanked again?"

"He sure did," Laurie said. "Look up," he said to his father.

"What?" his father said, looking up.

"Look down," Laurie said. "Look at my thumb. Gee, you're dumb." He began to laugh insanely.

"Why did Charles hit the teacher?" I asked quickly.

"Because she tried to make him color with red crayons," Laurie said. "Charles wanted to color with green crayons so he hit the teacher and she spanked him and said nobody play with Charles but everybody did."

The third day—it was Wednesday of the first week— Charles bounced a seesaw on the head of a little girl and made her bleed, and the teacher made him stay inside all during recess. Thursday Charles had to stand in a corner during story-time because he kept pounding his feet on the floor. Friday Charles was **deprived** of blackboard privileges because he threw chalk.

On Saturday I remarked to my husband, "Do you think kindergarten is too **unsettling** for Laurie? All this toughness and bad grammar, and this Charles boy sounds like such a bad influence."

"It'll be all right," my husband said reassuringly. "Bound to be people like

**deprived**
had things
taken away

**unsettling**
upsetting;
disturbing

---

1 **addressing**: speaking to

2 **fresh**: impudent; disrespectful

Charles in the world. Might as well meet them now as later."

On Monday Laurie came home late, full of news. "Charles," he shouted as he came up the hill; I was waiting anxiously on the front steps. "Charles," Laurie yelled all the way up the hill. "Charles was bad again."

"Come right in," I said, as soon as he came close enough. "Lunch is waiting."

"You know what Charles did?" he demanded, following me through the door. "Charles yelled so in school they sent a boy in from first grade to tell the teacher she had to make Charles keep quiet, and so Charles had to stay after school. And so all the children stayed to watch him."

"What did he do?" I asked.

"He just sat there," Laurie said, climbing into his chair at the table. "Hi, Pop, y'old dust mop."

"Charles had to stay after school today," I told my husband. "Everyone stayed with him."

"What does Charles look like?" my husband asked Laurie. "What's his other name?"

"He's bigger than me," Laurie said. "And he doesn't have any rubbers and he doesn't even wear a jacket."

Monday night was the first Parent-Teachers meeting, and only the fact that the baby had a cold kept me from going; I wanted passionately to meet Charles's mother. On Tuesday Laurie remarked suddenly, "Our teacher had a friend come to see her in school today."

"Charles's mother?" my husband and I asked **simultaneously**.

"Naaah," Laurie said **scornfully**. "It was a man who came and made us do exercises, we had to touch our toes. Look." He climbed down from his chair and squatted down and touched his toes. "Like this," he said. He got solemnly back into his chair and said, picking up his fork, "Charles didn't even *do* exercises."

"That's fine," I said heartily. "Didn't Charles want to do exercises?"

"Naaah," Laurie said. "Charles was so fresh to the teacher's friend he wasn't *let* do exercises."

"Fresh again?" I said.

"He kicked the teacher's friend," Laurie said. "The teacher's friend told Charles to touch his toes like I just did and Charles kicked him."

**simultaneously**
together

**scornfully**
with disrespect

"What are they going to do about Charles, do you suppose?" Laurie's father asked him.

Laurie shrugged elaborately. "Throw him out of school, I guess," he said.

Wednesday and Thursday were routine; Charles yelled during story hour and hit a boy in the stomach and made him cry. On Friday Charles stayed after school again and so did all the other children.

With the third week of kindergarten Charles was an institution[3] in our family; the baby was being a Charles when she cried all afternoon; Laurie did a Charles when he filled his wagon full of mud and pulled it through the kitchen; even my husband, when he caught his elbow on the telephone cord and pulled telephone, ashtray, and a bowl of flowers off the table, said, after the first minute, "Looks like Charles."

During the third and fourth weeks it looked like a reformation[4] in Charles; Laurie reported grimly[5] at lunch on Thursday of the third week, "Charles was so good today the teacher gave him an apple."

"What?" I said, and my husband added warily,[6] "You mean Charles?"

"Charles," Laurie said. "He gave the crayons around and he picked up the books afterward and the teacher said he was her helper."

"What happened?" I asked incredulously.[7]

"He was her helper, that's all," Laurie said, and shrugged.

"Can this be true, about Charles?" I asked my husband that night. "Can something like this happen?"

**cynically**
doubting the motives of others

"Wait and see," my husband said **cynically**. "When you've got a Charles to deal with, this may mean he's only plotting,"

He seemed to be wrong. For over a week Charles was the teacher's helper; each day he handed things out and he picked things up; no one had to stay after school.

---

3 **institution**: a well-known idea

4 **reformation**: a change

5 **grimly**: sadly

6 **warily**: cautiously

7 **incredulously**: in disbelief or amazement

"The PTA meeting's next week again," I told my husband one evening. "I'm going to find Charles's mother there."

"Ask her what happened to Charles," my husband said. "I'd like to know."

"I'd like to know myself," I said.

On Friday of that week things were back to normal. "You know what Charles did today?" Laurie demanded at the lunch table, in a voice slightly awed.[8] "He told a little girl to say a word and she said it and the teacher washed her mouth out with soap and Charles laughed."

"What word?" his father asked unwisely, and Laurie said, "I'll have to whisper it to you, it's so bad." He got down off his chair and went around to his father. His father bent his head down and Laurie whispered joyfully. His father's eyes widened.

"Did Charles tell the little girl to say *that?*" he asked respectfully.

"She said it *twice,*" Laurie said. "Charles told her to say it *twice.*"

"What happened to Charles?" my husband asked.

"Nothing," Laurie said. "He was passing out the crayons."

Monday morning Charles abandoned the little girl and said the evil word himself three or four times, getting his mouth washed out with soap each time. He also threw chalk.

My husband came to the door with me that evening as I set out for the PTA meeting. "Invite her over for a cup of tea after the meeting," he said. "I want to get a look at her."

"If only she's there," I said prayerfully.

"She'll be there," my husband said. "I don't see how they could hold a PTA meeting without Charles's mother."

At the meeting I sat restlessly, scanning each comfortable matronly[9] face,

> "I don't see how they could hold a PTA meeting without Charles's mother."

---

8 **awed**: amazed

9 **matronly**: wifely; womanly

trying to determine which one hid the secret of Charles. None of them looked to me haggard[10] enough. No one stood up in the meeting and apologized for the way her son had been acting. No one mentioned Charles.

After the meeting I identified and sought out Laurie's kindergarten teacher. She had a plate with a cup of tea and a piece of chocolate cake; I had a plate with a cup of tea and a piece of marshmallow cake. We **maneuvered** up to one another cautiously and smiled.

**maneuvered**
moved carefully

"I've been so anxious to meet you," I said. "I'm Laurie's mother."

"We're all so interested in Laurie," she said."

"Well, he certainly likes kindergarten," I said. "He talks about it all the time."

"We had a little trouble adjusting, the first week or so," she said primly,[11] "but now he's a fine little helper. With occasional lapses, of course."

"Laurie usually adjusts very quickly," I said. "I suppose this time it's Charles's influence."

"Charles?"

"Yes," I said, laughing, "you must have your hands full in that kindergarten, with Charles."

"Charles?" she said. "We don't have any Charles in the kindergarten."

---

10 **haggard**: worn out

11 **primly**: properly

# Reviewing

## Charles

### Discussing the Selection

1. Compare your own kindergarten experience with Laurie's. Does he remind you of anyone else you knew as a five-year-old? If so, describe that child.

2. When did you begin to infer that Laurie and Charles were probably the same little boy? List any clues from the story that hint at Charles's identity.

3. Laurie's teacher says to his mother, "We are all so interested in Laurie." What inference do you draw from this statement?

4. Do you think that this story was written recently? Why or why not?

### Writing with Adverbs

In her writing, Shirley Jackson uses adverbs to describe how someone acts or speaks. For example, find the following words in the first few paragraphs of "Charles": *clearly, suddenly, insolently, elaborately, coldly, enormously*. Find other examples of adverbs in the story. What does the use of such words add? Now, write a paper about your experiences in kindergarten. Use interesting adverbs to make your writing colorful.

### About Shirley Jackson (1916–1965)

Shirley Jackson started writing verse almost as soon as she could form letters. Jackson is admired for her horror stories as well as for her witty fiction. Both of these talents came together in her hilarious family memoirs, *Life Among the Savages* and *Raising Demons*. Her most famous short story, "The Lottery," provoked as much outrage as praise. A chilling, unforgettable tale of human cruelty, the story was adapted both for the stage and television. For years it was one of the most frequently performed plays in the country, particularly in high schools. Besides the memoirs, Jackson wrote six novels, plays, and countless short stories. She died in her sleep in 1965 when she was only forty-eight years old.

# Understanding Poetry

Most poets would agree that poetry is a rhythmic and condensed form of writing. It's a way to express thoughts and emotions as well as create word-pictures.

There are two basic poetry forms—rhymed verse and unrhymed, or free, verse.

**Rhymed verse** requires strict attention to set patterns of **rhythm** and **rhyme**. This kind of verse will always be popular. Young children love nursery rhymes, the first poetry that they hear. Older children enjoy jump rope rhymes, and all sorts of people enjoy raps. The energy of the rhythm and the pleasure of rhyme make traditional poetry a close cousin of music itself.

Poetry that doesn't rhyme or have a set rhythm is called **free verse**. Free verse sounds closer to the way we really speak. Unlike conversation, however, the words are carefully chosen.

What we remember most about a favorite poem are new images that tickle our senses and speak straight to our hearts. For example, the poet William Carlos Williams wrote a celebrated poem about eating some plums. Not just any plums, but some very "cold . . . sweet . . . and delicious" plums that he stole from the refrigerator and gobbled up. When you read this poem, the plums seem to burst in your own mouth.

If you ask a hundred poets what makes a good poem, you may get a hundred different answers. Generally, they will agree that a good poem:

- uses words in a fresh, vivid, and economical way.
- contains images or word-pictures that "show" readers something by making comparisons and appealing to our senses.
- may contain rhymes and rhythm like music, or, if it's free verse, sound closer to the rhythm of human conversation.
- may bring up feelings or questions that are not always traceable to logic and reason. In other words, a good poem is mysterious. Someone once said that a poem's words are "like a map to buried treasure."

No one can prove that a certain poem is good, of course. It's not the kind of thing that can be proven in a courtroom or tested in a lab experiment. A poem is what you make of it. If it makes you think about things in a new way, it succeeds.

# Previewing

## I'm Nobody! Who Are You?
by Emily Dickinson

## Primer Lesson
by Carl Sandburg

### Reading Connection

At first glance, 19th-century poet Emily Dickinson and 20th-century poet Carl Sandburg don't seem to have much in common. She was a celebrated loner; he was a poet of the people, sociable and outgoing to the end of his life. But both poets are identified with free verse—poetry that doesn't require regular patterns of rhythm, rhyme, or line length. Though she also wrote traditional poetry, Dickinson was a pioneer of less-structured forms, often experimenting with punctuation and phrasing. For Sandburg, the conversational rhythms of free verse were a natural way of showing his kinship with common Americans.

### Skill Focus: Personification

Both the Dickinson and Sandburg poems employ personification. This literary technique involves giving human characteristics or traits to nonhuman things. As you read each poem, notice what traits are assigned to things that aren't human. Think about how personification contributes to meaning.

# I'm Nobody!
## Who Are You?

Emily Dickinson

I'm Nobody! Who are you?
Are you—Nobody—Too?
Then there's a pair of us!
Don't tell! they'd advertise—you know—!

How dreary—to be—Somebody!                    5
How public—like a Frog—
To tell one's name—the livelong June—
To an admiring Bog!¹

---

1 **bog**: a stretch of wet, soggy ground

# Primer[1]
## Lesson

Carl Sandburg

Look out how you use proud words.
When you let proud words go, it is
    not easy to call them back.
They wear long boots, hard boots; they
    walk off proud; they can't hear you       5
    calling—
Look out how you use proud words.

TEEN PERSONAS, Diana Ong, 2002

---

1 **primer**: an elementary schoolbook for teaching children important lessons

# Reviewing

## I'm Nobody! Who Are You? / Primer Lesson

### Discussing the Selections

1. Why is it "dreary" to be "Somebody," according to the speaker of the Dickinson poem?

2. What is the "primer lesson" given by the speaker of the Sandburg poem?

3. How is personification used in both poems? Identify all of the words in each poem that give human characteristics to something nonhuman.

4. Reread the information about free verse on page 44. How is each poem typical of this form of poetry?

### Writing a Poem

Both of the poems you have just read use direct address. In other words, the speaker addresses the audience as "you," as if the reader were in the same room. Instead of focusing on something or somebody else, or telling a story, the speaker pretends to be familiar with the reader. Using these poems as models, try writing your own short poem of direct address. Remember the main theme of this unit, "Who Am I?" when choosing a subject.

### About Emily Dickinson (1830–1886)

Born in 1830 in Amherst, Massachusetts, Dickinson was a bright and outgoing child. However, after the age of twenty-three, she seldom ventured out from her family home. Dickinson composed more than eighteen hundred poems, though only a handful were published during her lifetime. Many of her poems were experimental in form and daring in their treatment of such universal themes as love, death, and social relationships.

### About Carl Sandburg (1878–1967)

Carl Sandburg is often called the poet of the American people. He was an old-fashioned man who believed in the American ideals of hard work and equality. Born in Illinois in 1878 to poor Swedish immigrants, he left school early to help support his family. At seventeen he began to hitch rides on freight trains, roaming the country and meeting the ordinary folks who would later inspire his writing. Well into his old age, Sandburg entertained crowds with the stories and songs he'd learned on the hobo circuit of his youth.

# Previewing

## Change
by Charlotte Zolotow

### Reading Connection

Many of Charlotte Zolotow's stories and poems call attention to her love of nature. As a child, she fell in love with the children's classic *The Secret Garden*, a story that illustrates how the natural world can nurture children's spirits. Zolotow took special pleasure in being outdoors as it was the one thing she could always rely on for comfort and inspiration. She never lost this passion and in later years became an avid gardener. To call attention to her love of nature, she always autographed her books for fans in green ink.

### Skill Focus: Repetition

Repetition is the practice of repeating elements throughout a poem. The repeated elements can be words and phrases, rhymes, and even pauses. By repeating things, poets can draw attention to something they find important. Sometimes the repetition is a clue to the poem's theme, or underlying meaning. As you read the poem "Change," notice what is repeated in each stanza. Then decide how that repetition may relate to the theme.

CELADINE, 16th Century

# Change

Charlotte Zolotow

The summer
still hangs
heavy and sweet
with sunlight
as it did last year.          5

The autumn
still comes
showering gold and crimson
as it did last year.

The winter                    10
still stings
clean and cold and white
as it did last year.

The spring
still comes                   15
like a whisper in the dark night.

It is only I
who have changed.

# Reviewing

## Change

### Discussing the Selection

1. What is the theme, or underlying meaning, of this poem?

2. How do you think the speaker feels about the changing of the seasons? Explain your answer.

3. Which description of a season do you like best?

4. Consider how repetition contributes to the theme of this poem. Would it be as effective if the poet did not repeat things? Explain.

### Writing a Poem

Write your own variation of "Change." Use the repeated elements and the basic structure to create your own version.

> The summer
> still _____
> The autumn
> still _____
> The winter
> still _____
> The spring
> still _____
> like a _____
> It is only I
> who have changed.

### About Charlotte Zolotow (1915–)

Charlotte Zolotow believes that when writing for young people, life should be from their point of view. Her understanding of this perspective comes from her own experiences as a troubled child. Her family moved often, and she was plagued by physical problems, making it difficult for her to make new friends. She said, "I loved the idea of not only expressing myself in words but, because I was very shy in conversation, reaching other people through my writing."

# Previewing

## Tuesday of the Other June

by Norma Fox Mazer

### Reading Connection

A national study says that three out of ten children in the United States are either bullies, victims of bullies, or both. Bullies operate by intimidating those whom they sense are weak. How can they tell? Bullies seem to have a sixth sense about this. Typical targets include those who are perceived as different, those without friends, and those who attract envy because of their superior looks, things, or accomplishments. Most schools work hard to discourage bullying. Still, far too many young people are exposed to the name-calling, aggressive teasing, and/or physical assault that are typical bullying tactics.

### Skill Focus: Climax

This story highlights a turning point, or climax, in the story of a young girl tormented by a bully. As you read, think about why the narrator, June, might be singled out for bullying by the other girl named June. Consider the narrator's home life, especially her relationship with her mother. Then look for the climax in the two girls' relationship. Consider what makes the narrator decide she won't put up with the bullying any longer.

### Vocabulary Words

Add these interesting words to your everyday vocabulary. They are defined on the pages of the story where they appear.

| | | | |
|---|---|---|---|
| slink | frisky | wheezed | droning |
| bureau | trouble-shooters | crest | |
| torment | tenant | mocked | |

Fifteen Girls With The Same Face In The Same Place, Ellen Harvey

Unit One   Who Am I?

# Tuesday of the Other June

Norma Fox Mazer

"Be good, be good, be good, be good, my Junie," my mother sang as she combed my hair; a song, a story, a croon, a plea. "It's just you and me, two women alone in the world, June darling of my heart; we have enough troubles getting by, we surely don't need a single one more, so you keep your sweet self out of fighting and all that bad stuff. People can be little-hearted, but turn the other cheek, smile at the world, and the world'll surely smile back."

We stood in front of the mirror as she combed my hair, combed and brushed and smoothed. Her head came just above mine; she said when I grew another inch, she'd stand on a stool to brush my hair. "I'm not giving up this pleasure!" And she laughed her long honey laugh.

My mother was April, my grandmother had been May, and I was June. "And someday," said my mother, "you'll have a daughter of your own. What will you name her?"

"January!" I'd yell when I was little. "February! No, November!" My mother laughed her honey laugh. She had little emerald eyes that warmed me like the sun.

Every day when I went to school, she went to work. "Sometimes I stop what I'm doing," she said, "lay down my tools, and stop everything, because all I can think about is you. Wondering what you're doing and if you need me. Now, Junie, if anyone ever bothers you—"

"—I walk away, run away, come on home as fast as my feet will take me," I recited.

"Yes. You come to me. You just bring me your trouble, because I'm here on this earth to love you and take care of you."

I was safe with her. Still, sometimes I woke up at night and heard footsteps slowly creeping up the stairs. It wasn't my mother, she was asleep in the bed across the room, so it was robbers, thieves, and murderers, creeping slowly . . . slowly . . . slowly toward my bed.

I stuffed my hand into my mouth. If I screamed and woke her, she'd be tired at work tomorrow. The robbers and thieves filled the warm darkness and slipped across the floor more quietly than cats. Rigid under the covers, I stared at the shifting dark and bit my knuckles and never knew when I fell asleep again.

In the morning we sang in the kitchen. "Bill Grogan's GOAT! Was feelin' FINE! Ate three red shirts, right off the LINE!" I made sandwiches for our lunches, she made pancakes for breakfast, but all she ate was one pancake and a cup of coffee. "Gotta fly, can't be late."

I wanted to be rich and take care of her. She worked too hard; her pretty hair had gray in it that she joked about. "Someday," I said, "I'll buy you a real house, and you'll never work in a pot factory again."

"Such delicious plans," she said. She checked the windows to see if they were locked. "Do you have your key?"

I lifted it from the chain around my neck.

"And you'll come right home from school and—"

"—I won't light fires or let strangers into the house, and I won't tell anyone on the phone that I'm here alone," I finished for her.

"I know, I'm just your old worrywart mother." She kissed me twice, once on each cheek. "But you are my June, my only June, the only June."

She was wrong; there was another June. I met her when we stood next to each other at the edge of the pool the first day of swimming class in the Community Center.

"What's your name?" She had a deep growly voice.

"June. What's yours?"

She stared at me. "June."

"We have the same name."

"No we don't. June is *my* name, and I don't give you permission to use it. Your name is Fish Eyes." She pinched me hard. "Got it, Fish Eyes?"

The next Tuesday, the Other June again stood next to me at the edge of the pool. "What's your name?"

"June."

"Wrong. Your—name—is—Fish—Eyes."

"June."

"Fish Eyes, you are really stupid." She shoved me into the pool.

The swimming teacher looked up, frowning, from her chart. "No one in the water yet."

Later, in the locker room, I dressed quickly and wrapped my wet suit in the towel. The Other June pulled on her jeans. "You guys see that bathing suit Fish Eyes was wearing? Her mother found it in a trash can."

"She did not!"

The Other June grabbed my fingers and twisted. "Where'd she find your bathing suit?"

"She bought it, let me go."

"Poor little stupid Fish Eyes is crying. Oh, boo hoo hoo, poor little Fish Eyes."

After that, everyone called me Fish Eyes. And every Tuesday, wherever I was, there was also the Other June—at the edge of the pool, in the pool, in the locker room. In the water, she swam alongside me, blowing and huffing, knocking into me. In the locker room, she stepped on my feet, pinched my arms, hid my blouse, and knotted my braids together. She had large square teeth; she was shorter than I was, but heavier, with bigger bones and square hands. If I met her outside on the street, carrying her bathing suit and towel, she'd walk toward me smiling a square, friendly smile. "Oh well, if it isn't Fish Eyes." Then she'd punch me, *blam!* her whole solid weight hitting me.

I didn't know what to do about her. She was training me like a dog. After a few weeks of this, she only had to look at me, only to growl, "I'm going to get you, Fish Eyes," for my heart to **slink** like a whipped dog down into my stomach. My arms were covered with bruises. When my mother noticed, I made up a story about tripping on the sidewalk.

**slink**
creep; sneak

My weeks were no longer Tuesday, Wednesday, Thursday, and so on. Tuesday was Awfulday. Wednesday was Badday. (The Tuesday bad feelings were still there.) Thursday was Betterday, and Friday was Safeday. Saturday was Goodday, but Sunday was Toosoonday, and Monday—Monday was nothing but the day before Awfulday.

I tried to slow down time. Especially on the weekends, I stayed close by my mother, doing everything with her, shopping, cooking, cleaning, going to the laundromat. "Aw, sweetie, go play with your friends."

"No, I'd rather be with you." I wouldn't look at the clock or listen to the radio (they were always telling you the date and the time). I did special magic things to keep the day from going away, rapping my knuckles six times on the bathroom door six times a day and never, ever touching the chipped place on my **bureau**. But always I woke up to the day before Tuesday, and always, no matter how many times I circled the worn spot in the living-room rug or counted twenty-five cracks in the ceiling, Monday disappeared and once again it was Tuesday.

**bureau**
a piece of bedroom furniture with drawers

The Other June got bored with calling me Fish Eyes. Buffalo Brain came next, but as soon as everyone knew that, she renamed me Turkey Nose.

Now at night it wasn't robbers creeping up the stairs, but the Other June, coming to **torment** me. When I finally fell asleep, I dreamed of kicking her, punching, biting, pinching. In the morning I remembered my dreams and felt brave and strong. And then I remembered all the things my mother had taught me and told me.

**torment**
torture

*Be good, be good, be good; it's just us two women alone in the world . . .* Oh, but if it weren't, if my father wasn't long gone, if we'd had someone else to fall back on, if my mother's mother and daddy weren't dead all these years, if my father's daddy wanted to know us instead of being glad to forget us—oh, then I would have punched the Other June with a **frisky** heart, I would have grabbed her arm at poolside and bitten her like the dog she had made me.

**frisky**
lively; playful

One night, when my mother came home from work, she said, "Junie, listen to this. We're moving!"

Alaska, I thought. Florida. Arizona. Someplace far away and wonderful, someplace without the Other June.

"Wait till you hear this deal. We are going to be caretakers, **trouble-shooters** for an eight-family apartment building. Fifty-six Blue Hill Street. Not janitors; we don't do any of the heavy work. April and June, Trouble-shooters, Incorporated. If a **tenant** has a complaint or a problem, she comes to us and we either take care of it or call the janitor for service. And for that little bit of work, we get to live rent free!" She swept me around in a dance. "Okay? You like it? I do!"

**trouble-shooter**
someone who solves problems

**tenant**
someone who rents a place to live

So. Not anywhere else, really. All the same, maybe too far to go to swimming class? "Can we move right away? Today?"

"Gimme a break, sweetie. We've got to pack, do a thousand things. I've got to line up someone with a truck to help us. Six weeks, Saturday the fifteenth." She circled it on the calendar. It was the Saturday after the last day of swimming class.

Soon, we had boxes lying everywhere, filled with clothes and towels and glasses wrapped in newspaper. Bit by bit, we cleared the rooms, leaving only what we needed right now. The dining-room table staggered on a bunched-up rug, our bureaus inched toward the front door like patient cows. On the calendar in the kitchen, my mother marked off the days until we moved, but the only days I thought about were Tuesdays—Awfuldays. Nothing else was real except the too fast passing of time, moving toward each Tuesday . . . away from Tuesday . . . toward Tuesday . . . .

And it seemed to me that this would go on forever, that Tuesdays would come forever and I would be forever trapped by the side of the pool, the Other June whispering *Buffalo Brain Fish Eyes Turkey Nose* into my ear, while she ground her elbow into my side and smiled her square smile at the swimming teacher.

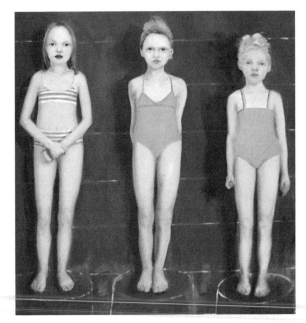

LINE-UP, Melora Kuhn, 2001

And then it ended. It was the last day of swimming class. The last Tuesday. We had all passed our tests, and, as if in celebration, the Other June only pinched me twice. "And now," our swimming teacher said, "all of you are ready for the Advanced Class which starts in just one month. I have a sign-up slip here. Please put your name down before you leave." Everyone but me crowded around. I went to the locker room and pulled on my clothes as fast as possible. The Other June burst through the door just as I was leaving. "Goodbye," I yelled, "good riddance to bad trash!" Before she could pinch me again, I ran past her and then ran all the way home, singing, "Goodbye . . . goodbye . . . good riddance to bad trash!"

Later, my mother carefully untied the blue ribbon around my swimming class diploma. "Look at this! Well, isn't this wonderful! You are on your way, you might turn into an Olympic swimmer, you never know what life will bring."

"I don't want to take more lessons."

"Oh, sweetie, it's great to be a good swimmer." But then, looking into my face, she said, "No, no, no, don't worry, you don't have to."

The next morning, I woke up hungry for the first time in weeks. No more swimming class. No more Baddays and Awfuldays. No more Tuesdays of the Other June. In the kitchen, I made hot cocoa to go with my mother's corn muffins. "It's Wednesday, Mom," I said, stirring the cocoa. "My favorite day."

"Since when?"

"Since this morning." I turned on the radio so I could hear the announcer tell the time, the temperature, and the day.

Thursday for breakfast I made cinnamon toast, Friday my mother made pancakes, and on Saturday, before we moved, we ate the last slices of bread and cleaned out the peanut butter jar.

"Some breakfast," Tilly said. "Hello, you must be June." She shook my hand. She was a friend of my mother's from work; she wore big hoop earrings, sandals, and a skirt as dazzling as a rainbow. She came in a truck with John to help us move our things.

John shouted cheerfully at me, "So you're moving." An enormous man with a face covered with little brown bumps. Was he afraid his voice wouldn't travel the distance from his mouth to my ear? "You looking at my moles?" he shouted, and he heaved our big green flowered chair down the stairs. "Don't worry, they don't bite. Ha, ha, ha!" Behind him came my mother and Tilly balancing a bureau between them, and behind them I carried a lamp and the round, flowered Mexican tray that was my mother's favorite. She had found it at a garage sale and said it was as close to foreign travel as we would ever get.

The night before, we had loaded our car, stuffing in bags and boxes until there was barely room for the two of us. But it was only when we were in the car, when we drove past Abdo's Grocery, where they always gave us credit, when I turned for a last look at our street—it was only then that I understood we were truly going to live somewhere else, in another apartment, in another place mysteriously called Blue Hill Street.

Tilly's truck followed our car.

"Oh, I'm so excited," my mother said. She laughed. "You'd think we were going across the country."

Our old car **wheezed** up a long, steep hill. Blue Hill Street. I looked from one side to the other, trying to see everything.

My mother drove over the **crest** of the hill. "And now—ta da!—our new home."

"Which house? Which one?" I looked out the window and what I saw was the Other June. She was sprawled on the stoop of a pink house, lounging back on her elbows, legs outspread, her jaws working on a wad of gum. I slid down into the seat, but it was too late. I was sure she had seen me.

**wheezed**
made a gasping sound as if struggling for breath

**crest**
the top or peak

My mother turned into a driveway next to a big white building with a tiny porch. She leaned on the steering wheel. "See that window there, that's our living-room window . . . and that one over there, that's your bedroom . . ."

We went into the house, down a dim, cool hall. In our new apartment, the wooden floors clicked under our shoes, and my mother showed me everything. Her voice echoed in the empty rooms. I followed her around in a daze. Had I imagined seeing the Other June? Maybe I'd seen another girl who looked like her. A double. That could happen.

"Ho yo, where do you want this chair?" John appeared in the doorway. We brought in boxes and bags and beds and stopped only to eat pizza and drink orange juice from the carton.

"June's so quiet, do you think she'll adjust all right?" I heard Tilly say to my mother.

"Oh, definitely. She'll make a wonderful adjustment. She's just getting used to things."

But I thought that if the Other June lived on the same street as I did, I would never get used to things.

That night I slept in my own bed, with my own pillow and blanket, but with floors that creaked in strange voices and walls with cracks I didn't recognize. I didn't feel either happy or unhappy. It was as if I were waiting for something.

Monday, when the principal of Blue Hill Street School left me in Mr. Morrisey's classroom, I knew what I'd been waiting for. In that room full of strange kids, there was one person I knew. She smiled her square smile, raised her hand, and said, "She can sit next to me, Mr. Morrisey."

"Very nice of you, June M. OK, June T., take your seat. I'll try not to get you two Junes mixed up."

I sat down next to her. She pinched my arm. "Good riddance to bad trash," she **mocked**.

**mocked**
made fun of

I was back in the Tuesday swimming class, only now it was worse, because every day would be Awfulday. The pinching had already started. Soon, I knew, on the playground and in the halls, kids would pass me, grinning. "Hiya, Fish Eyes."

**droning**
speaking in a boring or dull manner

The Other June followed me around during recess that day, **droning** in my ear, "You are my slave, you must do everything I say, I am your master, say it, say, 'Yes, master, you are my master.'"

I pressed my lips together, clapped my hands over my ears, but without hope. Wasn't it only a matter of time before I said the hateful words?

"How was school?" my mother said that night.

"OK."

She put a pile of towels in a bureau drawer. "Try not to be sad about missing your old friends, sweetie; there'll be new ones."

The next morning, the Other June was waiting for me when I left the house. "Did your mother get you that blouse in the garbage dump?" She butted me, shoving me against a tree. "Don't you speak anymore, Fish Eyes?" Grabbing my chin in her hands, she pried open my mouth. "Oh, ha ha, I thought you lost your tongue."

We went on to school. I sank down into my seat, my head on my arms. "June T., are you all right?" Mr. Morrisey asked. I nodded. My head was almost too heavy to lift.

The Other June went to the pencil sharpener. Round and round she whirled the handle. Walking back, looking at me, she held the three sharp pencils like three little knives.

Someone knocked on the door. Mr. Morrisey went out into the hall. Paper planes burst into the air, flying from desk to desk. Someone turned on a transistor radio.[1] And the Other June, coming closer, smiled and licked her lips like a cat sleepily preparing to gulp down a mouse.

I remembered my dream of kicking her, punching, biting her like a dog.

Then my mother spoke quickly in my ear: *Turn the other cheek, my Junie; smile at the world, and the world'll surely smile back.*

But I had turned the other cheek and it was slapped. I had smiled and the world hadn't smiled back. I couldn't run home as fast as my feet would take me. I had to stay in school—and in school there was the Other June. Every morning, there would be the Other June, and every afternoon, and every day, all day, there would be the Other June.

She frisked down the aisle, stabbing the pencils in the air toward me. A boy stood up on his desk and bowed. "My fans," he said, "I greet you." My

---

[1] **transistor radio**: a type of radio used before integrated circuit boards were developed

arm twitched and throbbed, as if the Other June's pencils had already poked through the skin. She came closer, smiling her Tuesday smile.

"No," I whispered, "*no*." The word took wings and flew me to my feet, in front of the Other June. "*Noooooo*." It flew out of my mouth into her surprised face.

The boy on the desk turned toward us. "You said something, my devoted fans?"

"No," I said to the Other June. "Oh, no! No. No. No. No more." I pushed away the hand that held the pencils.

The Other June's eyes opened, popped wide like the eyes of somebody in a cartoon. It made me laugh. The boy on the desk laughed, and then the other kids were laughing, too.

"No," I said again, because it felt so good to say it. "No, no, no, no." I leaned toward the Other June, put my finger against her chest. Her cheeks turned red, she squawked something—it sounded like "Eeeraaghyou!"—and she stepped back. She stepped away from me.

The door banged, the airplanes disappeared, and Mr. Morrisey walked to his desk. "OK. OK. Let's get back to work. Kevin Clark, how about it?" Kevin jumped off the desk, and Mr. Morrisey picked up a piece of chalk. "All right, class—" He stopped and looked at me and the Other June. "You two Junes, what's going on there?"

I tried it again. My finger against her chest. Then the words. "No—more." And she stepped back another step. I sat down at my desk.

"June M.," Mr. Morrisey said.

She turned around, staring at him with that big-eyed cartoon look. After a moment she sat down at her desk with a loud slapping sound.

Even Mr. Morrisey laughed.

And sitting at my desk, twirling my braids, I knew this was the last Tuesday of the Other June.

# Reviewing

## Tuesday of the Other June

### Discussing the Selection

1. What kind of person is June? Her mother? List some specific character traits that are described or hinted at in the story.

2. Why do you think the other June picks on the narrator? Point out some of the bullying techniques that she uses.

3. What is the turning point in this story? Find the place in the story where the narrator acts, after making a discovery.

4. Review the poems in this unit. How do their themes relate to the events and characters in this story?

### Writing a Letter of Advice

Write a letter of advice to someone who is being bullied. If you have been bullied yourself, what steps did you take to stop the bullying and recover from it?

### About Norma Fox Mazer (1931–)

At the age of thirteen, Norma Fox Mazer decided she would become a writer. Since that momentous decision, she has published over thirty books, including the Newbery Honor Book *After the Rain*. Mazer's admirers believe that she is able to tap into how adolescents think and feel. She creates sympathetic characters who draw on their relationships and inner strength to help them overcome problems. Authentic feelings are important in Mazer's fiction. According to the author, "Stories bring us the essential human emotions we all share."

# FAMILY MATTERS

*Call it a clan, call it a network, call it a tribe, call it a family. Whatever you call it, whoever you are, you need one.*

Jane Howard

The theme of the selections in Unit Two is family. How do those closest to you shape your life? How do you celebrate your family gatherings? What stories does your family tell and retell? In the 21st century, there are many recipes for "family." The traditional one includes a mother, father, and two children, all related by blood. The blended version may be made up of stepparents, half-siblings, or adopted and foster children. If you are lucky, your family is a source of pride and joy, always there when you need them. In unlucky circumstances, your family can be a barrier to your happiness and success. Literature offers a way to look at how families influence us in ways that can be comforting or troubling.

# Building Vocabulary

## Prefixes

A **prefix** is a word part added to the beginning of a root or base word to change its meaning in some way. The change made by a prefix may be slight. For example, you can *enlarge* a photo by making it just a little larger—say, from wallet-sized to a 5" x 7".

Adding a prefix to a word can also make a dramatic change in the word's meaning. An *unfriendly* person is the opposite of a *friendly* one. And if you don't know the difference between an *illegal* act and a *legal* one, you can get arrested. Knowing prefixes is vital to making sense of unfamiliar words.

Sometimes prefixes are added to whole words that you already know. You may not recognize the new word that has been created, but you can figure it out. To do that, first you need to realize that the word contains a prefix.

This table shows some common prefixes and their meanings.

| PREFIX | MEANING | EXAMPLES |
| --- | --- | --- |
| en | to make or cause | enlarge, encourage |
| il, im, in, ir, un | not | illegal, immature, inability, irregular, unprofessional |
| mis | bad | misfortune, mistreat |
| pre | before | precaution, prepay |
| re | again | rewrite, refresh |
| re | back | recall, repay |
| co | with | cowrite |
| in | in, into | invasion |
| hyper | overly | hypercritical |
| im | in, into | import |
| ad | addition, toward | addiction, administer |

Here's a helpful hint. In many cases, the meaning of the prefix will make more sense if you put it after the word in your mind.

Examples:     prepay: "pay before" (not "before pay")
              rewrite: "write again" (not "again write")
              repay: "pay back" (not "back pay")

# Previewing

## The Circuit
by Francisco Jiménez

### Reading Connection

A family of migrant laborers literally follows a circuit, or circular route. In an agricultural state like California, they might pick grapes in September, move on to the cotton harvest in winter, and after that pick lettuce. By fall, they are back in the grape-growing area, ready to help with that harvest again. And, as author Francisco Jiménez says, "It's a symbolic circuit. If you're a migrant worker, you're constantly living in poverty. It's very difficult to get out of it." Some experts believe that up to 800,000 children are part of the migrant labor force. Half of them never graduate from high school, their educations disrupted by the need to work and the need to follow the harvest.

### Skill Focus: Foreign Words

The following story includes many words and phrases in Spanish, including place names and bits of conversation. If not overdone, this technique gives fiction the feel of reality. As you read, see if you can guess the meaning of some of these words from the context of the story. If you cannot, a footnote will provide a translation.

### Vocabulary Builder

You'll find the following words are boldfaced and defined in the story. Before you read, see how many of these words you already know. Use this knowledge along with your imagination and any other information you might have to predict what the story will be about.

| | | | |
|---|---|---|---|
| jalopy | populated | instinctively | hesitantly |
| surplus | vineyard | murmured | |
| gasping | drone | savoring | |

# The **Circuit**

Francisco Jiménez

CAMPESINO, Daniel DeSiga, 1976

It was that time of year again. Ito, the strawberry sharecropper,[1] did not smile. It was natural. The peak of the strawberry season was over, and the last few days the workers, most of them *braceros*,[2] were not picking as many boxes as they had during the months of June and July.

As the last days of August disappeared, so did the number of *braceros*. Sunday, only one—the best picker—came to work. I liked him. Sometimes we talked during our half-hour lunch break. That is how I found out he was from Jalisco, the same state in Mexico my family was from. That Sunday was the last time I saw him.

When the sun had tired and sunk behind the mountains, Ito signaled us that it was time to go home. "*Ya esora,*"[3] he yelled in his broken Spanish. Those were the words I waited for twelve hours a day, every day, seven days a week, week after week. And the thought of not hearing them again saddened me.

As we drove home, Papa did not say a word. With both hands on the wheel, he stared at the dirt road. My older brother, Roberto, was also silent. He leaned his head back and closed his eyes. Once in a while he cleared from his throat the dust that blew in from outside.

Yes, it was that time of year. When I opened the front door to the shack, I stopped. Everything we owned was neatly packed in cardboard boxes. Suddenly I felt even more the weight of hours, days, weeks, and months of work. I sat down on a box. The thought of having to move to Fresno, and knowing what was in store for me there, brought tears to my eyes.

That night I could not sleep. I lay in bed thinking about how much I hated this move.

A little before five o'clock in the morning, Papa woke everyone up. A few minutes later, the yelling and screaming of my little brothers and sisters, for whom the move was a great adventure, broke the silence of dawn. Shortly, the barking of the dogs accompanied them.

---

1 **sharecropper**: a farmer who works someone else's land for a share of the profits

2 *braceros*: Spanish for Latino farm workers

3 *"Ya esora"*: Ito's mispronunciation of "Ya es hora"—Spanish for "It is time."

While we packed the breakfast dishes, Papa went outside to start the "Carcanchita." That was the name Papa gave his old '38 black Plymouth. He bought it in a used-car lot in Santa Rosa in the winter of 1949. "*Mi Carcanchita*," my little **jalopy**, he called it. He had a right to be proud of it. He spent a lot of time looking at other cars before buying this one. When he finally chose the "Carcanchita," he checked it thoroughly before driving it out of the car lot. He examined every inch of the car. He listened to the motor, tilting his head from side to side like a parrot, trying to detect any noises that spelled car trouble. After being satisfied with the looks and sounds of the car, Papa then insisted on knowing who the original owner was. He never did find out from the car salesman. But he bought the car anyway. Papa figured the original owner must have been an important man, because behind the rear seat of the car he found a blue necktie.

**jalopy**
a run-down automobile

Papa parked the car out in front and left the motor running. "*Listo,*"[4] he yelled. Without saying a word, Roberto and I began to carry the boxes out to the car. Roberto carried the two big boxes, and I carried the smaller ones. Papa then threw the mattress on top of the car roof and tied it with ropes to the front and rear bumpers.

Everything was packed except Mama's pot. It was an old, large, galvanized[5] pot she had picked up at an army **surplus** store in Santa Maria the year I was born. The pot was full of dents and nicks, and the more dents and nicks it had, the more Mama liked it. "*Mi olla,*"[6] she used to say proudly.

**surplus**
extra

I held the front door open as Mama carefully carried out her pot by both handles, making sure not to spill the cooked beans. When she got to the car, Papa reached out to help her with it. Roberto opened the rear car door, and Papa gently placed it on the floor behind the front seat. All of us then climbed in. Papa sighed, wiped the sweat off his forehead with his sleeve, and said wearily: "*Es todo.*"[7]

---

4 *"Listo"*: Spanish for "Ready"

5 **galvanized**: metal that has been coated with zinc to prevent rust

6 *"Mi olla"*: Spanish for "My pot."

7 *"Es todo"*: Spanish for "That's everything."

As we drove away, I felt a lump in my throat. I turned around and looked at our little shack for the last time.

At sunset we drove into a labor camp near Fresno. Since Papa did not speak English, Mama asked the camp foreman if he needed any more workers. "We don't need no more," said the foreman, scratching his head. "Check with Sullivan down the road. Can't miss him. He lives in a big white house with a fence around it."

When we got there, Mama walked up to the house. She went through a white gate, past a row of rose bushes, up the stairs to the front door. She rang the doorbell. The porch light went on, and a tall, husky man came out. They exchanged a few words. After the man went in, Mama clasped her hands and hurried back to the car. "We have work! Mr. Sullivan said we can stay there the whole season," she said, **gasping** and pointing to an old garage near the stables.

> As we drove away, I felt a lump in my throat. I turned around and looked at our little shack for the last time.

**gasping**
breathing with difficulty

The garage was worn out by the years. It had no windows. The walls, eaten by termites, strained to support the roof full of holes. The loose dirt floor, **populated** by earthworms, looked like a gray road map.

**populated**
lived in

That night, by the light of a kerosene lamp, we unpacked and cleaned our new home. Roberto swept away the loose dirt, leaving the hard ground. Papa plugged the holes in the walls with old newspapers and tin can tops. Mama fed my little brothers and sisters. Papa and Roberto then brought in the mattress and placed it in the far corner of the garage. "Mama, you and the little ones sleep on the mattress. Roberto, Panchito, and I will sleep outside under the trees," Papa said.

Early next morning Mr. Sullivan showed us where his crop was, and after breakfast, Papa, Roberto, and I headed for the **vineyard** to pick.

**vineyard**
an area where grapes grow

Around nine o'clock the temperature had risen to almost one hundred degrees. I was completely soaked in sweat, and my mouth felt as if I had been chewing on a handkerchief. I walked over to the end of the row, picked up the jug of water we had brought and began drinking. "Don't drink too much; you'll get sick," Roberto shouted. No sooner had he said that than I felt sick to my stomach. I dropped to my knees and let the jug roll off my hands. I remained motionless with my eyes glued on the hot, sandy ground. All I could hear was the **drone** of insects. Slowly I began to recover. I poured water over my face and neck and watched the black mud run down my arms and hit the ground.

**drone**
buzzing sound

I still felt a little dizzy when we took a break to eat lunch. It was past two o'clock, and we sat underneath a large walnut tree that was on the side of the road. While we ate, Papa jotted down the number of boxes we had picked. Roberto drew designs on the ground with a stick. Suddenly I noticed Papa's face turn pale as he looked down the road. "Here comes the school bus," he whispered loudly in alarm. **Instinctively**, Roberto and I ran and hid in the vineyards. We did not want to get in trouble for not going to school. The yellow bus stopped in front of Mr. Sullivan's house. Two neatly dressed boys about my age got off. They carried books under their arms. After they crossed the street, the bus drove away. Roberto and I came out from hiding and joined Papa. "*Tienen que tener cuidado*,"[8] he warned us.

**instinctively**
automatically

After lunch we went back to work. The sun kept beating down. The buzzing insects, the wet sweat, and the hot dry dust made the afternoon seem to last forever. Finally the mountains around the valley reached out and

8 *"Tienen que tener cuidado"*: Spanish for "You have to be careful."

swallowed the sun. Within an hour it was too dark to continue picking. The vines blanketed the grapes, making it difficult to see the bunches. *"Vámonos,"*[9] said Papa, signaling to us that it was time to quit work. Papa then took out a pencil and began to figure out how much we had earned our first day. He wrote down numbers, crossed some out, wrote down some more. *"Quince,"*[10] he **murmured**.

**murmured**
spoke in a low, quiet voice

When we arrived home, we took a cold shower underneath a waterhose. We then sat down to eat dinner around some wooden crates that served as a table. Mama had cooked a special meal for us. We had rice and tortillas with *carne con chile,*[11] my favorite dish.

The next morning I could hardly move. My body ached all over. I felt little control over my arms and legs. This feeling went on every morning for days until my muscles finally got used to the work.

It was Monday, the first week of November. The grape season was over, and I could now go to school. I woke up early that morning and lay in bed, looking at the stars and **savoring** the thought of not going to work and of starting sixth grade

It was Monday, the first week of November. The grape season was over, and I could now go to school.

**savoring**
enjoying

for the first time that year. Since I could not sleep, I decided to get up and join Papa and Roberto at breakfast. I sat at the table across from Roberto, but I kept my head down. I did not want to look up and face him. I knew he was sad. He was not going to school today. He was not going tomorrow, or next week, or next month. He would not go until the cotton season was over, and that was sometime in February. I rubbed my hands together and watched the dry, acid-stained skin fall to the floor in little rolls.

When Papa and Roberto left for work, I felt relief. I walked to the top of a

---

9 *"Vámonos"*: Spanish for "Let's go."

10 *"Quince"*: Spanish for "Fifteen."

11 *carne con chile*: Spanish for a peppery mixture of meat and beans

small grade[12] next to the shack and watched the "Carcanchita" disappear in the distance in a cloud of dust.

Two hours later, around eight o'clock, I stood by the side of the road waiting for school bus number twenty. When it arrived, I climbed in. No one noticed me. Everyone was busy either talking or yelling. I sat in an empty seat in the back.

When the bus stopped in front of the school, I felt very nervous. I looked out the bus window and saw boys and girls carrying books under their arms. I felt empty. I put my hands in my pants pockets and walked to the principal's office. When I entered, I heard a woman's voice say: "May I help you?" I was startled. I had not heard English for months. For a few seconds I remained speechless. I looked at the lady who waited for an answer. My first instinct was to answer her in Spanish, but I held back. Finally, after struggling for English words, I managed to tell her that I wanted to enroll in the sixth grade. After answering many questions, I was led to the classroom.

> I was so nervous and scared at that moment when everyone's eyes were on me that I wished I were with Papa and Roberto picking cotton.

Mr. Lema, the sixth-grade teacher, greeted me and assigned me a desk. He then introduced me to the class. I was so nervous and scared at that moment when everyone's eyes were on me that I wished I were with Papa and Roberto picking cotton. After taking roll, Mr. Lema gave the class the assignment for the first hour. "The first thing we have to do this morning is finish reading the story we began yesterday," he said enthusiastically. He walked up to me, handed me an English book, and asked me to read. "We are on page 125," he said politely. When I heard this, I felt the blood rush to my head. I felt dizzy. "Would you like to read?" he asked **hesitantly**. I opened the book to page 125. My mouth was dry. My eyes began to water. I could not begin. "You can read later," Mr. Lema said understandingly.

**hesitantly**
uncertainly;
cautiously

---

12 **grade**: hill

For the rest of the reading period, I kept getting angrier and angrier with myself. I should have read, I thought to myself.

During recess I went into the restroom and opened my English book to page 125. I began to read in a low voice, pretending I was in class. There were many words I did not know. I closed the book and headed back to the classroom. Mr. Lema was sitting at his desk correcting papers. When I entered he looked up at me and smiled. I felt better. I walked up to him and asked if he could help me with the new words. "Gladly," he said.

The rest of the month I spent my lunch hours working on English with Mr. Lema, my best friend at school.

One Friday during lunch hour, Mr. Lema asked me to take a walk with him to the music room. "Do you like music?" he asked me as we entered the building.

"Yes, I like Mexican *corridos*,[13]" I answered. He then picked up a trumpet, blew on it, and handed it to me. The sound gave me goose bumps. I knew that sound. I had heard it in many Mexican *corridos*. "How would you like to learn how to play it?" he asked. He must have read my face, because before I could answer, he added: "I'll teach you how to play it during our lunch hours."

That day I could hardly wait to get home to tell Papa and Mama the great news. As I got off the bus, my little brothers and sisters ran up to meet me. They were yelling and screaming. I thought they were happy to see me, but when I opened the door to our shack, I saw that everything we owned was neatly packed in cardboard boxes.

---

13 **corrido**: a Mexican ballad

# Reviewing

## The Circuit

### Discussing the Selection

1. Did the Spanish words in the story make your reading more difficult? Would the story have been as effective without them?

2. What is Panchito, the narrator, like? Find details in the story that show or suggest what kind of boy he is.

3. Describe how Panchito's family influences him, in both positive and negative ways.

4. Find all the references to time in "The Circuit." What purpose do you think they serve?

### Writing a Comparison/Contrast Paper

Compare your family life to the Jiménez family's. Describe both the (comparisons) and the differences (contrasts).

### About Francisco Jiménez (1943–)

The son of poor migrant workers, Francisco Jiménez was put to work in the fields when he was only six years old. Though he failed the first grade and struggled for years with the English language, he eventually graduated from prestigious Columbia University. Now he is a professor in the humanities at Santa Clara University and a leader in teacher education in California. The story in this book comes from his collection of autobiographical short stories, *The Circuit: Stories from the Life of a Migrant Child*. Jiménez claims that John Steinbeck's novel *The Grapes of Wrath*, also about migrant workers, was the first book he ever read that he could relate to. "For the first time, I realized the power of the written word—that an artist can write creatively and make a difference in people's lives."

# Previewing

## My Father's Hands Held Mine
Norman H. Russell

## Knoxville, Tennessee
Nikki Giovanni

### Reading Connection

Contemporary poets Norman H. Russell, a Native American, and Nikki Giovanni, an African American, are sometimes called "multicultural" poets. In their work, they celebrate their ethnic heritage and promote its values. For Russell, that means writing about the natural world. The Native American oral tradition—passing down stories from person to person—can be heard in his plainly worded poetry. Giovanni's poetry is as outgoing as her personality, prized for its bright ethnic details and sassy rhythms. Her own background is more political. She sees a connection between racial oppression and people's lack of knowledge about diverse cultures. Both poets believe that young people, especially, have much to gain by learning more about their own ethnic backgrounds.

### Skill Focus: Main Idea/Theme

Every piece of writing is created because the author has something to share with the reader. This message is called the main idea or theme. Don't confuse the main idea with the subject matter of the piece. The subject of some writing might be "Pets" but the main idea will say what the author thinks about them. For example, "Every family should have a pet." or "As long as people are starving in our world, we should not be giving food to pet animals."

# My Father's Hands Held Mine

Norman H. Russell

my father's hands held mine
the first flint[1]

now my hands alone
cut our arrows

the deer that dies from them      5
falls from both our hands

wife of my heart your mother's hands
help you sew my moccasins

my father speaks to me in many ways
i feel his hands on me      10

he is always with me
i will always touch my sons

HANDS FROM A FIGURE GROUP,
Egypt, c. 1350 B.C.

1 **flint**: a hard stone used in the past as a tool

# Knoxville, Tennessee

Nikki Giovanni

I always like summer
best
you can eat fresh corn
from daddy's garden
and okra[1]                        5
and greens
and cabbage
and lots of
barbecue
and buttermilk                    10
and homemade ice-cream
at the church picnic
and listen to
gospel[2] music
outside                           15
at the church
homecoming
and go to the mountains with
your grandmother
and go barefooted                 20
and be warm
all the time
not only when you go to bed
and sleep

GRANDDAUGHTER, Andrew Wyeth, 1956

1 **okra**: a green vegetable with edible pods, common in Southern cooking

2 **gospel**: based on the teachings of Christianity. Gospel music is lively and emotional.

# Reviewing

## My Father's Hands Held Mine / Knoxville, Tennessee

### Discussing the Selections

1. In your opinion, what is the main idea of each poem?

2. What do you think the last two lines of the Russell poem mean?

3. What attitude, or tone, does each writer take toward his or her subject? Explain your answer.

4. What words or other elements of these poems give you special insights into the cultures of the poets? Decide what, if anything, these poems have in common.

### Writing a Journal Entry

Choose to be the speaker from either of the poems you have just read. As that person, write a journal entry describing a day in the life of your family.

### Norman H. Russell (1921–)

Norman Hudson Russell is a scientist, poet, and longstanding member of the Cherokee Indian tribe. The Virginia-born writer obtained a Ph.D. from the University of Minnesota and became a respected professor and worldwide authority on violets. After 1970, he began to devote more time to poetry. He told an interviewer in 1978 that "the sort of science I studied—botany, outdoor work—is really the science of observation and how you observe nature. This is what the Indian does and this is what the poet does." His poem "The Tornado" was recently included in a collection of modern classics, noted for capturing "the horror and chaos of sudden disaster."

### About Nikki Giovanni (1943–)

Wit, honesty, passion . . . these three words come up often in the praise accorded Nikki Giovanni. Born in Knoxville, Tennessee, the African American writer and poet graduated from Fisk University, the University of Pennsylvania School of Social Work, and the Columbia University School of Fine Arts. Her poetry collections *Black Feeling, Black Talk* and *Black Judgment* capture the fiery attitude of the civil rights movement of the early 1960s. Her later poetry takes on more personal themes, echoing her life as a single mother. Among Giovanni's many honors is the Langston Hughes Medal for Outstanding Poetry. In 2003, a CD of her poetry was a Grammy contender in the spoken word category.

# Previewing

## The All-American Slurp
Lensey Namioka

### Reading Connection

In every culture, politeness is a virtue. However, what is considered polite can vary from place to place. This can create especially awkward moments when you are eating with people from other countries. The etiquette of eating has evolved over centuries in some cultures and often came about for practical reasons. For example, in cultures where people use their hands instead of utensils to eat, poverty and a lack of water may have made utensils too expensive and inconvenient. In the United States and many other countries, making noise while eating is strongly discouraged. But there are places where people consider a little slurping and burping a way to show a sense of gusto for the meal.

### Skill Focus: Tone

Tone refers to an author's attitude toward his or her subject. Tone is often described with the use of adjectives, for example "optimistic," "depressing," or "inspirational." As you read, consider what tone Lensey Namioka takes in "The All-American Slurp." Analyze how she achieves this by noticing the story's dialogue, situations, and character portrayals.

### Vocabulary Builder

Be on the lookout for the following words in the next story. They are printed in boldface type and defined on the page where they appear.

| | | | |
|---|---|---|---|
| immigrated | mortified | resolved | consumption |
| revolting | spectacle | systematic | urgency |
| lavishly | smugly | etiquette | coping |

THE STICKY RICE DUMPLING, Zhao Chuan Fang, 1998

# The **All-American** Slurp

By Lensey Namioka

The first time our family was invited out to dinner in America, we disgraced ourselves while eating celery. We had **immigrated** to this country from China, and during our early days here we had a hard time with American table manners.

In China we never ate celery raw, or any other kind of vegetable raw. We always had to disinfect the vegetables in boiling water first. When we were presented with our first relish tray, the raw celery caught us unprepared.

We had been invited to dinner by our neighbors, the Gleasons. After arriving at the house, we shook hands with our hosts and packed ourselves into a sofa. As our family of four sat stiffly in a row, my younger brother and I stole glances at our parents for a clue as to what to do next.

**immigrated**
moved to a
different country

Mrs. Gleason offered the relish tray to Mother. The tray looked pretty with its tiny red radishes, curly sticks of carrots, and long, slender stalks of pale green celery. "Do try some of the celery, Mrs. Lin," she said. "It's from a local farmer, and it's sweet."

Mother picked up one of the green stalks, and Father followed suit.[1] Then I picked up a stalk and my brother did too. So there we sat, each with a stalk of celery in our right hand.

Mrs. Gleason kept smiling. "Would you like to try some of the dip, Mrs. Lin? It's my own recipe: sour cream and onion flakes, with a dash of Tabasco sauce."

**revolting**
disgusting

Most Chinese don't care for dairy products, and in those days I wasn't even ready to drink fresh milk. Sour cream sounded perfectly **revolting**. Our family shook our heads in unison.[2]

Mrs. Gleason went off with the relish tray to the other guests, and we carefully watched to see what they did. Everyone seemed to eat the raw vegetables quite happily.

Mother took a bite of her celery. *Crunch.* "It's not bad!" she whispered.

Father took a bite of his celery. *Crunch.* "Yes, it *is* good," he said, looking surprised.

I took a bite, and then my brother. *Crunch, crunch.* It was more than good; it was delicious. Raw celery has a slight sparkle, a zingy taste that you don't get in cooked celery. When Mrs. Gleason came around with the relish tray, we each took another stalk of celery, except my brother. He took two.

There was only one problem: long strings ran through the length of the stalk, and they got caught in my teeth. When I help my mother in the kitchen, I always pull the strings out before slicing celery.

I pulled the strings out of my stalk. *Z-z-zip, z-z-zip.* My brother followed suit. *Z-z-zip, z-z-zip, z-z-zip.* To my left, my parents were taking care of their own stalks. *Z-z-zip, z-z-zip, z-z-zip.*

Suddenly I realized that there was dead silence except for the zipping.

---

1 **followed suit**: did the same

2 **in unison**: at the same time

Looking up, I saw that the eyes of everyone in the room were on our family. Mr. and Mrs. Gleason, their daughter Meg, who was my friend, and their neighbors the Badels—they were staring at us as we busily pulled the strings off our celery.

That wasn't the end of it. Mrs. Gleason announced that dinner was served and invited us to the dining table. It was **lavishly** covered with platters of food, but we couldn't see any chairs around the table. So we helpfully carried over some dining chairs and sat down. All the other guests just stood there.

**lavishly**
abundantly

Mrs. Gleason bent down and whispered to us, "This is a buffet dinner. You help yourselves to food and eat it in the living room."

Our family beat a retreat back to the sofa as if chased by enemy soldiers. For the rest of the evening, too **mortified** to go back to the dining table, I nursed[3] a bit of potato salad on my plate.

**mortified**
embarrassed

Next day Meg and I got on the school bus together. I wasn't sure how she would feel about me after the **spectacle** our family made at the party. But she was just the same as usual, and the only reference she made to the party was, "Hope you and your folks got enough to eat last night. You certainly didn't take very much. Mom never tries to figure out how much food to prepare. She just puts everything on the table and hopes for the best."

**spectacle**
a foolish or shameful scene

I began to relax. The Gleasons' dinner party wasn't so different from a Chinese meal after all. My mother also puts everything on the table and hopes for the best.

Our family beat a retreat back to the sofa as if chased by enemy soldiers.

Meg was the first friend I had made after we came to America. I eventually got acquainted with a few other kids in school, but Meg was still the only real friend I had.

My brother didn't have any problems making friends. He spent all his time with some boys who were teaching him baseball, and in no time he could

3 **nursed**: ate slowly, without appetite

speak English much faster than I could—not better, but faster.

I worried more about making mistakes, and I spoke carefully, making sure I could say everything right before opening my mouth. At least I had a better accent than my parents, who never really got rid of their Chinese accent, even years later. My parents had both studied English in school before coming to America, but what they had studied was mostly written English, not spoken.

Father's approach to English was a scientific one. Since Chinese verbs have no tense he was fascinated by the way English verbs changed form according to whether they were in the present, past imperfect, perfect, pluperfect, future, or future perfect tense. He was always making diagrams of verbs and their inflections,[4] and he looked for opportunities to show off his mastery of the pluperfect and future perfect tenses, his two favorites. "I shall have finished my project by Monday," he would say **smugly**.

**smugly**
in a conceited or self-satisfied way

Mother's approach was to memorize lists of polite phrases that would cover all possible social situations. She was constantly muttering things like "I'm fine, thank you. And you?" Once she accidentally stepped on someone's foot and hurriedly blurted, "Oh, that's quite all right!" Embarrassed by her slip, she **resolved** to do better next time. So when someone stepped on *her* foot, she cried, "You're welcome!"

**resolved**
decided

In our own different ways, we made progress in learning English. But I had another worry, and that was my appearance. My brother didn't have to worry, since Mother bought him blue jeans for school and he dressed like all the other boys. But she insisted that girls had to wear skirts. By the time she saw that Meg and the other girls were wearing jeans, it was too late. My school clothes were bought already, and we didn't have money left to buy new outfits for me. We had too many other things to buy first, like furniture, pots, and pans.

The first time I visited Meg's house, she took me upstairs to her room, and I wound up trying on her clothes. We were pretty much the same size, since Meg was shorter and thinner than average. Maybe that's how we became friends in the first place. Wearing Meg's jeans and T-shirt, I looked at myself in the mirror. I could almost pass for an American—from the back, anyway. At least the

---

4 **inflections**: additions to a word base, such as prefixes and suffixes, that change its meaning. For example, the inflection -ed changes a verb to its past tense.

kids in school wouldn't stop and stare at me in the hallways, which was what they did when they saw me in my white blouse and navy blue skirt that went a couple of inches below the knees.

When Meg came to my house, I invited her to try on my Chinese dresses, the ones with a high collar and slits up the sides. Meg's eyes were bright as she looked at herself in the mirror. She struck several sultry[5] poses, and we nearly fell over laughing.

The dinner party at the Gleasons' didn't stop my growing friendship with Meg. Things were getting better for me in other ways too. Mother finally bought me some jeans at the end of the month, when Father got his paycheck. She wasn't in any hurry about buying them at first, until I worked on her.

**"You can't go out in public like that! People can see all the way up to your thighs!"**

This is what I did. Since we didn't have a car in those days, I often ran down to the neighborhood store to pick up things for her. The groceries cost less at a big supermarket, but the closest one was many blocks away. One day, when she ran out of flour, I offered to borrow a bike from our neighbor's son and buy a ten-pound bag of flour at the big supermarket. I mounted the boy's bike and waved to Mother. "I'll be back in five minutes!"

Before I started pedaling, I heard her voice behind me. "You can't go out in public like that! People can see all the way up to your thighs!"

"I'm sorry," I said innocently. "I thought you were in a hurry to get the flour." For dinner we were going to have pot-stickers (fried Chinese dumplings), and we needed a lot of flour.

"Couldn't you borrow a girl's bicycle?" complained Mother. "That way your skirt won't be pushed up."

"There aren't too many of those around," I said. "Almost all the girls wear jeans while riding a bike, so they don't see any point buying a girl's bike."

We didn't eat pot-stickers that evening, and Mother was thoughtful. Next

---

5 **sultry**: exciting, passionate

day we took the bus downtown, and she bought me a pair of jeans. In the same week, my brother made the baseball team of his junior high school, Father started taking driving lessons, and Mother discovered rummage sales. We soon got all the furniture we needed, plus a dart board and a 1,000 piece jigsaw puzzle (fourteen hours later, we discovered that it was a 999-piece jigsaw puzzle). There was hope that the Lins might become a normal American family after all.

Then came our dinner at the Lakeview restaurant.

The Lakeview was an expensive restaurant, one of those places where a headwaiter dressed in tails[6] conducted you to your seat and the only light came from candles and flaming desserts. In one corner of the room, a lady harpist played tinkling melodies.

Father wanted to celebrate because he had just been promoted. He worked for an electronics company, and after his English started improving, his superiors decided to appoint him to a position more suited to his training. The promotion not only brought a higher salary but was also a tremendous boost to his pride.

Up to then we had eaten only in Chinese restaurants. Although my brother and I were becoming fond of hamburgers, my parents didn't care much for Western food, other than chow mein.

But this was a special occasion, and Father asked his co-workers to recommend a really elegant restaurant. So there we were at the Lakeview, stumbling after the headwaiter in the murky dining room.

At our table we were handed our menus, and they were so big that to read mine I almost had to stand up again. But why bother? It was mostly in French, anyway.

**systematic**
organized

Father, being an engineer, was always **systematic**. He took out a pocket French dictionary. "They told me that most of the items would be in French, so I came prepared." He even had a pocket flashlight, the size of a marking pen. While Mother held the flashlight over the menu, he looked up the items that were in French.

6 **tails**: a formal evening suit worn by men

"*Pâté en croûte*,"[7] he muttered. "Let's see .
. . *pâté* is paste . . . *croûte* is crust . . . hmm
. . . a paste in crust."

The waiter stood looking patient. I
squirmed and died at least fifty times.

At long last Father gave up. "Why
don't we just order four complete
dinners at random?" he suggested.

"Isn't that risky?" asked Mother.
"The French eat some rather peculiar
things, I've heard."

"A Chinese can eat anything a
Frenchman can eat," Father declared.

The soup arrived in a plate. How
do you get soup up from a plate? I
glanced at the other diners, but the
ones at the nearby tables were not on
their soup course, while the most distant
ones were invisible in the darkness.

Fortunately, my parents had studied books on
Western **etiquette** before they came to America. "Tilt your plate," whispered my
mother. "It's easier to spoon the soup up that way."

**etiquette**
manners

She was right. Tilting the plate did the trick. But the etiquette book didn't
say anything about what you did after the soup reached your lips. As any
respectable Chinese knows, the correct way to eat your soup is to slurp. This
helps to cool the liquid and prevent you from burning your lips. It also shows
your appreciation.

We showed our appreciation. *Shloop*, went my father. *Shloop*, went my
mother. *Shloop, shloop*, went my brother, who was the hungriest.

---

7 **"*Pâté en croûte*"**: French for a type of seasoned meat pie

The lady harpist stopped playing to take a rest. And in the silence, our

**consumption**
the amount
used or taken
in

family's **consumption** of soup suddenly seemed unnaturally loud. You know how it sounds on a rocky beach when the tide goes out and the water drains from all those little pools? They go *shloop, shloop, shloop*. That was the Lin family, eating soup.

At the next table, a waiter was pouring wine. When a large *shloop* reached him, he froze. The bottle continued to pour, and red wine flooded the table top and into the lap of a customer. Even the customer didn't notice anything at first, being also hypnotized by the *shloop, shloop, shloop*.

It was too much. "I need to go to the toilet," I mumbled, jumping to my

**urgency**
the need for
quickness

feet. A waiter, sensing my **urgency**, quickly directed me to the ladies' room.

I splashed cold water on my burning face, and as I dried myself with a paper towel, I stared into the mirror. In this perfumed ladies' room, with its pink-and-silver wallpaper and marbled sinks, I looked completely out of place. What was I doing here? What was our family doing in the Lakeview restaurant? In America?

The door to the ladies' room opened. A woman came in and glanced curiously at me. I retreated into one of the toilet cubicles and latched the door.

Time passed—maybe half an hour, maybe an hour. Then I heard the door open again, and my mother's voice. "Are you in there? You're not sick, are you?"

There was real concern in her voice. A girl can't leave her family just because they slurp their soup. Besides, the toilet cubicle had a few drawbacks as a permanent residence. "I'm all right," I said, undoing the latch.

Mother didn't tell me how the rest of the dinner went, and I didn't want to know. In the weeks following, I managed to push the whole thing into the back of my mind, where it jumped out at me only a few times a day. Even now, I turn hot all over when I think of the Lakeview restaurant.

But by the time we had been in this country for three months, our family was definitely making progress toward becoming Americanized. I remember my parents' first PTA meeting. Father wore a neat suit and tie, and Mother put on her first pair of high heels. She stumbled only once. They met my homeroom teacher and beamed as she told them that I would make the honor roll soon at the rate I was going. Of course Chinese etiquette forced Father to say that I was a very stupid girl and Mother to protest that the teacher was showing favoritism toward me. But I could tell they were both very proud.

The day came when my parents announced that they wanted to give a dinner party. We had invited Chinese friends to eat with us before, but this dinner was going to be different. In addition to a Chinese-American family, we were going to invite the Gleasons.

"Gee, I can hardly wait to have dinner at your house," Meg said to me. "I just *love* Chinese food."

That was a relief. Mother was a good cook, but I wasn't sure if people who ate sour cream would also eat chicken gizzards stewed in soy sauce.

Mother decided not to take a chance with chicken gizzards. Since we had Western guests, she set the table with large dinner plates, which we never used in Chinese meals. In fact we didn't use individual plates at all but picked up food from the platters in the middle of the table and brought it directly to our rice bowls. Following the practice of Chinese-American restaurants, Mother also placed large serving spoons on the platters.

The dinner started well. Mrs. Gleason exclaimed at the beautifully arranged dishes of food: the colorful candied fruit in the sweet-and-sour pork dish, the noodle-thin shreds of chicken meat stir-fried with tiny peas, and the glistening pink prawns in a ginger sauce.

At first I was too busy enjoying my food to notice how the guests were doing. But soon I remembered my duties. Sometimes guests were too polite to help themselves, and you had to serve them more food.

I glanced at Meg to see if she needed more food, and my eyes nearly popped out at the sight of her plate. It was piled with food: the sweet-and-sour meat pushed right against the chicken shreds, and the chicken sauce ran into the prawns. She had been taking food from a second dish before she finished eating her helping from the first!

Horrified, I turned to look at Mrs. Gleason. She was dumping rice out of her bowl and putting it on her dinner plate. Then she ladled prawns and gravy on top of the rice and mixed everything together, the way you mix sand, gravel, and cement to make concrete.

I couldn't bear to look any longer, and I turned to Mr. Gleason. He was chasing a pea around his plate. Several times he got it to the edge, but when he tried to pick it up with his chopsticks, it rolled back toward the center of the plate again. Finally he put down his chopsticks and picked up the pea with his fingers. He really did! A grown man!

All of us, our family and the Chinese guests, stopped eating to watch the activities of the Gleasons. I wanted to giggle. Then I caught my mother's eyes on me. She frowned and shook her head slightly, and I understood the message: the Gleasons were not used to Chinese ways, and they were just **coping** the best they could. For some reason, I thought of the celery strings.

**coping**
managing;
dealing with
difficulties

When the main courses were finished, Mother brought out a platter of fruit. "I hope you weren't expecting a sweet dessert," she said. "Since the Chinese don't eat dessert, I didn't think to prepare any."

"Oh, I couldn't possibly eat dessert!" cried Mrs. Gleason. "I'm simply stuffed!"

Meg had different ideas. When the table was cleared, she announced that she and I were going for a walk. "I don't know about you, but I feel like dessert," she told me when we were outside. "Come on, there's a Dairy Queen down the street. I could use a big chocolate milkshake!"

Although I didn't really want anything more to eat, I insisted on paying for the milkshakes. After all, I was still the hostess. Meg got her large chocolate milkshake, and I had a small one. Even so, she was finishing hers while I was only half done. Toward the end she pulled hard on her straws and went *shloop*, *shloop*.

"Do you always slurp when you eat a milkshake?" I asked before I could stop myself.

Meg grinned. "Sure. All Americans slurp."

# Reviewing

## The All-American Slurp

### Discussing the Selection

1. What kind of person is the narrator of "The All-American Slurp"? Choose a passage in the story—of dialogue, description, or thought—that makes her character come alive.

2. What words would you use to describe the tone of this story? Explain your answer using specific details from the text.

3. Compare some of the Lins' strategies for adapting to their new culture. Which of the family members do you think has the best strategies or attitude?

4. Have you ever experienced anything like one of the incidents in this story? Describe it to the class.

### Writing Dialogue

Dialogue is conversation between two people. Writers use quotation marks to show the exact words someone says. Look at how quotation marks and commas are used in the following example.

> "I'm really bummed," mumbled Alex, his head hanging low.
> "Why?" responded his friend Martin.
> "I studied really hard for the algebra test, but I only got a C."

Using correctly punctuated dialogue, write a conversation between two family members. They can be real people or imaginary characters.

### About Lensey Namioka (1929–)

Lensey Namioka showed an early talent for writing by self-publishing her first book when she was only eight. Born in Beijing, China, Namioka immigrated with her parents to the United States when she was nine years old. Despite her early love for literature, Namioka graduated from the University of California at Berkeley with a major in math. She taught mathematics for a time, but eventually decided she'd rather be an author. Namioka has written twenty-three books, ranging from picture books for toddlers to samurai tales for young adults. In many of them, she has captured her early childhood experiences in China. She especially likes to write about "what it's like to move to a new country and learn a new language."

# Understanding Nonfiction

Nonfiction sounds like it might be the opposite of fiction. Or that it might be anything *other* than fiction. In fact, much nonfiction uses many of the tools of fiction—vivid storytelling, characters, and settings—to write about true things. Like fiction, it relies on specific details, colorful images, and sometimes dialogue to make the writing come to life. Although it often reads like fiction, everything in it is expected to be true.

Nonfiction includes writing about the sciences, arts and culture, sports, adventure, travel, family, and personal life. Memoirs, biographies, and even literary book reviews fall under the heading of nonfiction. It comes in the shape of essays, diaries, and excerpts from longer works and can be either formal or informal. However, the most common kinds of nonfiction are listed below.

**Autobiography** An autobiography is the story of someone's life, written by the person him- or herself. Events in the writing are true, but they are colored by the author's memory as well as by the writer's wish to look "good" to readers. Autobiographers can emphasize incidents or leave them out entirely depending on the impression they want to create.

**Biography** This is also a true story about a person's life, but it is written by someone else. Usually, biographers do a great deal of research on their subject before they begin to write.

**Essay** An essay is a short multi-paragraph piece of writing that focuses on one topic or idea. Much of the writing you do for school will be essay writing. Essays differ depending on the writer's purpose. Some are **persuasive** and try to convince others to change their mind about an issue and accept the writer's point of view. **Personal** essays are informal pieces that present the writer's thoughts and feelings. An **expository** essay is more formal in tone and structure. The purpose of this type of essay is to present information and ideas.

**Articles** Articles may be long, short, humorous, serious, formal, or informal. Their purpose is to provide factual information to the reader. Examples include newspaper and magazine articles, textbooks, encyclopedias, and so forth.

Nonfiction writing is a product of the writers' unique voices and the choices they make when presenting their subjects. If two people write an essay about the same topic, the results will probably be very different. Imagine two essayists describing a chili cook-off. One writer thinks the event is absurd; the other takes it to heart. The first writer focuses on chili's weirdest ingredients—such as chocolate—and pokes fun at how seriously the competitors take themselves. The second writer depicts the event as a cooking Olympics of creativity.

# Previewing

## Power of the Powerless: A Brother's Lesson
Christopher de Vinck

### Reading Connection

In the sixty years since the author's severely retarded brother was born, more in-home health care providers have been trained to help families. But this kind of full-time assistance is costly. More quality institutions exist for the families who would like out-of-home care, but not nearly enough to meet the enormous need. Due to medical advances, many more extremely impaired babies are kept alive today. Who pays for the skyrocketing costs of their prescription drugs, special equipment, and other needs? Who stays with them when their parents must go to work? Many struggling parents exhaust their energy and savings in order to keep going or to qualify for government assistance. Doing the right thing for their severely impaired children demands a huge sacrifice from these families.

### Skill Focus: Using Persuasion

Authors write to inform, entertain, and persuade you of their point of view. While you read this essay, think about how the author describes growing up with a severely disabled brother at home. What does he think about his family life, and how does he try to get you to accept his view?

### Vocabulary Builder

Which of the following words have prefixes that you have studied? Does knowing the meaning of the prefix give you clues to the meaning of the word?

| | | | |
|---|---|---|---|
| stammered | institution | demanding | compassion |
| revived | insight | sheepishly | |

Das Kleine Zimmer (the little room), Karl Schmidt-Rottluff

# Power of the Powerless:
## A Brother's Lesson

By Christopher de Vinck

I grew up in the house where my brother was on his back in his bed for almost 33 years, in the same corner of his room, under the same window, beside the same yellow walls. Oliver was blind, mute. His legs were twisted. He didn't have the strength to lift his head nor the intelligence to learn anything.

Today I am an English teacher, and each time I introduce my class to the play about Helen Keller, *The Miracle Worker*,[1] I tell my students about Oliver. One day, during my first year teaching, a boy in the last row raised his hand and said, "Oh, Mr. de Vinck. You mean he was a vegetable."

I **stammered** for a few seconds. My family and I fed Oliver. We changed his diapers, hung his clothes and bed linen on the basement line in winter, and spread them out white and clean on the lawn in the summer. I always liked to watch the grasshoppers jump on the pillowcases.

**stammered**
stuttered;
hesitated

---

1 **Helen Keller/The Miracle Worker**: Born in 1880, Helen Keller overcame both deafness and blindness to become one of the country's most respected writers and lecturers. *The Miracle Worker* is a play about Helen and her teacher, Annie Sullivan.

We bathed Oliver. Tickled his chest to make him laugh. Sometimes we left the radio on in his room. We pulled the shade down over his bed in the morning to keep the sun from burning his tender skin. We listened to him laugh as we watched television downstairs. We listened to him rock his arms up and down to make the bed squeak. We listened to him cough in the middle of the night.

"Well, I guess you could call him a vegetable. I called him Oliver, my brother. You would have liked him."

One October day in 1946, when my mother was pregnant with Oliver, her second son, she was overcome by fumes from a leaking coal-burning stove. My oldest brother was sleeping in his crib, which was quite high off the ground, so the gas didn't affect him. My father pulled them outside, where my mother **revived** quickly.

On April 20, 1947, Oliver was born. A healthy-looking, plump, beautiful boy.

One afternoon, a few months later, my mother brought Oliver to a window. She held him there in the sun, the bright good sun, and there Oliver looked and looked directly into the sunlight, which was the first moment my mother realized that Oliver was blind. My parents, the true heroes of this story, learned, with the passing months, that blindness was only part of the problem. So they brought Oliver to Mt. Sinai Hospital in New York for tests to determine the extent of his condition.

The doctor said that he wanted to make it very clear to both my mother and father that there was absolutely nothing that could be done for Oliver. He didn't want my parents to grasp at false hope. "You could place him in an **institution**," he said. "But," my parents replied, "he is our son. We will take Oliver home of course." The good doctor answered, "Then take him home and love him."

Oliver grew to the size of a 10-year-old. He had a big chest, a large head. His hands and feet were those of a five-year-old, small and soft. We'd wrap a box of baby cereal for him at Christmas and place it under the tree; pat his head with a damp cloth in the middle of a July heat wave. His baptismal certificate[2] hung on

**revived**
recovered; felt better

**institution**
a group home or establishment devoted to special care

---

2 **baptismal certificate**: the paper affirming a legitimate Christian baptism. Baptism is a religious ceremony of initiation or welcome.

the wall above his head. A bishop came to the house and confirmed[3] him.

Even now, five years after his death from pneumonia on March 12, 1980, Oliver still remains the weakest, most helpless human being I ever met, and yet he was one of the most powerful human beings I ever met. He could do absolutely nothing except breathe, sleep, eat, and yet he was responsible for action, love, courage, **insight**. When I was small my mother would say, "Isn't it wonderful that you can see?" And once she said, "When you go to heaven, Oliver will run to you, embrace you, and the first thing he will say is 'Thank you.'" I remember, too, my mother explaining to me that we were blessed with Oliver in many ways that were not clear to her at first.

**insight**
a new understanding or idea

So often parents are faced with a child who is severely retarded, but who is also hyperactive,[4] **demanding** or wild, who needs constant care. So many people have little choice but to place their child in an institution. We were fortunate that Oliver didn't need us to be in his room all day. He never knew what his condition was. We were blessed with his presence, a true presence of peace.

**demanding**
needy; attention-seeking

When I was in my early 20s I met a girl and fell in love. After a few months I brought her home to meet my family. When my mother went to the kitchen to prepare dinner, I asked the girl, "Would you like to see Oliver?" for I had told her about my brother. "No," she answered.

Soon after, I met Roe, a lovely girl. She asked me the names of my brothers and sisters. She loved children. I thought she was wonderful. I brought her home after a few months to meet my family. Soon it was time for me to feed Oliver. I remember **sheepishly** asking Roe if she'd like to see him. "Sure," she said.

**sheepishly**
bashfully; meekly

I sat at Oliver's bedside as Roe watched over my shoulder. I gave him his first spoonful, his second. "Can I do that?" Roe asked with ease, with freedom, with **compassion**, so I gave her the bowl and she fed Oliver one spoonful at a time.

**compassion**
concern; sympathy

The power of the powerless. Which girl would you marry? Today Roe and I have three children.

---

3 **confirmed**: performed the Christian ceremony to make him a full member of his church

4 **hyperactive**: overly active

# Reviewing

## Power of the Powerless

### Discussing the Selection

1. What is the author's point of view regarding the care of severely disabled children? Explain how you know.

2. Why do you think the de Vinck family is able to care for Oliver at home for so long?

3. Explain what you think of how Oliver's family copes with his disabilities. Do you agree that he has been a blessing to them?

4. What does the writer mean when he says that Oliver "was one of the most powerful human beings I ever met"?

### Writing a Memoir

This essay is in a form called the memoir, a short account of an author's personal experiences. Write a short memoir about your family. You may want to write about hardships your family has withstood, family members who have influenced you in positive or negative ways, or some significant family event.

### About Christopher de Vinck (1951–)

In 1985, Christopher de Vinck wrote a moving essay about how his family had cared for his severely handicapped brother Oliver for thirty-two years. When *The Wall Street Journal* published it, people from across the country responded sympathetically. de Vinck interviewed many of those correspondents for his book *Power of the Powerless*. Since then de Vinck has won many awards for his essays and poems, which often draw on his personal experiences. He is a longtime teacher and language arts supervisor in the New Jersey school system and continues to write feature articles for publications such as *Reader's Digest, Guideposts*, and *The New York Times*.

# Previewing

## Beneath the Cherry Trees
### from *Marley and Me*
by John Grogan

## Reading Connection

Despite its large size and larger-than-life personality, the Labrador retriever has been Americans' favorite dog breed for the last sixteen years. Because of their intelligence and eagerness to please, they are often trained as guide dogs for the blind, helpers for disabled people, and trackers for the police. Labs are best suited to "active households," according to experts in the dog world. They love to go hunting, romp, and play all kinds of games. If well-trained, a Lab makes a wonderful family dog, friendly and loyal to the end.

## Skill Focus: Anecdote

An anecdote is a short, often humorous story. Good writers know that a punchy, well-chosen anecdote can liven up a longer work of writing. As you read the excerpt from John Grogan's book about Marley, notice the anecdotes he uses to portray his dog, Marley.

## Vocabulary Builder

This story has many challenging vocabulary words. While it is always important to preview the features of a piece of writing, you will find it especially helpful for this one. Look at the list of words below, noting any that you already know or think you know. Now check yourself by looking at the definitions of these words on the pages of the story. Also read the footnotes. This process will make the story of Marley even more memorable.

| | | | |
|---|---|---|---|
| inconvenience | depression | intuition | adversity |
| severed | equated | empathy | unwavering |
| massive | lethargic | shaft | illiterate |
| crevice | indulge | optimism | buoyant |
| intuitively | excursion | | |

A Labrador retriever similar to Marley

# Beneath the **Cherry Trees**
From *Marley and Me*

John Grogan

Ohe day in 1991, John Grogan and his wife Jenny
joyfully brought home an adorable little puppy. They named
him Marley. Little did they know that Marley would quickly
become "the world's worst dog"! Marley lived a long, happy,
and crazy life adoring his owners and being adored in
return. Sadly, pets don't live as long as humans do. In the
excerpt you are about to read, John grieves over the loss of
his friend and looks for a place to lay Marley to rest.

Sleep came fitfully that night, and an hour before dawn
I slid out of bed and dressed quietly so as not to wake
Jenny. In the kitchen I drank a glass of water—coffee
could wait—and walked out into a light, slushy drizzle.
I grabbed a shovel and pickax and walked to the pea
patch, which hugged the white pines. . . . It was here I
decided to lay him to rest.

The temperature was in the mid-thirties and the ground blessedly unfrozen. In the half dark, I began to dig. Once I was through a thin layer of topsoil, I hit heavy, dense clay studded with rocks. . . After fifteen minutes I peeled off my coat and paused to catch my breath. After thirty minutes I was in a sweat and not yet down two feet. At the forty-five-minute mark, I struck water. The hole began to fill. And fill. Soon a foot of muddy cold water covered the bottom. I fetched a bucket and tried to bail it, but more water just seeped in. There was no way I could lay Marley down in that icy swamp. No way.

Despite the work I had invested in it—my heart was pounding like I had just run a marathon—I abandoned the location and scouted the yard, stopping where the lawn meets the woods at the bottom of the hill. Between two big native cherry trees, their branches arching above me in the gray light of dawn like an open-air cathedral, I sunk my shovel. . . . Digging went easily, and I soon had an oval hole roughly two by three feet around and four feet deep. I went inside and found all three kids up, sniffling quietly. Jenny had just told them.

Seeing them grieving—their first up-close experience with death—deeply affected me. Yes, it was only a dog, and dogs come and go in the course of a human life, sometimes simply because they become an **inconvenience**. It was only a dog, and yet every time I tried to talk about Marley to them, tears welled in my eyes. I told them it was okay to cry, and that owning a dog always ended with this sadness because dogs just don't live as long as people do. I told them how Marley was sleeping when they gave him the shot and that he didn't feel a thing. He just drifted off and was gone. Colleen was upset that she didn't have a chance to say a real good-bye to him; she thought he would be coming home. I told her I had said good-bye for all of us. Conor, our budding author, showed me something he had made for Marley, to go in the grave with him. It was a drawing of a big red heart beneath which he had written: "To Marley, I hope you know how much I loved you all of my life. You were always there when I needed you. Through life or death, I will always love you. Your brother, Conor Richard Grogan." Then Colleen drew a picture of a girl with a big yellow dog and beneath it, with spelling help from her brother, she wrote, "P.S.—I will never forget you."

**inconvenience**
bother;
annoyance

I went out alone and wheeled Marley's body down the hill, where I cut an armful of soft pine boughs that I laid on the floor of the hole. I lifted the heavy body bag off the cart and down into the hole as gently as I could, though there was really no graceful way to do it. I got into the hole, opened the bag to see him one last time, and positioned him in a comfortable, natural way—just as he might be lying in front of the fireplace, curled up, head tucked around to his side. "Okay, big guy, this is it," I said. I closed the bag up and returned to the house to get Jenny and the kids.

As a family, we walked down to the grave. Conor and Colleen had sealed their notes back-to-back in a plastic bag, and I placed it right beside Marley's head. Patrick used his jackknife to cut five pine boughs, one for each of us. One by one, we dropped them in the hole, their scent rising around us. We paused for a moment, then all together, as if we had rehearsed it, said, "Marley, we love you." I picked up the shovel and tossed the first scoop of dirt in. It slapped heavily on the plastic, making an ugly sound, and Jenny began to weep. I kept shoveling. The kids stood watching in silence.

When the hole was half filled, I took a break and we all walked up to the house, where we sat around the kitchen table and told funny Marley stories. One minute tears were welling in our eyes, the next we were laughing. . . . I told about all the leashes he had **severed** and the time he peed on our neighbor's ankle. We described all the things he had destroyed and the thousands of dollars he had cost us. We could laugh about it now. To make the kids feel better, I told them something I did not quite believe. "Marley's spirit is up in dog heaven now," I said. "He's in a giant golden meadow, running free. And his hips are good again. And his hearing is back, and his eyesight is sharp, and he has all his teeth. He's back in his prime[1]—chasing rabbits all day long."

**severed**
cut (in Marley's case "chewed through")

"Marley's spirit is up in dog heaven now," I said. "He's in a giant golden meadow, running free."

Jenny added, "And having endless screen doors to crash through." The image of him barging his way oafishly[2] through heaven got a laugh out of everyone.

The morning was slipping away, and I still needed to go to work. I went back down to his grave alone and finished filling the hole, gently, respectfully, using my boot to tamp down the loose earth. When the hole was flush with the ground, I placed two large rocks from the woods on top of it, then went inside, took a hot shower, and drove to the office.

In the days immediately after we buried Marley, the whole family went silent. The animal that was the amusing target of so many hours of conversation and stories over the years had become a taboo[3] topic. We were trying to return our lives to normal, and speaking of him only made it harder. Colleen in particular could not bear to hear his name or see his photo. Tears would well in her eyes and she would clench her fists and say angrily, "I don't want to talk about him!"

---

1 **prime**: the most active part; short for "the prime of his life"

2 **oafishly**: clumsily; like a klutz

3 **taboo**: forbidden; prohibited

I resumed my schedule, driving to work, writing my column, coming home again. Every night for thirteen years he had waited for me at the door. Walking in now at the end of the day was the most painful part of all. The house seemed silent, empty, not quite a home anymore. Jenny vacuumed like a fiend, determined to get up the bucketsful of Marley fur that had been falling out in **massive** clumps for the past couple of years, insinuating[4] itself into every **crevice** and fold. Slowly, the signs of the old dog were being erased. One morning I went to put my shoes on, and inside them, covering the insoles, lay a carpet of Marley fur, picked up by my socks from walking on the floors and gradually deposited inside the shoes. I just sat and looked at it—actually petted it with two fingers—and smiled. I held it up to show Jenny and said, "We're not getting rid of him that easy." She laughed, but that evening in our bedroom, Jenny—who had not said much all week—blurted out: "I miss him. I mean I really, *really* miss him. I ache-inside miss him."

**massive**
huge

**crevice**
a crack

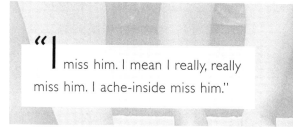

"I miss him. I mean I really, really miss him. I ache-inside miss him."

"I know," I said. "I do, too."

I wanted to write a farewell column to Marley, but I was afraid all my emotion would pour out into a gushy, maudlin piece of self-indulgence[5] that would only humiliate me. So I stuck with topics less dear to my heart. I did, however, carry a tape recorder with me, and when a thought came to me, I would get it down. I knew I wanted to portray him as he was and not as some impossibly perfect reincarnation[6] of Old Yeller or Rin Tin Tin,[7] as if there were any danger of that. So many people remake their pets in death, turning them

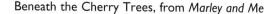

4 **insinuating**: slowly sneaking

5 **maudlin piece of self-indulgence**: something that is overly sentimental, done to make oneself feel better

6 **reincarnation**: the belief that one can be reborn into a new being

7 **Old Yeller, Rin Tin Tin**: names of heroic dogs in childhood novels

into supernatural,[8] noble beasts that in life did everything for their masters except fry eggs for breakfast. I wanted to be honest. Marley was a funny, bigger-than-life pain . . . who never quite got the hang of the whole chain-of-command thing. Honestly, he might well have been the world's worst-behaved dog. Yet he **intuitively** grasped from the start what it meant to be man's best friend.

> **intuitively**
> naturally;
> instinctively

During the week after his death, I walked down the hill several times to stand by his grave. Partly, I wanted to make sure no wild animals were coming around at night. The grave remained undisturbed, but already I could see that in the spring I would need to add a couple wheelbarrows of soil to fill the **depression** where it was settling. Mostly I just wanted to commune[9] with him. Standing there, I found myself replaying random snippets[10] from his life. I was embarrassed by how deep my grief went for this dog, deeper than for some humans I had known. It's not that I **equated** a dog's life with a human's, but outside my immediate family few people had given themselves so selflessly[11] to me. Secretly, I brought Marley's choker chain in from the car, where it had sat since his final ride to the hospital, and stashed it beneath the underwear in my dresser, where each morning I could reach down and touch it.

> **depression**
> hollow; dip

> **equated**
> compared;
> regarded as
> equal

I walked around all week with a dull ache inside. It was actually physical, not unlike a stomach virus. I was **lethargic**, unmotivated. I couldn't even muster[12] the energy to **indulge** my hobbies—playing guitar, woodworking, reading. I felt out of sorts, not sure what to do with myself. I ended up going to bed early most nights, at nine-thirty, ten o'clock.

> **lethargic**
> slow-moving;
> sluggish

> **indulge**
> find time for
> and enjoy

That weekend I took a long walk through the woods, and by the time I arrived at work on Monday, I knew what I wanted to say about the dog that touched my life, the one I would never forget.

---

8 **supernatural**: being more than what can be seen in nature

9 **commune**: communicate; connect

10 **snippets**: small pieces

11 **selflessly**: unselfishly

12 **muster**: collect; generate

I began the column by describing my walk down the hill with the shovel at dawn and how odd it was to be outdoors without Marley, who for thirteen years had made it his business to be at my side for any **excursion**. "And now here I was alone," I wrote, "digging him this hole."

I quoted my father who, when I told him I had to put the old guy down, gave the closest thing to a compliment my dog had ever received: "There will never be another dog like Marley."

I gave a lot of thought to how I should describe him, and this is what I settled on: "No one ever called him a great dog—or even a good dog. He was as wild as a banshee[13] and as strong as a bull. He crashed joyously through life with a gusto[14] most often associated with natural disasters. He's the only dog I've ever known to get expelled from obedience school." I continued: "Marley was a chewer of couches, a slasher of screens, a slinger of drool, a tipper of trash cans. As for brains, let me just say he chased his tail till the day he died, apparently convinced he was on the verge of a major canine breakthrough." There was more to him than that, however, and I described his **intuition** and **empathy**, his gentleness with children, his pure heart.

What I really wanted to say was how this animal had touched our souls and taught us some of the most important lessons of our lives. "A person can learn a lot from a dog, even a loopy one like ours," I wrote. "Marley taught me about living each day with unbridled exuberance[15] and joy, about seizing the moment and following your heart. He taught me to appreciate the simple things—a walk in the woods, a fresh snowfall, a nap in a **shaft** of winter sunlight. And as he grew old and achy, he taught me about **optimism** in the face of **adversity**. Mostly, he taught me about friendship and selflessness and, above all else, **unwavering** loyalty."

**excursion**
an adventure or trip

**intuition**
instinct; knowing something without thinking about it

**empathy**
sensitivity to others' feelings

**shaft**
a narrow beam of light

**optimism**
the feeling that things will turn out well

**adversity**
difficulty

**unwavering**
never changing

---

13 **banshee**: in folklore, a wailing female spirit

14 **gusto**: enthusiasm; passion

15 **unbridled exuberance**: uncontrolled enthusiasm

It was an amazing concept that I was only now, in the wake of his death, fully absorbing: Marley as mentor.[16] As teacher and role model. Was it possible for a dog—any dog, but especially a nutty, wildly uncontrollable one like ours—to point humans to the things that really mattered in life? I believed it was. Loyalty. Courage. Devotion. Simplicity. Joy. And the things that did not matter, too. A dog has no use for fancy cars or big homes or designer clothes. Status symbols[17] mean nothing to him. A waterlogged stick will do just fine. A dog judges others not by their color or creed[18] or class but by who they are inside. A dog doesn't care if you are rich or poor, educated or **illiterate**, clever or dull. Give him your heart and he will give you his. It was really quite simple, and yet we humans, so much wiser and more sophisticated, have always had trouble figuring out what really counts and what does not. As I wrote that farewell column to Marley, I realized it was all right there in front of us, if only we opened our eyes. Sometimes it took a dog with bad breath, worse manners, and pure intentions to help us see.

    I finished my column, turned it in to my editor, and drove home for the night, feeling somehow lighter, almost **buoyant**, as though a weight I did not even know I had been carrying was lifted from me.

**illiterate**
unable to read and write; uneducated

**buoyant**
cheerful; upbeat

---

16 **mentor**: advisor; guide

17 **status symbols**: items such as cars, jewelry, large homes, and so forth that present an image of wealth or importance

18 **creed**: faith; belief

# Reviewing

## Marley and Me

### Discussing the Selection

1. What are some of the things that Marley did that exasperated the Grogans? And what things endeared him to the family?

2. Point out some passages in the essay that show the extent of the Grogans' feelings about Marley.

3. What does the author mean when he says that Marley was his "mentor"?

4. What was your opinion of this selection? Did you find it funny, sad, challenging? Discuss your ideas with the class.

### Writing a Story

Is there anyone who doesn't have a funny pet story? Many pets have a talent for getting into trouble or have personalities that can make them a challenge. Write a story about a real or imaginary pet. First think about the plot of your story—how the story begins, what develops, and how it ends. Next, think about how you want the main character or characters to appear, and how you will describe them. Then—start writing!

### About John Grogan (1957–)

Michigan-born writer John Grogan started his career in high school, reporting for the school newspaper. After college, he worked as both a writer and editor before landing his dream job as a columnist for the *Philadelphia Inquirer*. His column about Marley, his family's unruly but large-hearted dog, attracted hundreds of letters from sympathetic readers. Inspired, he went on to write the bestselling memoir: *Marley and Me: Life and Love with the World's Worst Dog*. Grogan claims it is "not so much a 'dog book' as the story of a family in the making and the bigger-than-life animal that helped shape it." Grogan lives in the Pennsylvania countryside with his "three children, four chickens, and a surprisingly calm Labrador retriever puppy named Gracie."

# Understanding Drama

While plays are written to be performed, and this is certainly the best way to enjoy them, you can still experience drama by reading it. This is a great way to practice your visualizing skills. As you read a play, try to see the characters moving through the scenery and imagine how they sound.

In a good play, nothing is left to chance. Each character, change of scene, and line of dialogue is chosen carefully. Plays are more narrowly focused than novels and movies, with fewer characters, less action, and usually one dominant theme. Here are the main elements of drama.

**Cast of Characters**  The list of a play's characters is found at the beginning of a play. The playwright might add the briefest description; for example: **Lord Capulet,** *Juliet's father.* When you are reading the play, refer back to the cast of characters as often as necessary until you are familiar with everyone.

**Acts and Scenes**  An act is a large division of a full-length play, sometimes separated from the other act or acts by an intermission. A scene is a section of the play that occurs in one time and place. Each act may have one or several scenes. As you read a scene, try to visualize the set as well as the characters on the stage.

**Dialogue**  Dialogue refers to the words that characters speak to each other. In drama, great characters are defined by the quality of their dialogue—the juicier, the better. In a script, a character's words directly follow his or her name. This manuscript style helps the actors learn and keep their lines straight. When you are reading a character's lines, try to imagine what that person looks like and how he or she might speak.

**Stage Directions**  Stage directions are exactly that—instructions for the people who are putting on the play. The directions are usually printed in italic type. They describe the setting and tell actors where and how to move or say their lines. Some playwrights like to provide detailed descriptions of the scenery, lighting, costumes, and sound. Others leave such decisions for the play's director, actors, and production crew. Don't skip the stage directions when you are reading a play—they provide valuable information about the playwright's intent.

# Previewing

## These Shoes of Mine
by Gary Soto

## Reading Connection

Most Mexican Americans are very family-oriented. They believe they have a duty to help their immediate family as well as relatives in Mexico or those newly arrived in the United States. This strong support system has enabled them to survive poverty and difficult years. Working long, backbreaking hours in fields and factories, many recent immigrants from Mexico struggle to live on poverty-level wages.

## Skill Focus: Reading Plays

Reading a play requires some extra attention if you want to get the most out of it. Before you begin reading, review the Cast of Characters. In this play, you should also skim the setting, props, and costume details to get a sense of how the play should look when staged. Another element special to this play is the amount of Spanish the characters speak. Each speech in Spanish is followed by the English translation in brackets. If you have trouble with the pronunciation, ask a Spanish-speaking friend to help you.

## Vocabulary Builder
Here are a few good words to add to your writing and speaking vocabularies.

| | | | |
|---|---|---|---|
| moody | dejectedly | immigrant | absorbs |
| transfixed | | | |

# These **Shoes**
## of **Mine**

Gary Soto

## CAST OF CHARACTERS

MANUEL

MOTHER

ANGEL, *the school bully*

ELENA, *Manuel's sister*

MANUEL'S relatives

TÍO JOSÉ, *Manuel's uncle*

CECI, *the girl whom Manuel likes*

PARTYGOERS

## SETS

Living room of Manuel's house

A street in the neighborhood

Bedroom of Manuel's house

## PROPS

A sewing machine

A clunky pair of boy's shoes

A new pair of penny loafers

A letter

A wrapped birthday present

Two cots with pillows

## COSTUMES

Everyday clothes

•••••••••••••••••••••••••••••••

(MANUEL *paces back and forth in big clunky shoes while his mother sits at a table sewing patches onto a pair of pants.*)

**MANUEL**. (*indicating his shoes*). Look at them!

**MOTHER**. They're nice, *mi'jo* [my son].

**MANUEL**. Nice! They're too big! They're old! They're ugly. (*stomps his feet*) And can you hear them?

**MOTHER**. They're like drums.

(MANUEL *stomps louder.*)

**MOTHER**. No, like congas.[1]

---

1 **congas**: tall drums played with the hands

**MANUEL.** Everyone will hear me. They'll laugh and say, "Here comes Manuel in his big ugly shoes."

**MOTHER.** *Mi'jo*, it will be like music from your feet.

**MANUEL.** (*kicking up a shoe*). And look. There's a start of a hole on the bottom. Rain will get in. (*desperately*) And they're from the thrift store.

**MOTHER.** Sure, they're a little bit used, but these shoes are new for you.

**MANUEL.** Mom!

**MOTHER.** Manuel, new things cost money.

(MANUEL'S *sister enters stage left,[2] balancing three boxes of shoes and slowly walking across the stage.*)

**MANUEL.** But look at Elena! She's got new shoes. Lots of them!

**MOTHER.** She saved her money for them. And what did you do with your money?

**moody**
gloomy; in a
bad mood

(MANUEL *forces a **moody** face.*)

**MOTHER.** Come on. *Dime.* [Tell me.] Tell me.

**MANUEL.** (*low voice*). I bought a hundred ice creams.

**MOTHER.** Louder!

**MANUEL.** I bought a hundred ice creams for my friends. (*pause*) I should have bought a bicycle. Then I could ride by real fast and no one would see that I have ugly shoes.

(*Telephone rings, and the mother gets up to answer it. Her face brightens as she hears a relative's voice.*)

---

2 **stage left**: the area of the stage to the actor's left as he or she faces the audience

**MOTHER**. *¿Quién es? ¿Pablo? ¿Dónde está? En Chula Vista. Pues, Fresno no es muy lejos. Por Grehound dos días, no más.* [Who is this? Pablo? Where are you? In Chula Vista. Well, Fresno is not very far. No more than two days by Greyhound (bus).]

(*Her voice fades, but she keeps talking into the telephone.*)

**MANUEL**. (*to audience*). Mom's always helping relatives from Mexico. (*mocking*) "Please, stay with us. Don't worry. We have room for you." And me? I get stuck with old shoes or . . . (*looking at table piled with sewing, among it a patched-up pair of old pants*) or jeans like these.

(*Lights fade, then come up on* MANUEL *and his mother.* MANUEL *holds up a pair of brand-new loafers.*)

**MOTHER**. Take care of them. They're for your birthday, except early.

**MANUEL**. Thanks, mom! They're really nice.

(*He hugs his mother, kicks off his old shoes, and starts to put on the new loafers.*)

**MOTHER**. They're called loafers. *Mira* [Look], you can put pennies in them.

**MANUEL**. Where?

**MOTHER**. Here. In these slots. (*bends to put in pennies*) That's why they're called penny loafers.

(MANUEL *clicks the heels of his penny loafers;* MOTHER *leaves stage.*)

**MANUEL**. But why should I put pennies in? I'd rather have dimes!

(MANUEL *bends to insert two shiny dimes in the slots. He walks around the stage, admiring his shoes.* **Transfixed** *by the shoes, he doesn't notice* ANGEL, *the school bully, who has come onstage, "tagging"*[3] *walls.*)

**transfixed**
fascinated;
amazed

3 **"tagging"**: a slang term for applying graffiti

**ANGEL**. What's wrong with you, homes?[4] You *loco*?[5]

**MANUEL**. Oh, hi, Angel!

**ANGEL**. There's something different about you . . .
(*circles* MANUEL) How come you're wearing those kind of shoes? You look like a nerd, homes.

**MANUEL**. They're penny loafers. Stylish, huh?

**ANGEL**. (*pointing*). What's that?

**MANUEL**. What's what?

**ANGEL**. That shine! Looks like dimes. Give 'em up!

**MANUEL**. (*whining*). Angel.

**ANGEL**. Come on! Give 'em up. I could use a soda. Yeah, a root beer would make me feel real happy.

(MANUEL *squeezes the dimes from his shoes. He hands the dimes over to* Angel *who leaves, flipping the coins.* MANUEL *walks **dejectedly** back to his house. He takes the shoes off and throws them into a box.*)

**dejectedly**
sadly; unhappily

**MANUEL**. (*to audience*). Months pass. My mom keeps taking in relatives from Mexico, and I keep on wearing my old shoes.

(RELATIVES *march in a line across the stage; then his mother appears holding a letter. She sniffs the letter.*)

**MANUEL**. (*to audience*). And you know what else happens? I grow two inches. I get big. I can feel my shoulders rise like mountains . . . well, more like hills. But still, they get bigger . . . Then, I get an invitation.

**MOTHER**. Manuel, here's a letter . . . from a girl.

---

4 **homes**: shorthand slang for homeboy; friend

5 **loco**: Spanish for crazy

**MANUEL**.  A girl wrote to me?

**MOTHER**.  (*holding it under the light*). Yeah, it says—

**MANUEL**.  Mom! It's personal!

(MANUEL *takes the letter from his mother, who leaves stage.*)

**MANUEL**.  Wow! An invitation to Ceci's birthday party. "Games and dancing" and "Dress to impress."

(MANUEL *runs offstage.* MOTHER *and* TÍO [Uncle] JOSÉ, *a Mexican* **immigrant**, *enter.*)

**MOTHER**.  Let me show you your room. You'll share it with Manuel.

**TÍO JOSÉ**.  (*looking about*). Nice place, ¡Y que grande! [And how big!]

(*The two exit;* MANUEL *enters wearing a tie and holding a wrapped gift. He looks down at his old shoes.*)

**MANUEL**.  I can't wear these shoes.

(*He turns to the box holding his loafers. He takes out the loafers, fits in two dimes, and then struggles to put them on.*)

**MANUEL**.  Hmmm, kind of tight. Guess my feet were growing with the rest of me.

(Manuel *walks around stage, taking hurtful steps.*)

**MANUEL**.  But I got to go to the party! It's going to be a good one.

(MANUEL *walks painfully, crawls, swims, then gets back to his feet.*)

**MANUEL**.  Maybe if I walk backward, my toes won't feel so jammed.

(MANUEL *begins to walk backward, sighing with relief.*)

**MANUEL**.  Wow, the world looks different. The birds look different, and the cars, and those kids over there on their bikes.

> **immigrant**
> a person who goes to another country to live

THE GIFT, Diana Ong, 2003

**absorbs**
takes in

(*As* MANUEL **absorbs** *the world in his backward walk,* CECI *and* PARTYGOERS *come onstage.* MANUEL *bumps into* CECI.)

**MANUEL**. Sorry, Ceci.

**CECI**. That's okay. How come you're walking backward?

**MANUEL**. Oh, you know, to see how the world looks from the other direction. (paus*e*) Also, I'm inventing a dance.

**CECI**. You're what?

**MANUEL**. A new dance. It's called . . . the Backward Caterpillar.

(MANUEL *demonstrates by cha-chaing[6] backward.* CECI *and* PARTYGOERS *fall in line and cha-cha backward, too.*)

**CECI**.  Look at Manuel slide in his new shoes!

(PARTYGOERS *ad-lib[7]* "Cool shoes," "Look at the dude slide," "Manuel's the best!" PARTYGOERS *cha-cha off the stage. Lights dim, then come up on* MANUEL *and* TÍO JOSÉ *in their beds, ready to go to sleep, their hands folded behind their heads.*)

**MANUEL**.  Doesn't that crack in the ceiling look like lightning?

**TÍO JOSÉ**.  *Sí* [Yes], it does. And that one over there looks like a pair
    of scissors, *¿qué no* [doesn't it]? (*pause*)
    You have a good life, *muchacho* [boy]. A nice house and plenty
    to eat. Your mama's a good cook.

**MANUEL**.  I am lucky. And I had good luck at Ceci's party.

**TÍO JOSÉ**.  (*getting up*) Wish me luck tomorrow. I'm going to
    Modesto. I think I got a job in a restaurant there.

**MANUEL**.  How will you get there?

(TÍO JOSÉ *sits up.*)

**TÍO JOSÉ**.  (*hooking thumb into a "hitchhiking" manner*). *Un poquito de
    éste* [A little of this] and lots of walking. *Pero mira, mis huaraches
    son rasquachis.* [But look, my sandals are cheap, worn out.]
    (*laughing*) I hope they can make it to Modesto.

**MOTHER**.  (*offstage*). José! *¡Teléfono!* [Telephone]

(*When* TÍO JOSÉ *leaves*, MANUEL *examines his uncle's worn sandals.*
MANUEL *scribbles a note as lights dim. Lights come up on* TÍO JOSÉ *and*
MANUEL *asleep;* TÍO JOSÉ *rises, sleepily rubbing his face. A rooster crows
offstage.*)

---

6 **cha-chaing**: doing the cha-cha, a Latin-style dance

7 **ad-lib**: make up things to say on-the-spot

**TÍO JOSÉ**.  It's morning already. (*eyes* MANUEL'S *shiny shoes at foot of his bed*) What's this?

(TÍO JOSÉ *reads note and shakes his nephew awake.*)

**TÍO JOSÉ**.  These shoes? For me? They're too nice for a worker like me.

**MANUEL**.  You have a long way to go, Tío, and you need good shoes.

(TÍO JOSÉ *is touched by this gesture. He puts on shoes and walks a few steps as he tries them out.*)

**TÍO JOSÉ**.  They're perfect. *Adiós* [Goodbye], Manuel. These shoes will take me a long ways, and by the time they are worn out, you'll be as tall as your parents. They'll be looking up to you.

(TÍO JOSÉ *walks offstage and* MANUEL *lowers his head back onto the pillow.*)

# Reviewing

## These Shoes of Mine

### Discussing the Selection

1. How would you describe Manuel? Use examples from the play that display his true character.

2. What is Manuel's main problem? How well does he handle this situation?

3. Do all of the characters in this play come alive for you? Point out any dialogue that sounds especially authentic.

4. Both *These Shoes of Mine* and the short story "The Circuit" describe the difficulties of living in poor immigrant households. Compare and contrast Manuel with the narrator of "The Circuit."

### Writing a Character Analysis

Sometimes actors write out the back stories, or personal histories, of the characters they are going to play. Imagining their backgrounds can help them feel closer to the character and gives them some ideas about a character's motivation (what drives an individual to act a certain way). Write a back story for any of the main characters in the play. Keep it as realistic as possible.

### About Gary Soto (1952–)

When Gary Soto was five years old, his father died in a factory accident. Like many Mexican Americans in California's Central Valley, the Soto family worked as migrant laborers and had little time to encourage their children's reading. Soto developed into one of the nation's outstanding writers with the support of an inspiring college professor. Soto taught at the University of California, Berkeley, before retiring to write fiction, nonfiction, and film scripts for readers of all ages. His writing draws heavily on his Chicano heritage and the vivid street life of his youth. He has been recognized with a host of distinguished literary prizes including the National Book Award. His goal is to help the next generation of Mexican American writers.

## Unit Three

# BEST OF FRIENDS?

*The only way to have a friend is to be one.*

Ralph Waldo Emerson

A shared theme of friendship unites the selections in Unit Three. Some images of friends are easy to spot, and others ask you to test your imagination. For example, can animals be friends? Can soldiers fighting on different sides of a brutal war declare a friendly truce . . . for an hour or an evening of shared fun? What about a chance encounter on the street? The writers in this unit explore companionship—or its lack—in settings as diverse as city streets, Civil War battlefields, and an imaginary beach. Some of the relationships are permanent, others temporary, and others a figment of the imagination. Look for the value in all of them.

# Building Vocabulary

## Suffixes

A **suffix** is a word part added to the end of a root or base word to change its meaning in some way. This change in meaning is usually small. For example, *art* could change to *artist*, or *free* could change to *freedom*. Sometimes, however, a suffix makes a big difference. For example, adding *–less* to *hope* makes *hopeless*.

Sometimes suffixes are added to whole words that you already know. You can often figure out the meaning of an unfamiliar word if you see that it contains a suffix.

| SUFFIX | MEANING | EXAMPLES |
|--------|---------|----------|
| ant, ent | one who; likely to | complainant, resident |
| fy, ify | to make, form into, or become | comfy, beautify |
| ty, ity | quality, state, or condition | specialty, reality |
| ive | having the quality of; tending to | active, productive |
| ize | to cause to be, become, or make | alphabetize, fertilize |
| ous, eous | full of or having qualities of | dangerous, beauteous |

By adding a suffix to a base or root word, you often change its part of speech. Watch what happens to the base word *popular*, depending on what suffix is attached:

**Adjective**   popular, populous         **Noun**   population

**Verb**   populate, popularize           **Adverb**   popularly

Look at the following examples of words from this book.

*Suffixes That Indicate Nouns:* black*ness*, predictab*ility*, pedestr*ians*, handl*ers*, neighbor*hood*
*Suffixes That Indicate Verbs:* frigh*ten*, agit*ate*, custom*ize*, pur*ify*
*Suffixes That Indicate Adjectives:* heed*less*, practic*al*, monstr*ous*, supersti*tious*
*Adverbs* typically end in the suffix*–ly*: selfish*ly*, greed*ily*, sudden*ly*.

# Previewing

## The Dog of Pompeii
by Louis Untermeyer

### Reading Connection
The ancient Italian city of Pompeii was buried by the eruption of nearby Mount Vesuvius in 79 A.D. Two thousand residents were buried under tons of ashes and molten lava, and thousands of others fled for their lives. Pompeii lay undisturbed for nearly 1700 years. It was discovered in 1748, when a farm worker accidentally dug into one of its buried walls. As the ancient city was unearthed, scholars were able to piece together the daily lives of the citizens by studying the possessions and even clothing of these unfortunate victims.

### Skill Focus: Distinguishing Fact from Fiction
Historical fiction combines fact and fiction. By blending imaginary elements with real events from the past, authors can bring history to life. A fact is something that can be proved to be true. Fiction is anything that the author most likely made up—which might be parts of the plot, some or all of the characters, and probably all of the dialogue. As you read "The Dog of Pompeii," think about what is most likely true and what the author has probably invented.

### Vocabulary Builder
The following words are defined on the page of the story where they occur. Note that most have a suffix that indicates the word's part of speech.

| | | | |
|---|---|---|---|
| stodgy | corrupted | lurching | bellowed |
| romp | pondering | dislodging | thronging |
| ambitious | mock | bewildered | vapors |

The ruins of Pompeii with Mount Vesuvius in the background

# The **Dog** of **Pompeii**

Louis Untermeyer

Tito and his dog Bimbo lived (if you could call it living) under the wall where it joined the inner gate. They really didn't live there; they just slept there. They lived anywhere. Pompeii was one of the gayest of the old Latin towns, but although Tito was never an unhappy boy, he was not exactly a merry one. The streets were always lively with shining chariots and bright red trappings; the open-air theaters rocked with laughing crowds; sham[1] battles and athletic sports were free for the asking in the great stadium. Once a year the Caesar[2] visited the pleasure city, and the fireworks lasted for days; the sacrifices[3] in the forum were better than a show. But Tito saw none of these things. He was blind—had been blind from birth. He was known to everyone in the poorer quarters. But no one could say how old he was; no one remembered his parents; no one could tell where he came from. Bimbo was another mystery. As long as people could remember seeing Tito—about twelve or thirteen years—they had seen Bimbo. Bimbo had never left his side. He was not only dog but nurse, pillow, playmate, mother, and father to Tito.

---

1 **sham**: pretend; bogus
2 **Caesar**: the title of Roman emperor
3 **sacrifices**: rituals in which animals or objects were offered up to the gods

Did I say Bimbo never left his master? (Perhaps I had better say comrade, for if anyone was the master, it was Bimbo.) I was wrong. Bimbo did trust Tito alone exactly three times a day. It was a fixed routine, a custom understood between boy and dog since the beginning of their friendship, and the way it worked was this: Early in the morning, shortly after dawn, while Tito was still dreaming, Bimbo would disappear. When Tito woke, Bimbo would be sitting quietly at his side, his ears cocked, his stump of a tail tapping the ground, and a fresh-baked bread—more like a large round roll—at his feet. Tito would stretch himself; Bimbo would yawn; then they would breakfast. At noon, no matter where they happened to be, Bimbo would put his paw on Tito's knee, and the two of them would return to the inner gate. Tito would curl up in the corner (almost like a dog) and go to sleep, while Bimbo, looking quite important (almost like a boy), would disappear again. In half an hour he'd be back with their lunch. Sometimes it would be a piece of fruit or a scrap of meat; often it was nothing but a dry crust. But sometimes there would be one of those flat, rich cakes, sprinkled with raisins and sugar, that Tito liked so much. At suppertime the same thing happened, although there was a little less of everything, for things were hard to snatch in the evening with the streets full of people. Besides, Bimbo didn't approve of too much food before going to sleep. A heavy supper made boys too restless and dogs too **stodgy**—and it

**stodgy**
dull; slow

was the business of a dog to sleep lightly with one ear open and muscles ready for action.

But whether there was much or little, hot or cold, fresh or dry, food was always there. Tito never asked where it came from, and Bimbo never told him. There was plenty of rainwater in the hollows of soft stones; the old egg-woman at the corner sometimes gave him a cupful of strong goat's milk; in the grape season the fat winemaker let him have drippings of the mild juice. So there was no danger of going hungry or thirsty. There was plenty of everything in Pompeii if you knew where to find it—and if you had a dog like Bimbo.

**romp**
to play in a rough and noisy way

As I said before, Tito was not the merriest boy in Pompeii. He could not **romp** with the other youngsters and play hare and hounds and I spy and follow-your-master and ball-against-the-building and jackstones and kings and robbers with them. But that did not make him sorry for himself. If he could not see the sights that delighted the lads of Pompeii, he could hear and smell things they never noticed. He could really see more with his ears and his nose than they could with their eyes. When he and Bimbo went out walking, he knew just where they were going and exactly what was happening.

> He could really see more with his ears and his nose than they could with their eyes.

"Ah," he'd sniff and say as they passed a handsome villa, "Glaucus Pansa is giving a grand dinner tonight. They're going to have three kinds of bread, and roast pigling, and stuffed goose, and a great stew—I think bear stew—and fig pie." And Bimbo would note that this would be a good place to visit tomorrow.

Or, "H'm," Tito would murmur, half through his lips, half through his nostrils. "The wife of Marcus Lucretius is expecting her mother. She's shaking out every piece of goods in the house; she's going to use the best clothes—the ones she's been keeping in pine needles and camphor[4]—and there's an extra girl in the kitchen. Come, Bimbo, let's get out of the dust!"

Or, as they passed a small but elegant dwelling opposite the public baths, "Too bad! The tragic poet is ill again. It must be a bad fever this time, for they're trying smoke fumes instead of medicine. Whew! I'm glad I'm not a tragic poet!"

Or, as they neared the forum, "Mm-m! What good things they have in the macellum today!" (It really was a sort of butcher-grocer-marketplace, but Tito didn't know any better. He called it the macellum.) "Dates from Africa, and salt oysters from sea caves, and cuttlefish, and new honey, and sweet onions, and—ugh!—water buffalo steaks. Come, let's see what's what in the forum." And Bimbo, just as curious as his comrade, hurried on. Being a dog, he trusted his ears and nose (like Tito) more than his eyes. And so the two of them entered the center of Pompeii.

---

4 **camphor**: a strong-smelling substance used to protect clothes from moths

The forum was the part of the town to which everybody came at least once during each day. It was the central square, and everything happened here. There were no private houses; all was public—the chief temples, the gold and red bazaars,[5] the silk shops, the town hall, the booths belonging to the weavers and jewel merchants, the wealthy woolen market, the shrine of the household gods. Everything glittered here. The buildings looked as if they were new—which, in a sense, they were. The earthquake of twelve years ago had brought down all the old structures, and since the citizens of Pompeii were **ambitious** to rival Naples and even Rome, they had seized the opportunity to rebuild the whole town. And they had done it all within a dozen years. There was scarcely a building that was older than Tito.

**ambitious**
wanting honor
and success

Tito had heard a great deal about the earthquake, though being about a year old at the time, he could scarcely remember it. This particular quake had been a light one—as earthquakes go. The weaker houses had been shaken down; parts of the outworn wall had been wrecked; but there was little loss of life, and the brilliant new Pompeii had taken the place of the old. No one knew what caused these earthquakes. Records showed they had happened in the neighborhood since the beginning of time. Sailors said that it was to teach the lazy city folk a lesson and make them appreciate those who risked the dangers of the sea to bring them luxuries and protect their town from invaders. The priests said that the gods took this way of showing their anger to those who refused to worship properly and who failed to bring enough sacrifices to the altars and (though they didn't say it in so many words) presents to the priests. The tradesmen said that the foreign merchants had **corrupted** the ground and it was no longer safe to traffic[6] in imported goods that came from strange places and carried a curse with them. Everyone had a different explanation—and everyone's explanation was louder and sillier than his neighbor's.

**corrupted**
spoiled; ruined

They were talking about it this afternoon as Tito and Bimbo came out of the side street into the public square. The forum was the favorite promenade[7] for rich and poor. What with the priests arguing with the politicians, servants

---

5 **bazaar**: a marketplace with many small shops

6 **traffic**: to buy and sell

7 **promenade**: a public walkway or boulevard

doing the day's shopping, tradesmen crying their wares, women displaying the latest fashions from Greece and Egypt, children playing hide-and-seek among the marble columns, knots of soldiers, sailors, peasants from the provinces[8]—to say nothing of those who merely came to lounge and look on—the square was crowded to its last inch. His ears even more that his nose guided Tito to the place where the talk was loudest. It was in front of the shrine of the household gods that, naturally enough, the householders were arguing.

"I tell you," rumbled a voice which Tito recognized as bath master Rufus's, "there won't be another earthquake in my lifetime or yours. There may be a tremble or two, but earthquakes, like lightings, never strike twice in the same place."

"Do they not?" asked a thin voice Tito had never heard. It had a high, sharp ring to it, and Tito knew it as the accent of a stranger. "How about the two towns of Sicily that have been ruined three times within fifteen years by the eruptions of Mount Etna? And were they not warned? And does that column of smoke above Vesuvius mean nothing?"

"That?" Tito could hear the grunt with which one question answered another. "That's always there. We use it for our weather guide. When the smoke stands up straight, we know we'll have fair weather; when it flattens out, it's sure to be foggy; when it drifts to the east—"

"Yes, yes," cut in the edged voice. "I've heard about your mountain barometer.[9] But the column of smoke seems hundreds of feet higher than usual, and it's thickening and spreading like a shadowy tree. They say in Naples—"

"Oh, Naples!" Tito knew this voice by the little squeak that went with it. It was Attilio, the cameo[10] cutter. "*They* talk while we suffer. Little help we got from them last time. Naples commits the crimes, and Pompeii pays the price. It's become a proverb with us. Let them mind their own business."

"Yes," grumbled Rufus, "and others, too."

"Very well, my confident friends," responded the thin voice, which now

---

8 **provinces**: regions far from a country's capital or large cities

9 **barometer**: an instrument used to forecast changes in weather

10 **cameo**: a type of gem with a picture cut onto it

sounded curiously flat. "We also have a proverb—and it is this: Those who will not listen to men must be taught by the gods. I say no more. But I leave a last warning. Remember the holy ones. Look to your temples. And when the smoke tree above Vesuvius grows to the shape of an umbrella pine, look to your lives."

Tito could hear the air whistle as the speaker drew his toga[11] about him, and the quick shuffle of feet told him the stranger had gone.

"Now what," said the cameo cutter, "did he mean by that?"

"I wonder," grunted Rufus. "I wonder."

Tito wondered, too. And Bimbo, his head at a thoughtful angle, looked as if he had been doing a heavy piece of **pondering**. By nightfall the argument had been forgotten. If the smoke had increased, no one saw it in the dark. Besides, it was Caesar's birthday, and the town was in holiday mood. Tito and Bimbo were among the merry makers, dodging the charioteers who shouted at them. A dozen times they almost upset baskets of sweets and jars of Vesuvian wine, said to be as fiery as the streams inside the volcano, and a dozen times they were cursed and cuffed. But Tito never missed his footing. He was thankful for his keen ears and quick instinct—most thankful of all for Bimbo.

They visited the uncovered theater, and though Tito could not see the faces of the actors, he could follow the play better than most of the audience, for their attention wandered—they were distracted by the scenery, the costumes, the by-play, even by themselves—while Tito's whole attention was centered in what he heard. Then to the city walls, where the people of Pompeii watched a **mock** naval battle in which the city was attacked by the sea and saved after thousands of flaming arrows had been exchanged and countless colored torches had been burned. Though the thrill of flaring ships and lighted skies was lost to Tito, the shouts and cheers excited him as much as any, and he cried out with the loudest of them.

The next morning there were *two* of the beloved raisin and sugar cakes for his breakfast. Bimbo was unusually active and thumped his bit of a tail until

---

**pondering**
thinking;
meditating

**mock**
pretend

---

11 **toga**: a loose piece of clothing worn by Romans

Tito was afraid he would wear it out. The boy could not imagine whether Bimbo was urging him to some sort of game or was trying to tell him something. After a while, he ceased to notice Bimbo. He felt drowsy. Last night's late hours had tired him. Besides, there was a heavy mist in the air—no, a thick fog rather than a mist—a fog that got into his throat and scraped it and made him cough. He walked as far as the marine gate[12] to get a breath of the sea. But the blanket of haze had spread all over the bay and even the salt air seemed smoky.

> the blanket of haze had spread all over the bay and even the salt air seemed smoky.

He went to bed before dusk and slept. But he did not sleep well. He had too many dreams—dreams of ships **lurching** in the forum, of losing his way in a screaming crowd, of armies marching across his chest, of being pulled over every rough pavement of Pompeii.

**lurching**
rocking;
swaying

He woke early. Or, rather, he was pulled awake. Bimbo was doing the pulling. The dog had dragged Tito to his feet and was urging the boy along. Somewhere. Where, Tito did not know. His feet stumbled uncertainly; he was still half asleep. For a while he noticed nothing except the fact that it was hard to breathe. The air was hot. And heavy. So heavy that he could taste it. The air, it seemed, had turned to powder, a warm powder that stung his nostrils and burned his sightless eyes.

Then he began to hear sounds. Peculiar sounds. Like animals under the earth. Hissings and groanings and muffled cries that a dying creature might make **dislodging** the stones of his underground cave. There was no doubt of it now. The noises came from underneath. He not only heard them—he could feel them. The earth twitched; the twitching changed to an uneven shrugging of the soil. Then, as Bimbo half pulled, half coaxed him across, the ground jerked away from his feet and he was thrown against a stone fountain.

**dislodging**
removing;
freeing

The water—hot water—splashing in his face revived him. He got to his feet, Bimbo steadying him, helping him on again. The noises grew louder; they

12 **marine gate:** a gate in the wall separating the city from the sea

came closer. The cries were even more animal-like than before, but now they came from human throats. A few people, quicker of foot and more hurried by fear, began to rush by. A family or two—then a section—then, it seemed, an army broken out of bounds. Tito, **bewildered** though he was, could recognize Rufus as he **bellowed** past him, like a water buffalo gone mad. Time was lost in a nightmare.

It was then the crashing began. First a sharp crackling, like a monstrous snapping of twigs; then a roar like the fall of a whole forest of trees; then an explosion that tore earth and sky. The heavens, though Tito could not see them, were shot through with continual flickerings of fire. Lightnings above were answered by thunders beneath. A house fell. Then another. By a miracle the two companions had escaped the dangerous side streets and were in a more open space. It was the forum. They rested here awhile—how long he did not know.

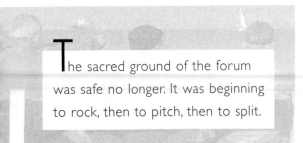

The sacred ground of the forum was safe no longer. It was beginning to rock, then to pitch, then to split.

Tito had no idea of the time of day. He could *feel* it was black—an unnatural blackness. Something inside—perhaps the lack of breakfast and lunch—told him it was past noon. But it didn't matter. Nothing seemed to matter. He was getting drowsy, too drowsy to walk. But walk he must. He knew it. And Bimbo knew it; the sharp tugs told him so. Nor was it a moment too soon. The sacred ground of the forum was safe no longer. It was beginning to rock, then to pitch, then to split. As they stumbled out of the square, the earth wriggled like a caught snake, and all the columns of the temple of Jupiter[13] came down. It was the end of the world—or so it seemed.

To walk was not enough now. They must run. Tito was too frightened to know what to do or where to go. He had lost all sense of direction. He started

---

13 **Jupiter**: also called Jove—the supreme god in Roman myth. He ruled the heavens and weather.

to go back to the inner gate; but Bimbo, straining his back to the last inch, almost pulled his clothes from him. What did the creature want? Had the dog gone mad?

Then, suddenly, he understood. Bimbo was telling him the way out— urging him there. The sea gate—and then the sea. Far from falling buildings, heaving ground. He turned, Bimbo guiding him across open pits and dangerous pools of bubbling mud, away from buildings that had caught fire and were dropping their burning beams. Tito could no longer tell whether the noises were made by the shrieking sky or the agonized people. He and Bimbo ran on—the only silent beings in a howling world.

> **S**uddenly it seemed too late for Tito. The red hot ashes blistered his skin; the stinging vapors tore his throat.

New dangers threatened. All Pompeii seemed to be **thronging** toward the marine gate; and, squeezing among the crowds, there was the chance of being trampled to death. But the chance had to be taken. It was growing harder and harder to breathe. What air there was choked him. It was all dust now—dust and pebbles, pebbles as large as beans. They fell on his head, his hands—pumice[14] stones from the black heart of Vesuvius. The mountain was turning itself inside out. Tito remembered a phrase that the stranger had said in the forum two days ago: "Those who will not listen to men must be taught by the gods." The people of Pompeii had refused to heed the warnings; they were being taught now—if it was not too late.

**thronging**
crowding; pressing together

Suddenly it seemed too late for Tito. The red hot ashes blistered his skin; the stinging **vapors** tore his throat. He could not go on. He staggered toward a small tree at the side of the road and fell. In a moment Bimbo was beside him. He coaxed him. But there was no answer. He licked Tito's hands, his feet, his face. The boy did not stir. Then Bimbo did the last thing he could—the last thing he wanted to do. He bit his comrade, bit him deep in the arm. With a

**vapors**
gases; fumes

---

14 **pumice:** a light rock that comes from cooled lava

cry of pain, Tito jumped to his feet, Bimbo after him. Tito was in despair, but Bimbo was determined. He drove the boy on, snapping at his heels, worrying his way through the crowd; barking, baring his teeth, heedless of kicks or falling stones. Sick with hunger, half dead with fear and sulphur[15] fumes, Tito pounded on, pursued by Bimbo. How long he never knew. At last he staggered through the marine gate and felt soft sand under him. Then Tito fainted. . . .

Someone was dashing seawater over him. Someone was carrying him toward a boat.

"Bimbo," he called. And then louder, "Bimbo!" But Bimbo had disappeared.

Voices jarred against each other. "Hurry—hurry!" "To the boats!" "Can't you see the child's frightened and starving!" "He keeps calling for someone!" "Poor boy, he's out of his mind." "Here, child—take this!"

They tucked him in among them. The oarlocks creaked; the oars splashed; the boat rode over toppling waves. Tito was safe. But he wept continually.

"Bimbo!" he wailed. "Bimbo! Bimbo!" He could not be comforted.

Eighteen hundred years passed. Scientists were restoring the ancient city; excavators were working their way through the stones and trash that had buried the entire town. Much had already been brought to light—statues, bronze instruments, bright mosaics, household articles; even delicate paintings had been preserved by the fall of ashes that had taken over two thousand lives. Columns were dug up, and the forum was beginning to emerge.

It was at a place where the ruins lay deepest that the director paused.

"Come here," he called to his assistant. "I think we've discovered the remains of a building in good shape. Here are four huge millstones[16] that were most likely turned by slaves or mules—and here is a whole wall standing with shelves inside it. Why! It must have been a bakery. And here's a curious thing. What do you think I found under this heap where the ashes were thickest? The skeleton of a dog!"

---

15 **sulphur**: a yellow chemical substance that produces a highly noxious fume when burned

16 **millstones**: large, heavy stones used to grind grain into flour

"Amazing!" gasped his assistant. "You'd think a dog would have had sense to run away at the time. And what is that flat thing he's holding between his teeth? It can't be a stone."

"No. It must have come from this bakery. You know it looks to me like some sort of cake hardened with the years. And, bless me, if those little black pebbles aren't raisins. A raisin cake almost two thousand years old! I wonder what made him want it at such a moment."

"I wonder," murmured the assistant.

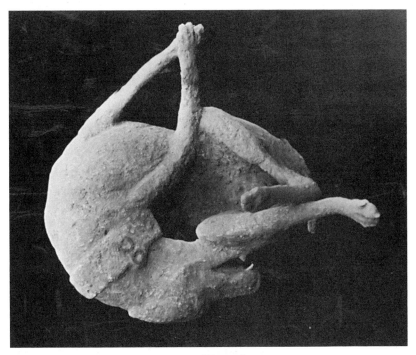

Plaster cast of a dog found in the ruins of Pompeii

# Reviewing

## The Dog of Pompeii

### Discussing the Selection

1. Skim the story briefly and note any elements that are probably true. Why do you think the author includes these particular facts?

2. In what ways does Tito compensate, or make up for, his blindness? Explain how his condition is important to this story.

3. The story ends in the future, when the ancient city of Pompeii is being restored by archaeologists. Why do you think the author ends with this flash-forward?

4. Think back to John Grogan's relationship with his dog Marley. How does it compare to Tito's relationship with Bimbo? Describe the qualities both dogs share, using specific examples to support your answer.

### Writing a Newspaper Account

Using large poster paper, prepare a mock-up of the front page of the *Pompeii Daily Forum*'s coverage of the day the city was buried. Include a banner headline, photos, and a couple of short articles. The stories should include some facts about the eruption, for historical accuracy, as well as some made-up quotes from on-the-scene witnesses.

### About Louis Untermeyer (1885–1977)

Although he never finished high school, Louis Untermeyer became a writer, editor, poet, and translator. Like many young men of his time, he quit school to work for his father, a jewelry manufacturer in New York. In 1911, he published a book of poems, *First Love*. He and other writers also published a journal that argued against U.S. involvement in World War I. When the country entered the war, the government forced the magazine out of business. In 1923, Untermeyer finally quit working in his father's company in order to write full-time. In 1956, he was awarded a gold medal from the Poetry Society of America and became a consultant for the Library of Congress.

# Previewing

## Elephants Cross Under River, Making Hearts Rise
by Michael Kaufman

### Reading Connection
Human beings' fascination with elephants is centuries old. Roman warriors first used them in triumphant processions. Later, trained elephants performed in the early beginnings of the modern circus. Around 1800, the English combined animal acts with human entertainers, and later still, businessmen like P.T. Barnum paid vast sums of money to buy elephants from abroad. In the 19th century, circuses were America's most popular form of entertainment. Herds of them traveled up and down the country in railroad cars, delighting people wherever they stopped for shows.

### Skill Focus: Titles
Authors usually choose titles carefully. A good title attracts a reader's attention and hints at the tone and subject of the writing. Consider the title of this essay, which first appeared as a column in *The New York Times*. What might it say about the author's purpose in writing this nonfiction article?

### Vocabulary Builder
The words below are defined on the pages where they occur. Which of these words do *not* have suffixes?

| | | | |
|---|---|---|---|
| blasé | adhered | procession | induce |
| pedestrian | introspective | maintained | |

# Elephants Cross Under River,
## Making Hearts Rise

Michael Kaufman

March 23, 2005. Elephants emerge from the Midtown Tunnel as they make their way to New York's Madison Square Garden.

The night was cool and the wind was churning as the eighteen elephants prepared to cross by foot into Manhattan from Queens. It was a little before midnight, and up ahead, the Empire State Building shone brightly as the mahouts[1] and keepers slid open the animal cars on the circus train.

Without a single snort of protest, without an elephant sneer, they emerged wallowing in grace like fat chorus girls happy to be back in town. Without anyone's saying a word to them, they lined up and bowed their heads to make it easier for their handlers to put on the red bridles with the Ringling Brothers and Barnum & Bailey insignia.[2]

For the elephants, it was a matter of routine. Sure, they were about to play the Apple,[3] but all of them have done that before and the fact is, walking into town is part of their act. It's what they do and they have done it all over the country. When they walk, people notice. They are good at it and they know it. But elephants once crossed the Alps with Hannibal,[4] so you can see how they might think that walking under the East River was no big deal.

But if the elephants were **blasé**, the handful of circus executives and their very few guests were atwitter as they waited. After all, how many among us have walked with elephants? Probably even fewer than have danced with wolves. Even the police were excited.

**blasé**
relaxed; laid back

"This is amazing," said Lieutenant John Rohe of the highway safety unit, who had helped plan the operation involving dozens of patrol cars and scores of uniformed men and women on both sides of the river. "It's the first time I've seen it."

Rodney Huey, a vice president of the circus who was on his first animal walk to Madison Square Garden, explained that not only were such parades

---

1 **mahouts**: elephant handlers

2 **insignia**: a label or emblem

3 **Apple**: nickname for New York City, the "Big Apple"

4 **Alps with Hannibal**: Hannibal (247–183 B.C.) was a general from Carthage, an ancient city-state in North Africa. Elephants accompanied his military expeditions across the Alps to attack the Romans in Europe.

"traditional" but also they were the most practical way to transport animals other than lions and tigers from the train.

Midnight came and Mark Oliver Gebel, the twenty-four-year-old lion tamer and chief animal trainer, said, "Go, Jenny, go." And Jenny, the pleasant lead elephant, led the way across Jackson Boulevard and down Fiftieth Avenue to the Queens Midtown Tunnel entrance. There were not many **pedestrians** around, but the drivers of cabs who had to stop as the animals crossed were all smiling. A few, who looked to be Indian, were really smiling, as if they had met Ganesh, the elephant-faced god, in Long Island City.

**pedestrian**
a person who is walking

the drivers of cabs who had to stop as the animals crossed were all smiling.

Jenny walked past the tollbooth. No one paid. Mr. Gebel said, "Hatri," a command that the elephants understand to mean "grab the tail of the elephant in front of you with your trunk." The trainer said, "Jaldi, jaldi," which Hindi[5] speakers and elephants understand to mean "step on it."

Jenny set the pace for the chain of elephants and for the twenty-three horses, four zebras, five camels, and two llamas that trailed behind them. For twenty-five minutes, the animals trudged in silence. Under the river, their surrealistic menagerie[6] formed a peaceable kingdom. And while no tolls had been paid, the circus people **adhered** carefully to pooper-scooper laws, with shovels speedily gathering the good luck that was being left behind.

**adhered**
obeyed; held on

As the bipeds[7] strained to keep up, the elephants glided, their lined faces and **introspective** eyes looking wise. One of the trainers said he thought they could probably get to where they were going without the guides. Another recalled an elephant he knew who, upon hearing a command that he had not heard for thirty years, immediately responded with the required trick.

**introspective**
thoughtful; reflective

When the **procession** came around the final bend in the tunnel to the

**procession**
march; parade

---

5 **Hindi**: the principal language spoken in India

6 **surrealistic menagerie**: a strange or bizarre group of animals

7 **biped**: an animal that has only two feet

Manhattan night, Mayor Rudolph W. Giuliani was waiting with his son, Andrew. The mayor urged Andrew to meet Jenny up close and personal, but Andrew **maintained** a more formal distance.

**maintained**
kept

Then the procession moved on, heading crosstown. Now there were people on every street. There were loud cheers for the animals. People started marching along on the sidewalks, shouting and yelling. At Stern College, hundreds of female students jumped up and down and danced to welcome the huge beasts. Clearly, elephants **induce** happiness. Are there people who do not like them? If so, should they be trusted?

**induce**
encourage;
cause

Among those who joined the elephant march were two brothers, Richard and Jonny Rosch, musicians who welcome the elephants every year. Along with a dozen friends all wearing elephant trunk noses, they wished long life to all elephants.

"I wasn't born an elephant fan," said Richard, who was wearing a Babar[8] shirt. "It was thrust upon me." Six years ago, while living near the tunnel, he first saw the march of the elephants. "I realized, what a great reason to party. Somebody had to welcome elephants. I saw my opening and I seized it.

"What else can I say? Everybody needs to celebrate elephants. They are not only big, they are compassionate and generous."

He was asked if he thought the city would be a better place if it had elephants on the street all the time.

"Definitely," he replied.

---

8 **Babar**: an elephant in a series of popular children's books

# Reviewing

## Elephants Cross Under River, Making Hearts Rise

### Discussing the Selection

1. Does the title of this essay, "Elephants Cross Under River, Making Hearts Rise," give you any clues about the content and purpose of the piece? Explain your answer.

2. This essay contains many vivid sensory details—details that appeal to the senses. Find such a passage and read it again. How do these details add to the story?

3. The author often uses personification—the literary device of giving human traits to nonhuman things. Find places in the story where the elephants are personified.

4. The mood of a piece of writing is its primary feeling or atmosphere. For example, a thriller is usually suspenseful and a comedy is often lighthearted. How would you describe the mood of this article?

### Writing a Personal Response

"Clearly, elephants induce happiness. Are there people who do not like them? Should they be trusted?" Write a short, personal response to the author's questions.

### About Michael Kaufman (1938–)

Michael Kaufman says, "For years before I came to write the 'About New York' column in *The New York Times,* I worked as a foreign correspondent covering wars and politics and cultural matters. In the years I lived and worked in Africa, India, and Sri Lanka, I grew aware of elephants who were part of the landscape. They had fascinated me ever since I saw my first circus. That was in New York City, some years after I arrived from Paris, where I was born in 1938. Anyway, when I was 54 years old and took over the column, I made sure to write a circus story whenever the clowns and animals came to town, and the very first of these involved accompanying the elephants on their march under the East River. Why? Because it seemed like a great idea."

# Previewing

## Thank You, M'am
by Langston Hughes

### Reading Connection

Like many other talented, ambitious African Americans of his time, Langston Hughes was drawn to Harlem in the 1920s. This thriving community in New York City was the place to be if you were an aspiring black poet or playwright. It was the "center of the universe" if you were a musician who wanted the best audiences in the world. Blues and jazz were all the rage, with such giants as Duke Ellington, Bessie Smith, and Cab Calloway composing and performing tunes that have become American classics. Feeding on one another's energy and creativity, black artists and intellectuals produced an amazing volume of work that changed American culture. Hughes was often called the "Poet Laureate of Harlem." His work captured the rhythms of the streets, as well as those of the people he so loved.

### Skill Focus: Making Connections

Good readers make connections as they read. That is, they link an idea, event, or reference from what they are reading with something they already know about or have experienced. For example, if you read about Vesuvius, the volcano in the story "The Dog of Pompeii," you might connect it with studying volcanoes in science class or making a model volcano. Or, if you read about students taking a field trip, it might remind you of something that happened on a field trip or vacation you took with your family. In either case, making the connection to real life deepens your understanding of the events and characters in what you read.

### Vocabulary Builder

There are probably only three words in this selection that you might wonder about; however many readers will already be familiar with one, two, or all of these.

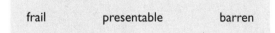

| frail | presentable | barren |

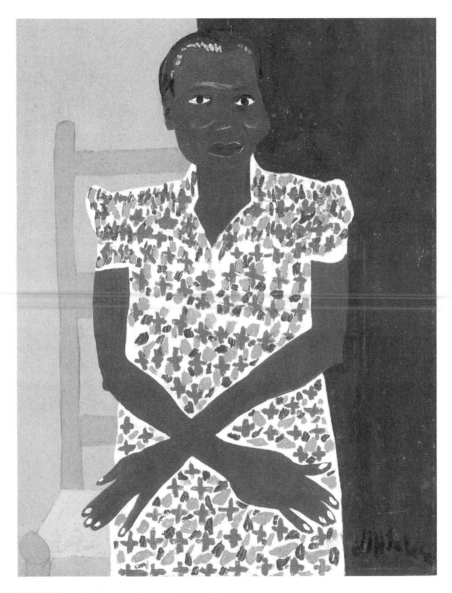

WOMAN IN CALICO, William Johnson, 1944

# Thank You, M'am

Langston Hughes

She was a large woman with a large purse that had everything in it but hammer and nails. It had a long strap, and she carried it slung across her shoulder. It was about eleven o'clock at night, and she was walking alone, when a boy ran up behind her and tried to snatch her purse. The strap broke with the single tug the boy gave it from behind. But the boy's weight and the weight of the purse combined caused him to lose his balance so, instead of taking off full blast as he had hoped, the boy fell on his back on the sidewalk, and his legs flew up. The large woman simply turned around and kicked him right square in his blue-jeaned sitter. Then she reached down, picked the boy up by his shirt front, and shook him until his teeth rattled.

After that the woman said, "Pick up my pocketbook, boy, and give it here." She still held him. But she bent down enough to permit him to stoop and pick up her purse. Then she said, "Now ain't you ashamed of yourself?"

Firmly gripped by his shirt front, the boy said, "Yes'm."

The woman said, "What did you want to do it for?"

The boy said, "I didn't aim to."

She said, "You a lie!"

By that time two or three people passed, stopped, turned to look, and some stood watching.

"If I turn you loose, will you run?" asked the woman.

"Yes'm," said the boy.

"Then I won't turn you loose," said the woman. She did not release him.

"I'm very sorry, lady, I'm sorry," whispered the boy.

"Um-hum! And your face is dirty. I got a great mind to wash your face for you. Ain't you got nobody home to tell you to wash your face?"

"No'm," said the boy.

"Then it will get washed this evening," said the large woman starting up the street, dragging the frightened boy behind her.

He looked as if he were fourteen or fifteen, **frail** and willow-wild, in tennis shoes and blue jeans.

**frail**
weak; thin

The woman said, "You ought to be my son. I would teach you right from wrong. Least I can do right now is to wash your face. Are you hungry?"

"No'm," said the being-dragged boy. "I just want you to turn me loose."

"Was I bothering *you* when I turned that corner?" asked the woman.

"No'm."

"But you put yourself in contact with *me*," said the woman. "If you think that that contact is not going to last awhile, you got another thought coming. When I get through with you, sir, you are going to remember Mrs. Luella Bates Washington Jones."

Sweat popped out on the boy's face and he began to struggle. Mrs. Jones stopped, jerked him around in front of her, put a half-nelson[1] about his neck,

---

1 **half-nelson:** a hold in which a wrestler hooks an arm under the arm of the opponent and places his hand on the back of the opponent's neck

and continued to drag him up the street. When she got to her door, she dragged the boy inside, down a hall, and into a large kitchenette-furnished room at the rear of the house. She switched on the light and left the door open. The boy could hear other roomers laughing and talking in the large house. Some of their doors were open, too, so he knew he and the woman were not alone. The woman still had him by the neck in the middle of her room.

She said, "What is your name?"

"Roger," answered the boy.

"Then, Roger, you go to that sink and wash your face," said the woman, whereupon she turned him loose—at last. Roger looked at the door—looked at the woman—looked at the door—*and went to the sink.*

"Let the water run until it gets warm," she said. "Here's a clean towel."

"You gonna take me to jail?" asked the boy, bending over the sink.

"**H**ere I am trying to get home to cook me a bite to eat and you snatch my pocketbook!"

"Not with that face, I would not take you nowhere," said the woman. "Here I am trying to get home to cook me a bite to eat and you snatch my pocketbook! Maybe, you ain't been to your supper either, late as it be. Have you?"

"There's nobody home at my house," said the boy.

"Then we'll eat," said the woman. "I believe you're hungry—or been hungry—to try to snatch my pocketbook."

"I wanted a pair of blue suede shoes,"[2] said the boy.

"Well, you didn't have to snatch *my* pocketbook to get some suede shoes," said Mrs. Luella Bates Washington Jones. "You could of asked me."

"M'am?"

The water dripping from his face, the boy looked at her. There was a long pause. A very long pause. After he had dried his face and not knowing what else to do dried it again, the boy turned around, wondering what next. The door

---

2 **blue suede shoes**: "Blue Suede Shoes" is the name of one of the first rock and roll songs ever recorded. Carl Perkins's and Elvis Presley's versions were especially popular in the fifties, the time of this story.

was open. He could make a dash for it down the hall. He could run, run, run, run, *run!*

The woman was sitting on the day-bed. After a while she said, "I were young once and I wanted things I could not get."

There was another long pause. The boy's mouth opened. Then he frowned, but not knowing he frowned.

The woman said, "Um-hum! You thought I was going to say *but*, didn't you? You thought I was going to say, *but I didn't snatch people's pocketbooks.* Well, I wasn't going to say that." Pause. Silence. "I have done things, too, which I would not tell you, son—neither tell God, if he didn't already know. So you set down while I fix us something to eat. You might run that comb through your hair so you will look **presentable**."

"I were young once and I wanted things I could not get."

**presentable**
respectable

In another corner of the room behind a screen was a gas plate[3] and an icebox. Mrs. Jones got up and went behind the screen. The woman did not watch the boy to see if he was going to run now, nor did she watch her purse which she left behind her on the day-bed. But the boy took care to sit on the far side of the room where he thought she could easily see him out of the corner of her eye, if she wanted to. He did not trust the woman *not* to trust him. And he did not want to be mistrusted now.

"Do you need somebody to go to the store," asked the boy, "maybe to get some milk or something?"

"Don't believe I do," said the woman, "unless you just want sweet milk yourself. I was going to make cocoa out of this canned milk I got here."

"That will be fine," said the boy.

She heated some lima beans and ham she had in the icebox, made the cocoa, and set the table. The woman did not ask the boy anything about where he lived, or his folks, or anything else that would embarrass him. Instead, as they ate, she told him about her job in a hotel beauty-shop that stayed open

---

3 **gas plate**: a single burner appliance used for cooking

late, what the work was like, and how all kinds of women came in and out, blondes, red-heads, and Spanish. Then she cut him a half of her ten-cent cake.

"Eat some more, son," she said.

When they were finished eating she got up and said, "Now, here, take this ten dollars and buy yourself some blue suede shoes. And next time, do not make the mistake of latching onto *my* pocketbook *nor nobody else's*—because shoes come by devilish like that will burn your feet. I got to get my rest now. But I wish you would behave yourself, son, from here on in."

She led him down the hall to the front door and opened it. "Good-night! Behave yourself, boy!" she said, looking out into the street.

The boy wanted to say something else other than "Thank you, m'am" to Mrs. Luella Bates Washington Jones, but he couldn't do so as he turned at the **barren** stoop[4] and looked back at the large woman in the door. He barely managed to say "Thank you" before she shut the door. And he never saw her again.

**barren**
bare; empty

---

4 **stoop**: porch

# Reviewing

## Thank You, M'am

### Discussing the Selection

1. Do you think it was a good idea for Mrs. Jones to give Roger ten dollars? Why do you think she does this?

2. List four things for which Roger might want to thank Mrs. Jones.

3. Do you think Roger will change as a result of his experience with Mrs. Jones? Explain your answer.

4. Does this seem like a realistic story to you? Why or why not?

### Writing a Thank-you Letter

When you receive a gift, it is good manners to send a thank-you note or letter to the giver. What gift or gifts has the boy in this story received? What kind of a thank-you letter do you believe he owes Mrs. Luella Bates Washington Jones? Write that letter using correct letter form. (Your teacher, your English textbook, or the Internet can help you with formatting a letter correctly.)

### About Langston Hughes (1902–1967)

Langston Hughes grew up in the Midwest in a family that had been active in the anti-slavery movement. By the time he enrolled at Columbia University, he was already dedicated to writing. In 1930, he won the Harmon gold medal for literature for his first novel. As a leader in the Harlem Renaissance, Hughes became friends with some of the most important writers, musicians, and social activists of his time. Hughes is beloved for his vivid depictions of black life in America from the twenties through the sixties and admired for his commitment to justice and equality for all people. He is one of the first African Americans to make a living from his writing, honored many times for his books of poetry and children's stories, plays, novels, essays, and song lyrics.

# Previewing

## Noodle Soup for Nincompoops
by Ellen Wittlinger

### Reading Connection
Writer Ellen Wittlinger is often asked how she stays tuned in to youth culture. She responds that when her own two teenagers were at home, it was "a huge help." These days she watches kid-friendly television and goes on Meet-the-Author visits to classrooms, where she can study young people even more closely. She believes that one of the themes linking almost all of her writing is "how art can save you." And art can mean anything from playing in the middle school orchestra to writing the advice column for the school newspaper. If you pursue your passions, you discover your very best self—a wonderful recipe for confidence.

### Skill Focus: First-person Narrator
When "I" is the voice of the narrator, it is called the first-person point of view. A story told in this manner lets you inside the mind of the storyteller. You learn what this individual's reactions are to other characters and events in the story. First-person point of view can make a story seem very personal and real. The disadvantage is that you see the story *only* from one character's point of view, which may be biased.

### Vocabulary Builder
Look for the following words as you read. Many of them are extremely descriptive of the characters you will meet in this humorous story.

| | | | |
|---|---|---|---|
| asset | nonchalant | spoof | diverged |
| anticipation | sauntered | dawdle | scalded |
| pompous | ecstatic | dithering | |

HOMEWORK, Milton Avery, 1946

# Noodle Soup
## for
# Nincompoops

Ellen Wittlinger

**E**verybody else in seventh-grade honors English had groaned at the assignment, "I Am a Camera," but I thought it would be fun—three pages about anything your invisible "camera" noticed over the weekend. After spending most of Saturday at David Segal's bar mitzvah[1] and Sunday afternoon at the mall with Liza and Harper, it didn't take me long to write "How to Flirt Without Showing Your Braces." Even Liza thought it was funny, and it was mostly about her. Actually, that's probably why she liked it; Liza is her own favorite subject these days.

---

1 **bar mitzvah**: a Jewish coming-of-age ceremony for boys; it takes place at age thirteen

I guess I notice things other kids don't. I like watching people. Most kids I know don't shut up long enough to notice anybody else; they're constantly yelling and wiggling around so *they* get noticed. David Segal's bar mitzvah party was so loud, I saw three grown-ups popping ibuprofen[2] before they even served lunch. Liza, who's been my best friend since birth, or possibly earlier, is always right in the middle of the action. I'm usually standing on the edge of the crowd, hoping *not* to be noticed. It's always been that way, and neither of us has ever minded.

But now, according to Liza, I do way too much watching and not nearly enough flirting. Up until this year, neither of us had talked to boys. We agreed they were aliens. But ever since Harper showed up, Liza is suddenly all about the opposite sex. "Who likes who" takes up three quarters of her conversation.

When Mr. Chrisman asked me to stay after class for a few minutes, I figured he wanted to talk to me about my essay. Mr. C is always complimenting me on my writing. Sure enough, he waved it in front of me and smiled. "Maggie, I knew you were a good writer," he said, "but I had no idea until now how funny you could be!" Even if I *did* have braces, I'd smile at Mr. Chrisman, who, in my opinion, is the best teacher at South Hadfield Middle School (and also really cute).

"You're such a natural writer—why is it you've never written anything for the *Newsflash*?" he asked me. Mr. C is the advisor for the school newspaper, the *Weekly Newsflash*, and he's always trying to recruit kids to write stuff for it. I guess it's hard to fill four pages every week with sports scores, lunch menus, and articles about how much toilet paper gets stolen from the girls' bathroom.

I shrugged. "I'm not that interested in writing *facts*. You know. I like to make things up."

He nodded. "Well your essay gave me an idea. How would you like to write an advice column for the newspaper?"

I had to laugh. "What kind of advice could *I* give anybody? How to be invisible?"

Mr. C's smile disappeared. "Do you really think you're invisible?"

---

2 **ibuprofen**: a medicine similar to aspirin

I shrugged. "To most kids. I don't care, though."

"I think of you as quiet, but certainly not invisible. Anyway, for this job keeping a low profile[3] is an **asset**." Mr. C motioned for me to sit down in the chair next to his desk. "Here's my idea. You wouldn't be writing a *real* advice column; it would be funny, something to get more kids interested in reading the paper. To begin with, I'd write a few letters with silly questions, and you could come up with funny answers. We'd tell kids that if they want to ask you questions, they can leave them in my box in the main office, and I can give them to you after class. That way, no one will know who you are."

**asset**
benefit;
advantage

"You mean, I wouldn't be answering the questions as Maggie Cluny? I'd make up a name? I'd be somebody else?"

"That's right. Make up a name. You can name the whole column whatever you want, just so it's funny. I think if we set it up as humorous from the beginning, kids will get the idea and write you funny questions."

The idea crept around in my mind. I could say whatever I wanted to as long as I wasn't Maggie Cluny. I'd have an alter ego,[4] like Clark Kent and Superman. "But won't people find out it's me?"

"Well, that's the thing. In order to keep it secret, you couldn't tell *anybody*. Not even your best friends. I think the mystery aspect will add to the fun of it—everybody will be guessing who it is." Mr. Chrisman sat forward, his hands on his knees. "So, what do you think? Interested?"

"Yeah, I am. Can I think about it overnight?"

"Sure, sure. Meanwhile, I'll try my hand at a few letters, in **anticipation**!"

**anticipation**
hope;
expectation

Why didn't anybody *my* age ever smile at me like Mr. C did? Sometimes I felt like I must already be thirty. I'd skipped right over the so-called "best years of my life" right into elderly boredom.

By the time I got to my locker, Liza was sitting on the floor, her head drooping over her books, her long blond-streaked hair hiding her face. She looked up when she heard me coming.

---

3 **keeping a low profile**: avoiding notice by others

4 **alter ego**: a different identity

"Where have you *been*? Everybody left already. Robbie Piersall's mother picked him up, and he asked me if I needed a ride home, but you weren't here!"

"Sorry. I was talking to Mr. . . . Meadows . . . about the geography test."

"Ugh, geography." She got to her feet and dusted off the butt of her low-rise jeans, then readjusted her shirt so her belly button peeked out. You aren't allowed to have your stomach bare in school, but Liza always wears that stretchy material you can pull down or push up, depending on the occasion.

"Why did you want a ride?" I asked her, carefully changing the subject from my recent whereabouts. "It only takes us fifteen minutes to walk, and the weather's nice."

Liza sighed. "Maggie, I don't care about the *ride*. Robbie wanted me in his car! Don't you get it?"

"Oh." I hated it when Liza acted like I was the dumbest geek on earth. "Well, how was I supposed to know you liked Robbie Piersall? I thought you were crazy about David Segal—you were yesterday!" The turnover in Liza's boyfriends was hard to keep up with; she fell in love more often than most people brushed their teeth.

"I *am*. I don't think I even like Robbie, but maybe he likes *me*. Now I'll never know."

"I don't see how one car ride would have proved anything," I grumbled.

"That's because you just don't *get* stuff, Maggie. Honestly, sometimes you don't even seem like you're really thirteen!"

I guess she hadn't heard the news that I was actually thirty in disguise. "Well, sometimes you don't either," I said. "Sometimes you seem like you're about eighteen!"

Liza's pout turned up at the corners. "You really think so? Because of my hair?" She hooked her arm through mine and turned into my best friend again. "Wait till you hear what David said to me after math today. . . ."

"How's this?" I said, handing Mr. Chrisman a sheet of paper. I'd been working on the idea since I left school the day before, and I was proud of the final product.

"Noodle Soup for Nincompoops; by Faustina Intelligentsia. No question too stupid to answer." He gave me his big, full-of-teeth smile. "You're going to do the column!"

"Do you like the name?" I asked.

"I love Faustina Intelligentsia—it's silly and **pompous**—perfect for a humor column. But I'm not sure I get 'Noodle Soup—'"

**pompous**
arrogant;
self-important

"I was trying to think of a name that would get people's attention, so I checked the paper to see what books were on the best-seller lists. There were all these books for 'dummies' and 'idiots,' and then there were a couple of Chicken Soup books, so I thought if I combined both of them . . ."

He threw his head back and laughed, his brown hair falling in his face. If only there were *boys* as cool as Mr. C. "'Noodle Soup for Nincompoops'! It's great. You're going to be

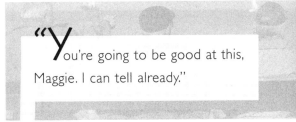

"You're going to be good at this, Maggie. I can tell already."

good at this, Maggie. I can tell already." He handed me some papers. "Take a look at these and see if you can come up with funny answers. You don't have to do them all, just two or three. And remember, don't let anyone see what you're doing!"

If popularity at school had anything to do with how much teachers liked you, I'd have a posse. Unfortunately, it seemed to work the opposite way. Liza and Harper were both standing in the hallway when I came around the corner. As I said, Liza had been my friend forever, but Harper was a new addition. She was really Liza's friend more than mine, although I didn't hate her or anything. She hung around with more of the popular kids than Liza and I did; it was because of her we got invited to David Segal's bar mitzvah. But sometimes I felt like Liza and Harper were the best friends and I was just a dark, silent shadow following them around.

At least Liza looked happy to see me today. "There you are. Harper's mom is going to drive us to the mall."

"How come? Wasn't Robbie Piersall's mother available?"

"Ha-ha. Let's go—she's waiting."

I hung back. "You're really going to the mall again? We were just there on Sunday?"

Liza narrowed her eyes and stared at me as if she was trying to send me a coded message. "So? It's *fun*."

"Oh, yeah, if your idea of fun is watching boys pick out jeans at Abercrombie."

Harper was studying the white crescents of her cuticles, staying out of the debate.

Liza sighed. "Come on Maggie. We'll go to the food court and get sweet-potato fries."

"Can we go to the bookstore?" I asked.

Harper looked up. "No! When you go into the bookstore, you want to stay forever, and we have to wait for you!"

"Oh, like I didn't wait half an hour for you two to try on fifty shades of nail polish!"

Liza gave me a tight smile. "Maybe we could meet you someplace if you want to go to the bookstore."

I shook my head. "That's okay. You guys go. I don't feel like being inside this afternoon anyway. I might go home and rake leaves."

Harper rolled her eyes. "You're kidding. *Rake leaves?*"

"I like doing it. It's relaxing."

"So is going to the mall!" Liza said.

"Don't beg her," Harper said, heading for the stairs.

Liza looked disappointed. "Okay, go do your chores. Maybe you can come over tomorrow or something."

"Yeah, maybe," I said. Liza ran to catch up with Harper, which I hated to see. When had Harper become so very important?

**nonchalant**
casual; relaxed

**sauntered**
strolled; walked in a slow, relaxed way

Robbie Piersall set two boxes of the *Weekly Newsflash* on a table in the hallway outside the Little Theater, where kids usually picked up their copies. I tried to be **nonchalant** as I **sauntered** over and reached into a box. Several other kids were right behind me.

"This is a really good issue," Robbie announced. I had the feeling he was looking at me, so I didn't look up. Actually, I almost never look at Robbie; he's the kind of person who looks you right in the eyeballs, even if you hardly know him. It makes me so nervous, I can't think straight.

"You're the editor; you have to think it's good," some eighth grader said as he walked past without grabbing a copy.

"No, really. There's a new column on page three—it's really funny."

I took my skinny newspaper and stood back against the wall, where I could see people's reactions without them noticing. Not that they ever noticed me anyway. This morning, though, my heart was beating so loud, I was afraid they'd look around to see where all the noise was coming from.

I opened the paper to page three, like everybody else. There it was:

Noodle Soup for Nincompoops
    *by Faustina Intelligentsia*
"No question too stupid to answer!"

"Ha! Did you read this?" Jillie Randolph said. "Listen!" And she began to read my column out loud to the assembled group:

"Dear Faustina,
    I am madly in love with my boyfriend, but my mother keeps calling it 'puppy love.' I hate that! How can I get her to stop?
    —Teenager in Love

Dear Teenager in Love,
    Poor you. Have you considered chewing up her bedroom slippers?
    —Faustina Intelligentsia"

As Jillie was reading the column some kids had come up to look over her shoulder while others stood nearby, listening. They all laughed at my answer. Or rather, *Faustina's* answer.

"Who wrote that?" Adam Levine asked as he grabbed a paper out of the box.

"It doesn't say." Patrick Deveraux, an eighth grader, was sharing a paper with his girlfriend, Ellie Something-or-Other. "There's more." He read the second letter aloud:

"Dear Faustina,

I'm crazy about a girl who's two years older than me. I lied to her about my age, but now I'm afraid she'll find out and hate me for lying to her. What should I do?
—Tangled Web

Dear Tangled Web,

Well, dearie, you have two choices: Keep lying until she tells everybody what a big phony you are, or find a girl two years younger and let her do the lying.
—Faustina Intelligentsia"

The first bell rang, but nobody moved. Jillie started in again, reading the last letter:

"Dear Faustina,

I have a crush on my sister's boyfriend, and I think he likes me too. Is it okay for me to go for it? "
—Better-Looking Sister

Dear Better-Looking Sister,

Sure, sweetheart, go right ahead. Of course, it's also okay for your sister to kick your butt from here to Tuscaloosa. Duh.
—Faustina Intelligentsia"

"These are funny!" Ellie said. "Somebody must know who wrote them."
"Here's a clue," Patrick said. "It says, 'If you have questions for Faustina Intelligentsia, please leave them in Mr. Chrisman's mailbox in the main office.' So it must be somebody who's on the staff."

"Who wrote this, Robbie?" Melanie Cross said. "You must know."

Robbie shrugged. "It's a secret."

"Oh, come on," Ben Anders said. "You're the editor."

"I don't know. Really. Mr. Chrisman is the only one who knows."

Everybody was talking about my column and trying to guess who'd written it. They were guessing all the obviously funny kids—the guys who can break up the teachers, the girls whose sarcasm can drop an enemy at fifty feet. When the second bell rang, I folded up my newspaper and walked off down the hall, invisible as ever. It was wonderful, but it was frightening, too. All these kids wanted to know who I was! Now I *really* didn't want them to find out because I knew they'd be disappointed that it was just me, Maggie Cluny.

Everybody was talking about my column and trying to guess who'd written it.

It was almost impossible for Mr. Chrisman to get our class to settle down.

"Come on, Mr. C. Who is it?"

"Why does it have to be a secret, anyway?"

"We won't tell anybody!"

He smiled and shook his head. "Give it up," he said. "I am an excellent keeper of secrets."

I turned into a piece of petrified wood, afraid to move so much as a finger lest I call attention to myself. I didn't dare even glance at Mr. Chrisman.

"I would think whoever is writing the column would *want* people to know who he is. He's good!"

"It's not necessarily a *he*, Robbie," Liza said. "It could be any of us."

"Yes, it could. Isn't a little mystery fun?" Mr. C said. "And now on to the mystery of your vocabulary tests."

After school I saw little knots of kids huddled over the *Newsflash*, laughing. Amazingly, I was a hit.

"Who do you think it is?" Liza asked me while we were walking home.

Mr. C had told me not to tell even my best friends, but I wouldn't have told Liza anyway. Her record for secret keeping is about twelve seconds.

"Who do you think?" I asked her back, hoping not to have to tell another out-and-out lie.

"At first I thought Robbie had probably written it himself—he was making such a big deal out of it—but now I don't think so." She gave me a sideways glance.

"No?" I picked a yellowing leaf from a tree and studied it carefully.

"No. Who do you think it is?"

"How should I know?" I said.

"Is it *you*?" Liza said, suddenly turning in front of me so I had to stop walking.

I was so surprised, I jumped. "*Me*? You really think I could write something like that?" I could feel my pupils jumping around in my eyes.

"You can be funny sometimes. Around me. Besides, you're all buddy-buddy with Mr. Chrisman."

I didn't say anything. I just stared at Liza like she was a skunk in my path while I tried to decide how on earth to convince her I was not Faustina Intelligentsia. It turned out silence was the right move.

"Oh, don't look so shocked!" she said. "I guess it couldn't really be you, could it? I mean, you wouldn't do anything as outrageous as that, would you?"

My silence began to heat up as we continued walking.

"I mean, I wish you *were* Faustina Intelligentsia. That would be so cool."

"And I'm not cool enough as I am? Is that what you mean?"

"Don't get mad about it. You're just not the kind of person who's funny in public." She gave my arm a little punch. "It's okay. *I* know you're funny."

I wished I could tell her the truth, that everybody at school was laughing at *my* writing. But I couldn't, and it didn't seem fair that she was ragging on me again, so I said, "At least we know it isn't Harper who's writing it. I've never heard her say anything in the least *bit* funny."

We stopped to pet Mrs. Grayson's collie so we wouldn't have to talk anymore.

**ecstatic**
thrilled;
overjoyed

Mr. Chrisman was **ecstatic** about the reaction kids were having to my column.

During the next few weeks, we got two dozen letters in the box. Most kids understood that the column was supposed to be a **spoof**, and they wrote silly questions about things like whether or not to cut their hair and whether you should kiss on the first date. Questions Faustina could have fun with.

spoof
parody; a humorous imitation

While I was playing with Faustina, Liza began to spend more time with Harper. Sometimes they invited me along, and sometimes they didn't, which was fine. Shopping is boring. Besides, I never really felt comfortable with Harper, anyway. I missed Liza, though—I missed her a lot.

Meanwhile, the kids were still trying to figure out who Faustina was. For a while they were evenly divided between those who thought Robbie Piersall was writing the column and those who thought it might be Pam Ackerman, a girl with a big attitude who'd transferred to our school this year from a school in New York City. The idea was that anybody who'd lived in New York was automatically funny, although I'd personally never seen her crack a smile. Except for Liza, nobody suspected me, not for a moment. I pretended to Mr. C that this was great, but secretly, I was getting a little depressed about it. Nobody had a clue that Faustina Intelligentsia could live inside somebody like me.

Now I was always the last person to leave English class. Mr. C would put the letters on a corner of his desk so I could whisk them up without attracting too much attention, even if he was talking with somebody. One afternoon there was a single letter lying there. I scooped it up and dumped it in my backpack to read when I got home. Liza and Harper had plans after school with another girl, Annie, whom I didn't know very well, so I walked home alone. It was starting to get cold now, which made me remember walking home with Liza on wintry days, how we'd put our hoods up over our ears and run until we got warmed up, then **dawdle** the rest of the way, as usual.

dawdle
to move slowly and without a purpose

By the time I got home, I'd forgotten about the letter. I did my Spanish and geography homework, then went downstairs to help Mom make potato latkes[5] for dinner. It wasn't until nine o'clock that I remembered Faustina's letter. I dug it out of my backpack, opened the envelope, and got ready to laugh.

---

5 **latkes**: a thin pancake made of potatoes

The question was neatly typed with no errors and run out on a sheet of canary yellow paper. I shivered the minute I saw it.

> "Dear Faustina,
>
> I'm having a problem with my best friend. I've made some new friends lately, and I don't think she likes them. I feel like I'm stuck in the middle between my old friend, who's sort of quiet, and the new ones, who like to party. What should I do?
> —Stuck"

There was no doubt in my mind—it was from Liza. For one thing, she was a very good typist, and I happened to know that her mother kept a big stack of yellow computer paper in her desk drawer. Liza certainly had new friends, who liked to party. And one old dull one. Suddenly, I felt sick to my stomach and lay down on my bed. Liza was having a "problem" with me. She wanted to hang out with her new friends and I was holding her back. It never occurred to me that Liza wanted to dump me, but I could see she was asking Faustina Intelligentsia for permission to do just that.

And then I wondered if Liza had figured out who Faustina Intelligentsia really was. If so, she'd know that *I'd* know she sent the letter. We'd used that yellow paper ourselves lots of times. Maybe she was warning me: Either go along with my new friends, or get out of the way.

My best friend since forever was getting ready to throw me overboard, and I was supposed to write something funny about it and *publish it in the school newspaper*! It was impossible—I couldn't do it. I couldn't even think about it! Except I couldn't *stop* thinking about it either.

**dithering**
indecisiveness;
wavering

After an hour of **dithering**, I decided I wasn't going to get anything else done anyway, so I crawled into bed and turned out the light, even though I knew it was going to be impossible to go to sleep. In the dark I started wondering what Faustina Intelligentsia would say to Liza.

It was funny. I had a picture in my mind of who Faustina was, and she was nothing like me. She had wild red hair piled up on her head like a messy bird's nest, with pencils and feathers and beads all wound around it. She was about twenty-five years old and wore granny boots and thrift-store clothes and black lipstick. And her laugh was loud enough to make everybody look at her, even in the middle of someplace as noisy as David Segal's bar mitzvah party. She was very cool and definitely *not* invisible.

Every time I sat down to think of an answer to a question, I imagined her putting her boots up on the table and cackling over the smart-aleck answer. It wasn't that I wanted to *be* like her, but I really liked having her inside my head, letting me see things the way she saw them. I wondered what Mr. C would think of her. He'd probably like Faustina more than me, since she was funny *and* a grown-up. He probably liked red hair.

When I finally fell asleep, I dreamed I lived in the custodian's closet at school. Mr. Chrisman was the only person who knew I was there, and he brought me bowls of noodle soup for every meal. I didn't mind at all. When I woke up in the morning, I knew what Faustina Intelligentsia would say to Liza.

"Dear Stuck,

What you should do, dearie, is *get out of the middle*! Two roads **diverged**,[6] and all that. You can't go both ways, unless you're a real split personality. Here's the question: Do you want to end up eating noodle soup with the nincompoop, or do you want to have a good time? Do you really have to ask?

—Faustina Intelligentsia"

**diverged**
split or
departed from
each other

It was the right answer. Faustina was always right.

The rest of that week Liza acted the same as she always did, nice to me one minute, then running off with Harper the next. Until Friday, the day the *Weekly Newsflash* came out.

Once again everybody was giggling at the column. They couldn't believe they still didn't know who wrote it. I caught up with Liza as she headed into Mr. C's room for English.

---

6 **Two roads diverged**: a reference to the first line of the Robert Frost poem, "The Road Not Taken"

"Got your *Newsflash*, I see." I wondered if she'd read her answer yet, if she'd take Faustina's advice.

Liza turned and glared at me. "Yes, I do."

Her look **scalded** my cheeks. "So, after school do you want to—"

"I'm busy after school," she said, flinging her half-and-half hair in my face as she turned away from me. "I'm going to Harper's. She's having a party tonight."

"Oh, okay." But she wasn't hanging around to hear my response. She'd already *had* a response, from Faustina Intelligentsia, and she was obviously following the advice to the letter.

I couldn't concentrate very well in English; I kept sneaking looks at Liza, who had taken the seat farthest away from mine, even though it meant sitting in the front row. Could this really be happening? Would Liza really stop being my friend after all these years because of some silly newspaper column? But no, I reminded myself, she'd wanted to get rid of me before that. The column just gave her permission.

I let Liza fly out of class before I gathered my books and trudged to the door. Mr. C gave me a big smile, and I gave him a halfhearted one in return. Then, just as I got to the door, Robbie Piersall came up behind me and bent his head close to my ear.

"It's you, isn't it?" he whispered. "I know it is."

"What?" I was so shocked to see his grinning mouth and blue eyes so close to mine.

He pulled me off to the side of the hall, so we were out of the traffic flow. "You're Faustina, aren't you? I know it." When I still struggled to speak, he added, "Don't worry. I'm not going to tell anybody. The column is great—it's the best thing in the *Newsflash*!"

I dared to glance into his eyes as they bored into mine. Finally, I found my voice. "Thanks. How did you—"

"Two reasons. First of all, most of the bigmouths around here would have already told people if they were writing it. You aren't like that. And secondly, I saw your 'I Am a Camera' essay. Mr. C left a stack of papers lying around the newspaper office, and yours was on top, so I read it. I didn't put two and two together right away, but suddenly, it hit me. If there was anybody else who could write that well, I'd know about them."

My mouth fell open. "I didn't think anybody would figure it out. I mean, I'm sort of invisible around here."

"You just think you are. I've noticed you before."

Then we both turned red and looked at the floor.

I wanted to run away, but the only excuse I could think of, that I had to meet Liza to walk home, was a lie. Finally, I just said. "I should get going."

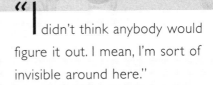

"I didn't think anybody would figure it out. I mean, I'm sort of invisible around here."

Robbie nodded. "If you ever need a ride home or anything . . . I mean, my mom drives me and . . . you don't live that far away."

He knew where I *lived*?

"I told Liza a few weeks ago we'd give you guys a ride, but I guess she didn't tell you."

She *told* me, she just made it sound more like *her* invitation than mine.

"Actually, if your mom doesn't mind . . . I would kind of like a ride."

"Great!" Robbie smiled as we walked to the seventh-grade lockers. We walked together, like it was a normal thing to do.

I didn't hear from Liza on Friday night, but who cared? Let her go to some dumb party with Harper. Robbie called and we talked on the phone for a while. Actually, we ran out of stuff to say to each other after about five minutes, so then we just sort of *breathed* together and laughed for another five.

On Saturday, Mom offered to take me to the mall for new shoes, but I was afraid I'd run into the new best friends there, so I said I didn't feel like it. I sat at my desk doing homework and writing next week's "Noodle Soup for Nincompoops."

Robbie called Saturday night and wanted to know if I could go out with him, like to the movies. I couldn't believe this was happening to me! I got so nervous—what would we talk about for a whole evening?—that I told him my mother wouldn't let me go out alone with boys yet. I don't even know if that's true; I never had to ask her about it before. He said that was okay, that maybe next weekend we could get a group of kids to go!

As soon as I hung up the phone, I missed Liza terribly. It looked like I might just have my first boyfriend ever, and I didn't even have a best friend to talk to about it! Liza would know what to say if somebody asked her to the movies. I needed her! Twice I dialed her phone number, all but the last digit, then hung up. If she didn't want to be my friend, I wasn't going to beg her.

I slept late Sunday—Robbie had to work on a project for a science class, so I knew he wouldn't call until the evening. There wasn't much to do until then except to read the Sunday papers and avoid my mother's questions about who that boy was who "keeps calling."

Just after noon the doorbell rang. Mom and Dad were in the backyard mulching[7] the roses for winter, so I hauled myself off the couch and opened the door. There stood Liza, her lips pursed, her eyes blazing.

"I can't believe you, Maggie!" She started right in yelling. "Doesn't our friendship mean *anything* to you? After all these years? You just tell me to 'get out of the middle' and go to parties with my new friends. You just wipe me out of your life like . . . like you're erasing a chalkboard!" The anger melted off her face, and before I knew it, she was standing there with her hands over her eyes, crying.

I pulled her inside the house, and she sniffed and rubbed her face on her sleeve, trying to get the mad back.

"Did you know it was me all along?"

"Of course I knew. Well, not immediately, but I kept thinking about it. Who else can write that funny? And I know you and Mr. Chrisman are crazy about each other, so of course he got you to do it. You thought your best friend wouldn't figure it out?"

"If you're my best friend, why did you write that letter to me?"

"I don't know. You've been so weird since we started hanging around with Harper . . . ."

---

7 **mulching**: covering the ground with something to improve the soil and stop weeds

"You're the one who started hanging around with Harper."

She shrugged. "Whatever. I wrote the letter to tell you . . . it's hard for me that you don't like my new friends that much. And I thought it would be a funny way to do it in a letter to your column. I knew you'd know it was me because of the yellow paper and all, but I didn't think you'd say, 'Fine, just go off with your new friends'!"

"But I thought you were saying I had to go along with all your new friends or . . . get out of your way. I thought you were dumping me."

"You dumped me! You said, 'two roads diverge' and all that stuff." Her tears had finally dried up.

"I thought that was what Faustina Intelligentsia would tell you. You should get rid of your boring friend and hang out with the ones who want to party. It's not what *I* wanted you to do."

Liza stared at me, her mouth hanging slightly open. Then she took her fist and punched me on the arm. "You're nuts, Maggie. You're a crazy person. You told me to go hang out with other people even though you still want to be my best friend?"

"Of course I do. Who else would I hang out with?"

She hit me again, and then we hugged each other, briefly. Liza isn't really the huggy type. "If you ever do anything this dumb again, Maggie Cluny, you can be best friends with Faustina Intelligentsia or the nincompoop or whoever you are at the moment."

"I won't," I promised as we sank down onto the sofa. "So I guess this means you're stuck in the middle again."

She sighed. "The middle isn't so bad. At least I won't have to spend another entire weekend with Harper. Here I was all upset, and all she wanted to talk about was whether or not she should get her hair cut. I guess your weekend wasn't so hot either, huh?"

I smiled. "Liza, you won't even believe it."

# Reviewing

## Noodle Soup for Nincompoops

### Discussing the Selection

1. What do you learn about Maggie Cluny, the narrator, in the first two paragraphs? Make and fill in a chart like the one below.

| CHARACTERISTICS OF MAGGIE CLUNY | DETAIL FROM STORY |
| --- | --- |
| Likes to write | Considers a school writing assignment "fun" |
|  |  |
|  |  |
|  |  |
|  |  |

2. Is the first-person voice important to your enjoyment of this story? Explain.

3. How is Maggie's altar ego, Faustina Intelligentsia, different from her? Similar?

4. What does "Noodle Soup for Nincompoops" suggest about friendships?

### Writing Epigrams

An epigram is a short, witty saying, such as "Rules are the solution to yesterday's problems." Imagine that you work in marketing for a candy company that is about to launch a new brand of candy targeted at young people. Your candy will have "personalized" packaging, wrappers containing bits of short and snappy wisdom. Alone or with a partner, write as many "candy-grams" as you can.

### About Ellen Wittlinger (1948–)

Ellen Wittlinger is a former children's librarian who decided to try her hand at writing for young people. A poet and playwright, she knows the value of choosing the precise word and writing jazzy dialogue to give her stories impact. "I find myself drawn to characters who are slightly oddball—the artists, the outsiders, those who don't quite fit in." She believes that most middle school students think of themselves as outsiders, even those who "appear to be in the thick of things." Many of the characters in her fiction turn to some form of art, from singing to videos to dance and writing, to express themselves and in so doing find a source of comfort, joy, and esteem.

# Previewing

## The Walrus and the Carpenter

by Lewis Carroll

### Reading Connection

"The Walrus and the Carpenter" is a nonsense poem that appears in Lewis Carroll's novel *Through the Looking-Glass*, the sequel to *Alice's Adventures in Wonderland*. A nonsense poem is verse that is silly or absurd. It can make sense but it doesn't have to. In such verse, actual words are used in unusual ways or new words are invented and put to use wherever the poet likes the sound and look of them. Lewis Carroll's poem "Jabberwocky" is the purest nonsense, and also one of the most famous poems in the world. Its first line is lively and inviting: "Twas brillig and the slithy toves did gyre and gimble in the wabe." However, it is completely open to interpretation! Some of the most beloved children's poets—Dr. Seuss, Ogden Nash, A. A. Milne (author of Winnie the Pooh books)—were masters of the art of nonsense poetry.

### Skill Focus: Consonance

Consonance in a line of poetry is when similar consonant sounds are repeated close together. For example, "**t**wo **t**iny **tad**poles **d**arted **d**ownstream" contains many variations of the "t" and "d" sounds. Read aloud the first stanza of "The Walrus and the Carpenter," listening for examples of consonance. List any repeated sounds.

### Vocabulary Builder

Although this is a nonsense poem, there are only a few words that might be unfamiliar.

| | | |
|---|---|---|
| billows | sulkily | dismal |

# The **Walrus** and the **Carpenter**

Lewis Carroll

The sun was shining on the sea,
Shining with all his might:
He did his best to make

**billows**
large or
surging waves

The **billows** smooth and bright—
And this was odd, because it was          5
The middle of the night.

**sulkily**
in a moody or
sullen way

The moon was shining **sulkily**,
Because she thought the sun
Had got no business to be there
After the day was done—          10
"It's very rude of him," she said,
"To come and spoil the fun!"

The sea was wet as wet could be,
The sands were dry as dry.
You could not see a cloud, because                    15
No cloud was in the sky:
No birds were flying overhead—
There were no birds to fly.

The Walrus and the Carpenter
Were walking close at hand;                           20
They wept like anything to see
Such quantities of sand:
"If this were only cleared away,"
They said, "it *would* be grand!"

"If seven maids with seven mops                 25
Swept it for half a year,
Do you suppose," the Walrus said,
"That they could get it clear?"
"I doubt it," said the Carpenter,
And shed a bitter tear.                          30

"O Oysters, come and walk with us!"
The Walrus did beseech.[1]
"A pleasant walk, a pleasant talk,
Along the briny[2] beach:
We cannot do with more than four,                35
To give a hand to each."

The eldest Oyster looked at him
But never a word he said:
The eldest Oyster winked his eye,
And shook his heavy head—                         40
Meaning to say he did not choose
To leave the oyster-bed.

But four young Oysters hurried up,
All eager for the treat:
Their coats were brushed, their faces washed,    45
Their shoes were clean and neat—
And this was odd, because, you know,
They hadn't any feet.

---

1 **beseech**: beg; plead
2 **briny**: salty

Four other Oysters followed them,
And yet another four:                                  50
And thick and fast they came at last,
And more, and more, and more—
All hopping through the frothy waves,
And scrambling to the shore.

The Walrus and the Carpenter                           55
Walked on a mile or so,
And then they rested on a rock
Conveniently low:
And all the little Oysters stood
And waited in a row.                                   60

"The time has come," the Walrus said,
"To talk of many things:
Of shoes— and ships— and sealing wax—$^3$
Of cabbages— and kings—
And why the sea is boiling hot—                        65
And whether pigs have wings."

"But wait a bit," the Oysters cried,
"Before we have our chat;
For some of us are out of breath,
And all of us are fat!"                                70
"No hurry!" said the Carpenter.
They thanked him much for that.

---

3 **sealing wax**: a substance that was melted and used to seal envelopes

"A loaf of bread," the Walrus said,
"Is what we chiefly need:
Pepper and vinegar besides                    75
Are very good indeed—
Now if you're ready, Oysters dear,
We can begin to feed."

"But not on us!" the Oysters cried,
Turning a little blue.                        80
"After such kindness, that would be

**dismal**
gloomy; dreary

A **dismal** thing to do!"
"The night is fine," the Walrus said.
"Do you admire the view?"

"It was so kind of you to come!                    85
And you are very nice!"
The Carpenter said nothing but
"Cut us another slice.
I wish you were not quite so deaf—
I've had to ask you twice!"                        90

"It seems a shame," the Walrus said,
"To play them such a trick,
After we've brought them out so far,
And made them trot so quick!"
The Carpenter said nothing but                     95
"The butter's spread too thick!"

"I weep for you," the Walrus said:
"I deeply sympathize."
With sobs and tears he sorted out
Those of the largest size,                         100
Holding his pocket-handkerchief
Before his streaming eyes.

"O Oysters," said the Carpenter,
"You've had a pleasant run!
Shall we be trotting home again?"                  105
But answer came there none—
And this was scarcely odd, because
They'd eaten every one.

# Reviewing

## The Walrus and the Carpenter

### Discussing the Selection

1. What is the plot—the chain of events—of this poem? Try to sum it up in one or two sentences.

2. Who feels guiltier for eating the oysters, the Walrus or the Carpenter? Explain, giving evidence from the poem to support your answer.

3. Do you think there is a message in this poem? If so, state it briefly.

4. The Walrus says to the Oysters: "I weep for you, I deeply sympathize" but secretly plans to eat "Those of the largest size." Who are the Walruses in our own society, pretending to be sympathetic but taking advantage of the weak and unsuspecting?

### Writing a Nonsense Poem

Try your hand writing some nonsense poetry. Start by reading some other nonsense verse, such as Lewis Carroll's poem "Jabberwocky," or anything by Shel Silverstein or Ogden Nash. Make up new words—ones that sound good or simply look good. Or use "real" words in any odd way you wish. For example:

Silly putty kittie,

swimming in her spool,

hit a riddle hiccup

purped and mewed a fool.

### About Lewis Carroll (1832–1898)

Lewis Carroll was the pen name of Charles Lutwidge Dodson, universally famous for his Alice books: *Alice's Adventures in Wonderland* and *Through the Looking-Glass and What Alice Found There*. He was born third among eleven children, the brilliant son of a British country parson. Carroll is considered "among the immortals of literature" for writing that blends fantastic word play with intriguing ideas about nature and human behavior. The author was equally talented at mathematics, photography, art, and science. In his time, he was considered a clever game and puzzle maker, hobbies which also demonstrated his keen wit.

# Previewing

## What Do Fish Have to Do with Anything?
by Avi

### Reading Connection
The following short story comes from Avi's collection with the same title, *What Do Fish Have to Do with Anything?* The seven stories in the collection all center on turning points in the lives of the young characters. One critic said, "These short stories affirm the ability of their main characters to choose their fate." The theme of survival has always entered into Avi's writing. In the title story here, the main character's father has lost his job and left the family. Home alone while his mother works, the young boy seeks answers from a surprising source.

### Skill Focus: Symbol
A symbol is an object that stands for a broader idea. For example, a heart often indicates romance, and an eagle can represent freedom. In the following story the author has used cave-dwelling fish as a symbol. As you read, think about what this symbol represents.

### Vocabulary Builder
After you read the selection, try using at least three of these vocabulary words in a conversation with a teacher, parent, or friend.

| | | | |
|---|---|---|---|
| inevitably | vaguely | urgency | intently |
| preoccupied | interval | contemplated | |

THREE WORLDS, M. C. Escher, 1955

# What Do Fish Have to Do with Anything?

Avi

Every day at three o'clock Mrs. Markham waited for her son, Willie, to come out of school. They walked home together. If asked why she did it, Mrs. Markham would say, "Parents need to watch their children."

As they left the schoolyard, Mrs. Markham **inevitably** asked, "How was school?"

Willie would begin to talk, then stop. He was never sure his mother was listening. She seemed **preoccupied** with her own thoughts. She had been like that ever since his dad had abandoned them six months ago. No one knew where he'd gone. Willie had the feeling that his mother was lost too. It made him feel lonely.

**inevitably**
unavoidably; predictably

**preoccupied**
lost or absorbed in thought

One Monday afternoon, as they approached the apartment building where they lived, she suddenly tugged at him. "Don't look that way," she said.

"Where?"

"At that man over there."

Willie stole a look over his shoulder. A man, whom Willie had never seen before, was sitting on a red plastic milk crate near the curb. His matted, streaky gray hair hung like a ragged curtain over his dirty face. His shoes were torn. Rough hands lay upon his knees. One hand was palm up. No one seemed to pay him any mind. Willie was certain he had never seen a man so utterly alone. It was as if he were some spat-out piece of chewing gum on the pavement.

"What's the matter with him?" Willie asked his mother in a hushed voice.

Keeping her eyes straight ahead, Mrs. Markham said, "He's sick." She pulled Willie around. "Don't stare. It's rude."

"What kind of sick?"

As Mrs. Markham searched for an answer, she began to walk faster. "He's unhappy," she said.

"What's he doing?"

"Come on, Willie, you know perfectly well. He's begging."

"Do you think anyone gave him anything?"

"I don't know. Now, come on, don't look."

"Why don't you give him anything?"

"We have nothing to spare."

When they got home, Mrs. Markham removed a white cardboard box from the refrigerator. It contained pound cake. Using her thumb as a measure, she carefully cut a half-inch piece of cake and gave it to Willie on a clean plate. The plate lay on a plastic mat decorated with images of roses with diamondlike dew-drops. She also gave him a glass of milk and a folded napkin. She moved slowly.

Willie said, "Can I have a bigger piece of cake?"

Mrs. Markham picked up the cake box and ran a manicured pink fingernail along the nutrition information panel. "A half-inch piece is a portion, and a portion contains the following health requirements. Do you want to hear them?"

"No."

"It's on the box, so you can believe what it says. Scientists study people, then write these things. If you're smart enough you could become a scientist. Like this." Mrs. Markham tapped the box. "It pays well."

Willie ate his cake and drank the milk. When he was done he took care to wipe the crumbs off his face as well as to blot his milk mustache with the napkin. His mother liked him to be neat.

His mother said, "Now go on and do your homework. Carefully. You're in sixth grade. It's important."

Willie gathered up his books that lay on the empty third chair. At the kitchen entrance he paused and looked back at his mother. She was staring sadly at the cake box, but he didn't think she was seeing it. Her unhappiness made him think of the man on the street.

"What *kind* of unhappiness do you think he has?" he suddenly asked.

"Who's that?"

"That man."

Mrs. Markham looked puzzled.

"The begging man. The one on the street."

"Oh, could be anything," his mother said, **vaguely**. "A person can be unhappy for many reasons." She turned to stare out the window, as if an answer might be there.

"Is unhappiness a sickness you can cure?"

"I wish you wouldn't ask such questions."

"Why?"

After a moment she said, "Questions that have no answers shouldn't be asked."

"Can I go out?"

"Homework first."

Willie turned to go again.

"Money," Mrs. Markham suddenly said. "Money will cure a lot of unhappiness. That's why that man was begging. A salesman once said to me, 'Maybe you can't buy happiness, but you can rent a lot of it.' You should remember that."

**vaguely**
unclearly

"How much money do we have?"

"Not enough."

"Is that why you're unhappy?"

"Willie, do your homework."

Willie started to ask another question, but decided he would not get an answer. He left the kitchen.

The apartment had three rooms. The walls were painted mint green. Willie walked down the hallway to his room, which was at the front of the building. By climbing up on the windowsill and pressing against the glass he could see the sidewalk five stories below. The man was still there.

It was almost five when he went to tell his mother he had finished his school assignments. He found her in her dim bedroom, sleeping. Since she had begun working the night shift at a convenience store—two weeks now—she took naps in the late afternoon.

For a while Willie stood on the threshold,[1] hoping his mother would wake up. When she didn't, he went to the front room and looked down on the street again. The begging man had not moved.

Willie returned to his mother's room.

"I'm going out," he announced—softly.

**interval**
pause; space of time

Willie waited a decent **interval** for his mother to waken. When she did not, he made sure his keys were in his pocket. Then he left the apartment.

By standing just outside the building door, he could keep his eyes on the man. It appeared as if he had still not moved. Willie wondered how anyone could go without moving for so long in the chill October air. Was staying still part of the man's sickness?

During the twenty minutes that Willie watched, no one who passed looked in the beggar's direction. Willie wondered if they even saw the man. Certainly no one put any money into his open hand.

A lady leading a dog by a leash went by. The dog strained in the direction of the man sitting on the crate. His tail wagged. The lady pulled the dog away. "Heel!" she commanded.

---

I **threshold**: doorsill or entrance

The dog—tail between his legs—scampered to the lady's side. Even so, the dog twisted around to look back at the beggar.

Willie grinned. The dog had done exactly what Willie had done when his mother told him not to stare.

Pressing deep into his pocket, Willie found a nickel. It was warm and slippery. He wondered how much happiness you could rent for a nickel.

> He wondered how much happiness you could rent for a nickel.

Squeezing the nickel between his fingers, Willie walked slowly toward the man. When he came before him, he stopped, suddenly nervous. The man, who appeared to be looking at the ground, did not move his eyes. He smelled bad.

"Here." Willie stretched forward and dropped the coin into the man's open right hand.

"God bless you," the man said hoarsely as he folded his fingers over the coin. His eyes, like high beams on a car, flashed up at Willie, then dropped.

Willie waited for a moment, then went back up to his room. From his window he looked down on the street. He thought he saw the coin in the man's hand, but was not sure.

After supper Mrs. Markham readied herself to go to work, then kissed Willie good night. As she did every night, she said, "If you have regular problems, call Mrs. Murphy downstairs. What's her number?"

"274-8676," Willie said.

"Extra bad problems, call Grandma."

"369-6754."

"Super special problems, you can call me."

"962-6743."

"Emergency, the police."

"911."

"Lay out your morning clothing."

"I will."

"Don't let anyone in the door."

"I won't."

"No television past nine."

"I know."

"But you can read late."

"You're the one who's going to be late," Willie reminded her.

"I'm leaving," Mrs. Markham said.

After she went, Willie stood for a long while in the hallway. The empty apartment felt like a cave that lay deep below the earth. That day in school Willie's teacher had told the class about a kind of fish that lived in caves. These fish could not see. They had no eyes. The teacher had said it was living in the dark cave that made them like that.

Willie had raised his hand and asked, "If they want to get out of the cave, can they?"

"I suppose."

"Would their eyes come back?"

"Good question," she said, but did not give an answer.

Before he went to bed, Willie took another look out the window. In the pool of light cast by the street lamp, Willie saw the man.

On Tuesday morning when Willie went to school, the man was gone. But when he came home from school with his mother, he was there again.

"*Please* don't look at him," his mother whispered with some **urgency**.

During his snack, Willie said, "Why shouldn't I look?"

"What are you talking about?"

"That man. On the street. Begging."

"I told you. He's sick. It's better to act as if you never saw him. When people are that way they don't wish to be looked at."

"Why not?"

Mrs. Markham pondered for a while. "People are ashamed of being unhappy."

Willie looked thoughtfully at his mother. "Are you sure he's unhappy?"

"You don't have to ask if people are unhappy. They tell you all the time."

"How?"

"The way they look."

"Is that part of the sickness?"

"Oh, Willie, I don't know. It's just the way they are."

Willie **contemplated** the half-inch slice of cake his mother had just given him. A year ago his parents seemed to be perfectly happy. For Willie, the world seemed easy, full of light. Then his father lost his job. He tried to get another but could not. For long hours he sat in dark rooms. Sometimes he drank. His parents began to argue a lot. One day, his father was gone.

**contemplated**
studied;
considered

For two weeks his mother kept to the dark. And wept.

Willie looked at his mother. "You're unhappy," he said. "Are *you* ashamed?"

His parents began to argue a lot. One day, his father was gone.

Mrs. Markham sighed and closed her eyes. "I wish you wouldn't ask that."

"Why?"

"It hurts me."

"But are you ashamed?" Willie persisted. He felt it was urgent that he know. So that he could do something.

She only shook her head.

Willie said, "Do you think Dad might come back?"

She hesitated before saying, "Yes, I think so."

Willie wondered if that was what she really thought.

"Do you think Dad is unhappy?" Willie asked.

"Where do you get such questions?"

"They're in my mind."

"There's much in the mind that need not be paid attention to."

"Fish who live in caves have no eyes."

"What are you talking about?"

"My teacher said it's all that darkness. The fish forget how to see. So they lose their eyes."

"I doubt she said that."

"She did."

"Willie, you have too much imagination."

After his mother went to work, Willie gazed down onto the street. The man was there. Willie thought of going down, but he knew he was not supposed to leave the building when his mother worked at night. He decided to speak to the man the next day.

That afternoon—Wednesday—Willie stood before the man. "I don't have any money," Willie said. "Can I still talk to you?"

The man lifted his face. It was a dirty face with very tired eyes. He needed a shave.

"My mother," Willie began, "said you were unhappy. Is that true?"

"Could be," the man said.

"What are you unhappy about?"

e looked down from the window. The man was still there.

**intently**
with great
concentration

The man's eyes narrowed as he studied Willie **intently**. He said, "How come you want to know?"

Willie shrugged.

"I think you should go home, kid."

"I am home." Willie gestured toward the apartment. "I live right here. Fifth floor. Where do you live?"

"Around."

"*Are* you unhappy?" Willie persisted.

The man ran a tongue over his lips. His Adam's apple bobbed. "A man has the right to remain silent," he said, and closed his eyes.

Willie remained standing on the pavement for a while before retreating back to his apartment. Once inside he looked down from the window. The man was still there. For a moment Willie was certain the man was looking at the apartment building and the floor where Willie lived.

The next day, Thursday—after dropping a nickel in the man's palm—Willie said, "I've never seen anyone look so unhappy as you do. So I figure you must know a lot about it."

The man took a deep breath. "Well, yeah, maybe."

Willie said, "And I need to find a cure for it."

"A *what*?"

"A cure for unhappiness."

The man pursed his cracked lips and blew a silent whistle. Then he said, "Why?"

"My mother is unhappy."

"Why's that?"

"My dad went away."

"How come?"

"I think because he was unhappy. Now my mother's unhappy too—all the time. So if I found a cure for unhappiness, it would be a good thing, wouldn't it?"

"I suppose. Hey, you don't have anything to eat on you, do you?"

Willie shook his head, then said, "Would you like some cake?"

"What kind?"

"I don't know. Cake."

"Depends on the cake."

On Friday Willie said to the man, "I found out what kind of cake it is."

"Yeah?"

"Pound cake. But I don't know why it's called that."

"Long as it's cake it probably don't matter."

Neither spoke. Then Willie said, "In school my teacher said there are fish who live in caves and the caves are so dark the fish don't have eyes. What do you think? Do you believe that?"

"Sure."

"You do? How come?"

"Because you said so."

"You mean, just because someone *said it* you believe it?"

"Not someone. You."

Willie was puzzled. "But, well, maybe it *isn't* true."

The man grunted. "Hey, do you believe it?"

Willie nodded.

"Well, you're not just anyone. You got eyes. You see. You ain't no fish."

"Oh." Willie was pleased.

"What's your name?" the man asked.

"Willie."

"That's a boy's name. What's your grown-up name?"

"William."

"And that means another thing."

"What?"

"I'll take some of that cake."

Willie started. "You will?" he asked, surprised.

"Just said it, didn't I?"

Willie suddenly felt excited. It was as if the man had given him a gift. Willie wasn't sure what it was except that it was important and he was glad to have it. For a moment he just gazed at the man. He saw the lines on the man's face, the way his lips curved, the small scar on the side of his chin, the shape of his eyes, which he now saw were blue.

"I'll get the cake," Willie cried and ran back to the apartment. He snatched the box from the refrigerator as well as a knife, then hurried back down to the street. "I'll cut you a piece," he said, and he opened the box.

"Hey, that don't look like a pound of cake," the man said.

Willie, alarmed, looked up.

"But like I told you, it don't matter."

Willie held his thumb against the cake to make sure the portion was the right size. With a poke of the knife he made a small mark for the proper width.

Just as he was about to cut, the man said, "Hold it!"

Willie looked up. "What?"

"What were you doing there with your thumb?"

"I was measuring the size. The right portion. A person is supposed to get only one portion."

"Where'd you learn that?"

"It says so on the box. You can see for yourself."

He held out the box.

The man studied the box then handed it back to Willie. "That's just lies," he said.

"How do you know?"

"William, how can a box say how much a person needs?"

"But it does. The scientists say so. They measured, so they know. Then they put it there."

"Lies," the man repeated.

Willie began to feel that this man knew many things. "Well, then, how much should I cut?" he asked.

The man said, "You have to look at me, then at the cake, and then you're going to have to decide for yourself."

"Oh." Willie looked at the cake. The piece was about three inches wide. Willie looked up at the man. After a moment he cut the cake into two pieces, each an inch and a half wide. He gave one piece to the man and kept the other in the box.

"God bless you," the man said as he took the piece and laid it in his left hand. He began to break off pieces with his right hand and put them in his mouth one by one. Each piece was chewed thoughtfully. Willie watched him eat.

> "What a person needs is always more than they say."

When the man was done, he licked the crumbs on his fingers.

"Now I'll give you something," the man said.

"What?" Willie said, surprised.

"The cure for unhappiness."

"You know it?" Willie asked, eyes wide.

The man nodded.

"What is it?"

"It's this: What a person needs is always more than they say."

"Who's *they*?" Willie asked.

The man pointed to the cake box. "The people on the box," he said.

In his mind Willie repeated what he had been told, then he gave the man the second piece of cake.

The man took it, saying, "Good man," and he ate it.

Willie grinned.

The next day was Saturday. Willie did not go to school. All morning he kept looking down from his window for the man, but it was raining and he did not appear. Willie wondered where he was, but could not imagine it.

Willie's mother woke about noon. Willie sat with her while she ate her breakfast. "I found the cure for unhappiness," he announced.

"Did you?" his mother said. She was reading a memo from the convenience store's owner.

"It's 'What a person needs is always more than they say.'"

His mother put her papers down. "That's nonsense. Where did you hear that?"

"That man."

"What man?"

"On the street. The one who was begging. You said he was unhappy. So I asked him."

"Willie, I told you I didn't want you to even look at that man."

"He's a nice man. . . ."

"How do you know?"

"I've talked to him."

"When? How much?"

Willie shrank down, "I did, that's all."

"Willie, I forbid you to talk to him. Do you understand me? Do you? Answer me!" She was shrill.

"Yes," Willie said, but he'd already decided he would talk to the man one more time. He needed to explain why he could not talk to him anymore.

On Sunday, however, the man was not there. Nor was he there on Monday.

"That man is gone," Willie said to his mother as they walked home from school.

"I saw. I'm not blind."

"Where do you think he went?"

"I couldn't care less. But you might as well know, I arranged for him to be gone."

Willie stopped short. "What do you mean?"

"I called the police. We don't need a nuisance like that around here. Pestering kids."

"He wasn't pestering me."

"Of course he was."

"How do you know?"

"Willie, I have eyes. I can see."

Willie glared at his mother. "No, you can't. You're a fish. You live in a cave."

"Fish?" retorted Mrs. Markham. "What do fish have to do with anything? Willie, don't talk nonsense."

"My name isn't Willie. It's William. And I know how to keep from being unhappy. I do!" He was yelling now. "What a person needs is always more than they say! *Always!*"

He turned on his heel and walked back toward the school. At the corner he glanced back. His mother was following. He kept on going. She kept following.

# Reviewing

## What Do Fish Have to Do with Anything?

### Discussing the Selection

1. What words would you use to describe Mrs. Markham? Point out passages that support your choices.

2. Why does Mrs. Markham say, "Questions that have no answers shouldn't be asked"?

3. Find and jot down all the words and phrases in this story that refer to sight. What do you think is the author's purpose?

4. In what ways are the narrator's parents like the cave-dwelling fish mentioned in the story?

### Writing an Explanation

In this story the homeless man says, "What a person needs is always more than they say." What do you think he means by this? Write a short essay explaining your answer.

### About Avi Wortis (1937–)

When he was one year old, Avi's twin sister called him the name he has gone by ever since. In school, he suffered from poor grades and a severe writing impairment called dysgrafia. After graduating from college, he worked many years as a children's librarian. Finally, upon having children of his own, he was inspired to pursue his writing dream. Avi is a fearless writer, tackling all kinds of topics in nearly all the genres: adventure, fantasy, mystery, thrillers, historical, comic, and realistic fiction. He has won many prestigious literature awards, including the Newbery Honor Award for his novels *The True Confessions of Charlotte Doyle* and *Nothing But the Truth*. Avi enjoys writing about complex issues while entertaining his readers "with the sheer pleasure of a good story."

# Previewing

## Homeless
by Anna Quindlen

### Reading Connection

Government experts say that from five to eight million people—two to three percent of the U.S. population—will experience at least one night of homelessness. Amazingly, between 25 and 40 percent of the homeless are employed. Unfortunately, their jobs do not pay well enough for them to buy or rent an apartment. And there is a nationwide shortage of affordable housing. Many of the homeless suffer from mental illness, substance abuse, and abuse at the hands of family. They survive by living under road overpasses, in alleys, bus stations, and abandoned buildings. Many refuse to go to shelters, fearing too many rules or, even worse, too much chaos.

### Skill Focus: Contrast

Some writers use contrast to explain a concept by showing its opposite. In the following essay, Anna Quindlen describes what *home* means in order to show you what is missing in the lives of homeless people. As you read, think about how her description of *home* helps you understand the true feelings of people who do not have one.

### Vocabulary Builder

Anna Quindlen writes for adult readers, but the ideas in this essay can be understood by readers of any age. If you are unfamiliar with the following words, they are defined on the page where they occur.

| | | | |
|---|---|---|---|
| rummaged | legacy | stability | compassionate |
| anonymous | ferocity | compromise | customary |

# Homeless

Anna Quindlen

Her name was Ann, and we met in the Port Authority Bus Terminal several Januarys ago. I was doing a story on homeless people. She said I was wasting my time talking to her; she was just passing through, although she'd been passing through for more than two weeks. To prove to me that this was true, she **rummaged** through a tote bag and a manila envelope and finally unfolded a sheet of typing paper and brought out her photographs.

They were not pictures of family, or friends, or even a dog or cat, its eyes brown-red in the flashbulb's light. They were pictures of a house. It was like a thousand houses in a hundred towns, not suburb, not city, but somewhere in between, with aluminum siding and a chain-link fence, a narrow driveway running up to a one-car garage, and a patch of backyard. The house was yellow. I looked on the back for a date or a name, but neither was there. There was no need for discussion. I knew what she was trying to tell me, for it was something I had often felt. She was not adrift, alone, **anonymous**, although her bags and her raincoat with the grime shadowing its creases had made me believe she was. She had a house, or at least once upon a time had had one. Inside were curtains, a couch, a stove, potholders. You are where you live. She was somebody.

**rummaged**
hunted;
searched

**anonymous**
nameless;
unidentified

**legacy**
inheritance;
hand-me-down

**ferocity**
fierceness;
intensity

**stability**
permanence;
solidness

I've never been very good at looking at the big picture, taking the global view, and I've always been a person with an overactive sense of place, the **legacy** of an Irish grandfather. So it is natural that the thing that seems most wrong with the world to me right now is that there are so many people with no homes. I'm not simply talking about shelter from the elements, or three square meals a day, or a mailing address to which the welfare people can send the check—although I know that all these are important for survival. I'm talking about a home, about precisely those kinds of feelings that have wound up in cross-stitch and French knots on samplers[1] over the years.

Home is where the heart is. There's no place like it. I love my home with a **ferocity** totally out of proportion to its appearence or location. I love dumb things about it: the hot-water heater, the plastic rack you drain dishes in, the roof over my head, which occasionally leaks. And yet it is precisely those dumb things that make it what it is—a place of certainty, **stability**, predictability, privacy, for me and for my family. It is where I live. What more can you say about a place than that? That is everything.

Yet it is something that we have been edging away from gradually during my lifetime and the lifetimes of my parents and grandparents. There was a time when where you lived often was where you worked and where you grew the food you ate and even where you were buried. When that era passed, where you lived at least was where your parents had lived and where you would live with your children when you became enfeebled.[2] Then, suddenly, where you lived was where you lived for three years, until you could move on to something else and something else again.

And so we have come to something else again, to children who do not understand what it means to go to their rooms because they have never had a room, to men and women whose fantasy is a wall they can paint a color of their own choosing, to old people reduced to sitting on molded plastic chairs, their skin blue-white in the lights of a bus station, who pull pictures

---

1 **cross-stitch and French knots on samplers**: fancy hand-stitches on embroidered cloth

2 **enfeebled**: weakened

of houses out of their bags. Homes have stopped being homes. Now they are real estate.[3]

People find it curious that those without homes would rather sleep sitting up on benches or huddled in doorways than go to shelters. Certainly some prefer to do so because they are emotionally ill, because they have been locked in before and they are determined not to be locked in again. Others are afraid of the violence and trouble they may find there. But some seem to want something that is not available in shelters, and they will not **compromise**, not for a cot, or oatmeal, or a shower with special soap that kills the bugs. "One room," a woman with a baby who was sleeping on her sister's floor once told me, "painted blue." That was the crux[4] of it; not the size or location, but pride of ownership. Painted blue.

**compromise**
settle for less than originally wanted

This is a difficult problem, and some wise and **compassionate** people are working hard at it. But in the main I think we work around it, just as we walk around it when it is lying on the sidewalk or sitting in the bus terminal—the problem, that is. It has been **customary** to take people's pain and lessen our own participation in it by turning it into an issue, not a collection of human beings. We turn an adjective into a noun: the poor, not poor people; the homeless, not Ann or the man who lives in the box or the woman who sleeps on the subway grate.

**compassionate**
kind; caring

**customary**
usual; commonly done

Sometimes I think we would be better off if we forgot about the broad strokes and concentrated on the details. Here is a woman without a bureau.[5] There is a man with no mirror, no wall to hang it on. They are not the homeless. They are people who have no homes. No drawer that holds the spoons. No window to look out upon the world. My God. That is everything.

---

3 **real estate**: property

4 **crux**: the main point

5 **bureau**: a piece of bedroom furniture with drawers

# Reviewing

## Homeless

### Discussing the Selection

1. Compare the treatment of the homeless people in Quindlen's essay and Avi's short story, "What Do Fish Have to Do with Anything?" In what ways do the woman in the essay and the man in the short story seem similar? Different?

2. What does the author mean when she says, "You are where you live. She was somebody"?

3. What does the author hope to gain by focusing on only one homeless person?

4. How does Quindlen say "home" has changed in recent times?

### Writing an Opinion Essay

The author of "Homeless" says "the thing that seems most wrong with the world to me right now" is homelessness. In your opinion what seems most wrong with the world today? Explore this question in a short essay, giving reasons and examples for your opinion.

### About Anna Quindlen (1953–)

New Yorker Anna Quindlen won a 1992 Pulitzer Prize for her popular newspaper column, "Public and Private." With a frank, sympathetic voice, she took on big issues—homelessness and poverty—as well as ones closer to home, such as parenting. She considers herself lucky to be able to write about things that trouble her. "What could make you happier than to make a better world, a world that is fairer, more egalitarian, that works better for all?" Quindlen continues to write a column every other week for *Newsweek* magazine. All of her novels and nonfiction books have been best-sellers, and two of her novels have been made into movies.

# Previewing

## from *Reflections on the Civil War*

by Bruce Catton

### Reading Connection

The American Civil War (1861–1865) was fought between the northern states (the Union) and the eleven states in the South (the Confederacy) that decided they no longer wished to be part of the United States. Although there were many reasons for the war, one of the most important was the practice of slavery in the South, which the North opposed. More than 600,000 young men died during this bloody confrontation that the North eventually won.

### Skill Focus: Drawing Conclusions

The historian Bruce Catton spent a lifetime researching and writing about the U.S. Civil War. His work is popular because he is able to combine historical facts with a feel for the flesh-and-blood experiences of soldiers in battle. He wrote in order to share his hard-earned wisdom on this vital subject—war. In particular, a civil war. As you read, consider what each example adds to the general point he is trying to make about war. What idea, if any, do they have in common?

### Vocabulary Builder

This is a challenging piece about a topic that you may know little about. To help make reading easier, preview the vocabulary definitions and the footnotes on the pages of the selection.

| | | | |
|---|---|---|---|
| unsophisticated | self-reliant | devastating | discharging |
| patriotism | ardent | stagnant | appalling |
| aroused | abominably | soberly | |
| recruiting | infested | laudable | |

The flagbearer of the 8th Pennsylvania Reserves

# from
# *Reflections* on
# the *Civil War*

Bruce Catton

In the Civil War, the common soldiers of both sides were the same sort of people: untrained and untaught young men, mostly from the country. There weren't many cities then, and they weren't very large, so the average soldier generally came either from a farm or from some very small town or rural area. He had never been anywhere; he was completely **unsophisticated**. He joined up because he wanted to, because his **patriotism** had been **aroused**. The bands were playing, the **recruiting** officers were making speeches, so he got stirred up and enlisted.[1] Sometimes, he was not altogether dry behind the ears.[2]

**unsophisticated**
simple; unrefined

**patriotism**
devotion
to country;
nationalism;

**aroused**
stirred up;
awakened

**recruiting**
enrolling or
signing up

---

1 **enlisted**: joined the armed services
2 **dry behind the ears**: grown-up

When the boy joined the army, he would, of course, be issued clothing. He would get his uniform—pants, coat, shoes, and underwear. In the frontier regions, the quartermasters[3] discovered that quite a lot of these young men picked up the underwear and looked at it and said, "What is this?" They had never seen any before. They hadn't worn it back home. Well, they caught on. They were fresh out of the backwoods, most of them.

The boys from the country and the very small towns seemed to have made better soldiers than the boys from the cities. In the North, for instance, the boys from the rural areas, and especially from the Middle West, which they then called the Northwest, were a little tougher than the boys from the big cities. They could stand more; they were more **self-reliant**; perhaps they were more used to handling weapons. In any case, they made very good soldiers. On the Southern side, the same was true—even more so. A larger percentage of the men came from rural areas because there were fewer cities in the South. A number of them didn't even bother with shoes, but they were very, very bad boys to get into a fight with.

The war was greeted in its first few weeks almost as a festival. Everybody seemed relieved. People went out and celebrated, both in the North and in the South. There were parades, bands playing, flags flying; people seemed almost happy. Large numbers of troops were enlisted; as a matter of fact, again in both the North and the South, more men offered themselves than could be handled. Neither the Union nor the Confederate government had the weapons, uniforms, or anything else to equip all of the men who tried to enlist.

Both armies contained a number of very **ardent** teenagers who had lied about their age in order to get into the army in the first place. Legal age, of course, was eighteen. It turned out that, in the North at least, a very common

T he war was greeted in its first few weeks almost as a festival. Everybody seemed relieved.

**self-reliant**
independent;
self-sufficient

**ardent**
enthusiastic;
passionate

---

3 **quartermaster**: military officer in charge of supplies

little gag had been developed. A boy who was under eighteen and wanted to enlist would take a piece of paper and scribble the figure eighteen on it. Then he would take off his shoe, placing the piece of paper into the sole of his shoe, put it back on and tie it up. He would go to the recruiting station, and since he would obviously be looking rather young, sooner or later the recruiting officer would look at him and say, "How old are you, son?" Then the boy, in perfect honesty, could say, "I am over eighteen."

The point about that is not so much that young men were lying about their age in order to get into the army but that they would go to the trouble of working out a gag like that. A man simply wouldn't dream of taking an oath that he was eighteen when he wasn't. Lying to the government was a little beyond him, but he would work out a thing like this and could say honestly, "I'm over eighteen," and that made it quite all right.

A set of statistics were compiled about the average Northern soldier that are rather interesting. They apply pretty much to the South as well. An average soldier was 5 feet 8¼ inches tall; he weighed just over 143 pounds. Forty-eight percent were farmers, 24 percent were mechanics, 15 percent were laborers, 5 percent were businessmen, and 3 percent were professional men. That was really a kind of cross-section of the population of the United States at that time: about one-half farmers, about 40 percent working men, and 10 percent businessmen or professionals.

When a man joined the Union army, he was given shoes that must have been a little bit of a trial to wear. In a great many cases, army contractors simply made the right and left shoes identical. They were squared off at the toe, and it didn't matter which one you put on which foot; they were supposed to work either way. They must have been very uncomfortable, and I imagine they account for a great many of the cases of footsore soldiers who fell out on the march and stumbled into camp long after everybody else had gone to bed.

The Civil War soldier, on the Northern side at least, got a great deal to eat; the trouble was that most of it was not very good. The Union army enlisted no cooks or bakers during the entire war. Originally, each man was supposed to cook for himself. It happened, of course, practically immediately that company kitchens were established. Men were detailed from the ranks[4] to act as cooks; some of them cooked fairly well, and some of them, of course, cooked **abominably**. But whatever they cooked, the boys ate.

The basic ration[5] for the Civil War soldier, particularly on the march, where it was not possible to carry along vegetables, was salt pork or bacon and hardtack. The hardtack was a big soda cracker, quite thick and, as the name implies, very tough—made tough so that it wouldn't fall into pieces while it was joggling about in a man's haversack.[6] When the hardtack was fresh, it was apparently quite good to eat. The trouble is that it was very rarely fresh. Boxes of hardtack would sit on the railroad platforms or sidetracked in front of warehouses for weeks and months at a time, and by the time the soldier got them, they were often **infested** and not very good.

Every soldier carried some sort of a tin can in which he could boil coffee. Coffee was issued in the whole bean, for when the government issued ground coffee, they could never quite trust the contractors not to adulterate[7] it. When the soldier made coffee, he would put a handful of beans in a bucket and grind them with the butt of his musket. In the morning, in camp, you could tell when the boys were getting up by the rhythmic clinking, grinding noise that came up from in front of every tent.

The soldier also had sugar to go with his coffee, and he would boil his coffee in his little tin can and then dump in some sugar. He would usually have a skillet in which to fry his bacon. Sometimes he would crumble up hardtack and drop the crumbs in the sizzling bacon fat and make a rather indescribable mess—I guess a healthy young man who got a good deal of exercise could digest it without too much difficulty.

In the Civil War, which lasted four years, about 600,000 young Americans,

---

4 **detailed . . . ranks**: selected from the enlisted troops

5 **ration**: food for one day

6 **haversack**: an over-the-shoulder bag for carrying supplies and personal items

7 **adulterate**: spoil; contaminate

North and South together, lost their lives. That is not the total casualty[8] list; it is the number that actually went under the sod.[9] The wounded, the missing, the prisoners, were in another list. Six hundred thousand is the number of lives that were actually lost.

If you want to understand what a terrible drain that was on the country, reflect that the total population in the United States in the 1860s was about an eighth or a ninth of what it is today. The number of men killed in that war, if you interpret it in today's terms, would come to something between four and four and one-half million. In other words, a perfectly frightful toll of American lives was taken.

> **S**ix hundred thousand is the number of lives that were actually lost.

There are a good many reasons why the toll was so high. More than *one-half* of the men who died were not killed in action; they simply died of camp diseases: typhoid fever, pneumonia, dysentery, and childhood diseases like measles and chicken pox.

To begin with, medical science then was woefully inadequate. Doctors simply did not know what caused such **devastating** camp diseases as typhoid fever, which accounted for about one-fourth of all deaths in army hospitals. Malaria, a plague of the Virginia swamp country, was attributed to "miasmic vapors" arising from **stagnant** waters and not to the pestiferous[10] mosquitoes bred therein. (The vapors were also largely blamed for typhoid and dysentery.) Nothing was known about how and why wounds became infected, and so nothing much was done to prevent infection; surgeons talked **soberly** about "**laudable** pus" which was expected to appear a few days after an operation or a gunshot wound, its laudable character arising because it showed that the body was **discharging** poisons.

**devastating**
destructive

**stagnant**
unmoving;
moving slowly

**soberly**
seriously;
solemnly

**laudable**
worthy of
praise

**discharging**
letting go of

---

8 **casualty**: injured person; victim

9 **went under the sod**: died and were buried ("were laid under the grass")

10 **pestiferous**: disease-carrying

**appalling**
terrible;
horrifying

The number of men who simply got sick and died, or who got a minor scratch or cut and then could do nothing to check the infection, was **appalling**. Just to be in the army in the 1860s was much more dangerous than anything we know about today, even though many a man in the army never got into action. It was a very common thing—in fact, almost a rule—for a Civil War regiment[11] on either side to lose about half of its strength in men who either became sick and died or became so ill they had to get medical discharges before the regiment ever saw action. Whereas a Civil War regiment, on paper, contained about one thousand men, in actual fact, a regiment that went into battle with as many as five hundred men was quite fortunate.

> Just to be in the army in the 1860s was much more dangerous than anything we know about today . . .

Not long after the war began, whenever a Northern army and a Southern army were camped fairly close to each other, the men on the picket lines[12] would get acquainted with one another and would call little informal truces.[13] The Northern soldiers would bring in coffee to trade. Along the Rappahannock River, they made quite a thing of constructing little toy boats out of planks. A boat would be maybe two feet long, with a mast and a sail. Loaded with coffee, it would be sent out into the stream, pointed south, and when it would get across the river, the Confederate soldiers would unload the coffee, stock it with tobacco, and send it back.

This led to some rather odd happenings, since men who are stopping to trade with each other are apt to get a little friendly along the way. There was one rather famous occasion, again along the Rappahannock River, when in a building not far behind the Confederate lines back of the outposts,[14] there

---

11 **regiment**: military troop or division

12 **picket lines**: guards posted around the edge of military encampments

13 **truces**: ceasefires; agreements to stop fighting

14 **outposts**: outlying settlements or stations of troops

was going to be a dance one evening, and the Confederate pickets invited their Yankee friends to come over and go to the dance.

Half a dozen Yankee soldiers, leaving their guns behind them, crossed the river in the darkness, went to the dance, and had a very good time—until a Confederate officer appeared just when festivities were at their height. He was, of course, horrified and ordered the Yankee soldiers arrested and thrown into prison, at which point the Confederates begged him not to do this. They said they had given the Yankees their word that everything would be all right if they came to the dance, and asked that the officer let them go.

Well, the officer saw some point to that appeal. He couldn't violate or cause his men to violate their honor, so after giving all hands a don't-let-it-happen-again lecture, he released the Yankee prisoners, and they went home with a good long dance under their belts.

Along the Rapidan River during the winter of 1863 and 1864, the armies for a number of miles had outposts that were drawn up very close to each other. In fact, in one or two places, they actually overlapped. The Yankees had a way of advancing their picket lines in the night and pulling them back in the daytime. The Confederates did it just the other way around; their picket lines were a little farther forward by day than by night. Pretty soon it turned out that there was a picket post, with a log cabin and a fireplace, that was used at night by the Yankees and in the daytime by the Confederates. The boys worked out a deal: Each party would leave a stack of firewood on hand and be sure to get out before the other one got there. They kept on that way quite pleasantly for some months.

At the great Battle of Fredericksburg, down at the far end of the line where the fighting was not very heavy, there was a woodland stretch held by the Confederates on one side and the Yankees on the other. The pickets, again, were quite close together, and the skirmish lines[15] not much farther apart. The men got to catcalling[16] and jeering at each other and making insulting remarks. This went on for quite a while in much the same way that a couple of high school

---

15 **skirmish lines**: lines of troops attacking each other
16 **catcalling**: harsh sounds expressing disapproval

football cheering sections might yell back and forth at each other. Finally, a couple of soldiers, a Confederate and a Yankee, got really angry. They got so angry that they had to have a fight. So all along the line in this particular section of the woodland, the soldiers called an informal truce, and the riled-up Yankee and Southerner got out and had a very fine, soul-satisfying fistfight. I don't know who came out on top, but at last the fight ended, as all such fights do, and the men went to a nearby stream and washed the blood off their faces and shook hands. Then both sides went back, picked up their weapons, and started shooting at each other again.

It was that kind of war—rather informal, and fought between men who, when left alone, got along together beautifully. You've often heard it spoken of as the War Between Brothers. Actually, it really was that.

The siege[17] of Vicksburg was another case where the picket lines were so close together that on one occasion the Southerners and the Northerners had a little meeting and came to an agreement as to just where the picket lines ought to go, so they wouldn't trespass on each other's territory.

During this siege, one of the Confederates out on the picket line asked if there were any Missouri regiments in the army immediately opposing his section. He was a Missourian himself and was looking for his brother. The Yankees made inquiry, and pretty soon they came forward with the Confederate soldier's brother—both boys from Missouri, one of them in Confederate gray and the other in Federal blue. The Confederate had a roll of bills in his hand and gave them to his brother to send to their mother, who was peaceably at home in Missouri. He couldn't get things out from Vicksburg through the Union lines, Vicksburg being completely surrounded, so he asked his brother to send them to her, and the brother did. There was no shooting while these arrangements were made, then the brothers shook hands and retired to their individual lines, and the shooting started up again.

During the fighting at Crampton's Gap in Maryland in the fall of 1862, the Confederates were slowly withdrawing. They were fighting a rear-guard

---

17 **siege**: the act of cutting off a city from water, food, and supplies

action rather than a regular battle. One Yankee soldier got a little too far forward, slipped, and accidentally slid down the side of the steep hill on which he had been posted, winding up at the bottom of the hill in a thicket.[18] There he confronted a Confederate soldier who wasn't ready to retreat yet. The two men grabbed their guns. But eventually they figured there was no point in shooting each other here, off in a quiet corner where there wasn't much going on, so they laid down their weapons and made an agreement. They would stay where they were with no shooting. At the end of the day if the Confederates had advanced,

> The two men grabbed their guns. But eventually they figured there was no point in shooting each other . . .

the Yankee would be the Confederate soldier's prisoner. If the Yankees had advanced, then the Confederate would be the Yankee's prisoner. Meanwhile, there wasn't any sense in getting shot. The Confederates eventually withdrew, and the Yankee soldier found he had taken a prisoner.

One of the most touching stories I know involving this acquaintanceship— friendship, really—between the rival soldiers took place at Fredericksburg, Virginia, along the Rappahannock, a couple of months after the big battle there. The Rappahannock River is not very wide, and the men on the northern bank could easily talk with the men on the southern bank if they raised their voices a little. One winter afternoon when nothing much was going on, a number of the Federal army bands were massed on the hillside overlooking the river valley to give a little informal concert. They played all of the Northern patriotic songs, and the Northern soldiers crowded around to listen. On the opposite shore, the Confederate soldiers gathered to enjoy the concert.

After a while, the band had pretty well run through its repertoire,[19] and there was a pause, whereupon some of the Confederates shouted, "Now play some of ours." So the band began to play Southern tunes. They played "Dixie"

---

18 **thicket**: a small, thick patch of bushes

19 **repertoire**: list of selections

and "Bonnie Blue Flag" and "Yellow Rose of Texas" and I don't know what all. They played Southern tunes while the Southern and Northern armies sat in the quiet and listened.

It was getting on toward dusk by this time, so the band, to signal the end of the concert, went into "Home, Sweet Home." Both armies together tried to sing it, and it was rather a sentimental occasion. After all, these boys were a long way from home. They knew perfectly well that a great many of them were never going to see home again; as soon as the warm weather came, they would be fighting each other. The song got to be a little too much for them, and pretty soon they choked up and couldn't sing, and the band finished the music all by itself.

A couple of months later, the troops faced each other in the terrible Battle of Chancellorsville.

# Reviewing

## from *Reflections on the Civil War*

### Discussing the Selection

1. From this account, draw some conclusions about what the average Civil War soldier was like.

2. "The war was greeted in its first few weeks almost as a festival. Everybody seemed relieved." Why might people have had this reaction?

3. Describe some of the hardships the enlisted men endured. How do you think this contributes, if at all, to their feelings about each other?

4. Does the author show any favoritism for one side or the other, Union or Confederacy? Support your answer with evidence from the essay.

### Writing an Informative Report

Find out more about the Civil War by choosing one of the details mentioned in this selection and writing a short report on what you learn. Make sure that the topic you choose is limited enough to be covered in just a few paragraphs. Some examples might be hardtack, uniforms, songs of the North or South, and so forth.

### About Bruce Catton  (1899–1978)

Born in Michigan to a Congregationalist minister and his family, Bruce Catton became one of America's most respected and popular Civil War historians. Catton's books are not just "doorstops" thick with facts and footnotes, but solid storytelling filled with details about real people's lives. Catton's writing has been described as having "a near-magic power of imagination." As a young man, Catton served in the navy during World War I, afterwards writing for a variety of news services. His book about the final military campaign in the Civil War, *A Stillness at Appomattox*, received two of America's most celebrated writing prizes: a Pulitzer Prize and the National Book Award. In 1954 Catton helped found *American Heritage* magazine.

# Unit Four

# **D**ECISIONS,
## DECISIONS

*It is our choices . . . that show what we truly are, far more than our abilities.*

J. K. Rowling

Each decision you make—or don't make—is a true test of who you are and what you value. It's never easy. Most important decisions include both positive and negative consequences. Sometimes you must make a decision that goes against your personal wishes. And sometimes it is simply out of your hands. Someone—or something—makes a decision that affects you. The literature in Unit Four offers you the opportunity to view others' decisions and learn from them. As in real life, some of the outcomes are tragic, and others are simply funny.

# Building Vocabulary

## Context Clues

There are many ways to figure out the meaning of a new word. You can, of course, look it up in a dictionary. You can ask someone who is familiar with the word. And you can use what you already know about root and base words, prefixes and suffixes.

For example, look at the word *disjoined*. If you don't know what it means, try figuring it out by using word parts.

> *disjoined* = *dis* + *joined*
> *joined* means "put together"
> *dislike* means "not like"
> *disjoined* means "not put together"

Words you know can often help you figure out words you don't know. When you see an unfamiliar word, ask yourself if it contains any familiar parts.

When word parts can't help you, try using context. The **context** of a word is the phrase, sentence, or paragraph in which it appears. Context always supplies some clue or clues to a word's meaning, but the amount of help varies. Sometimes all the context tells you is what part of speech the word is, but at other times it provides a great deal of information. For example:

> He's a *curmudgeon*!
> [The structure of this sentence tells you that *curmudgeon* is a noun.]

> I don't want to act like a *curmudgeon*.
> [Now you can determine that *curmudgeon* is a noun and probably not something good.]

> Her bad temper, rudeness, and grumpiness soon gave her a reputation as a *curmudgeon*.
> [Not only is *curmudgeon* a noun, it apparently means someone who has several bad qualities.]

The last example for *curmudgeon* actually provides a definition of the word. The reader doesn't usually get this much help.

# Building Vocabulary *continued*

## Synonyms

A common kind of context clue is a synonym, a word that means the same, or almost the same, thing as the unfamiliar word. For example:

> She has a *prickly* personality and irritates everyone she meets.
> [This suggests that *prickly* and *irritates* are similar in meaning.]

> Of course I *denounce* that action! Who wouldn't disapprove?
> [It is clear that someone who *denounces* something disapproves of it.]

> When he *berated* the child, I said that she had already been scolded enough.
> [This suggests that *berated* and *scolded* are similar.]

> Ramsey's *exertion* left him gasping, for he was not used to making such a considerable effort.
> [This makes it clear that an *exertion* is a considerable effort.]

## Antonyms

Another useful kind of context clue tells you that something is the opposite of something else, or at least quite different. For example:

> Unlike Matt, who was cowardly, Terry was *plucky*.
> [*Plucky* means something quite different from *cowardly*.]

> Some of my problems are important, but some are *piddling*.
> [*Piddling* means something that is the opposite of *important*.]

> Marsha meant to help me, but her efforts *hindered* me instead.
> [To *hinder* is obviously something very different from to *help*.]

> Antoine tried to *dissuade* me, but everyone else encouraged me.
> [To *dissuade* someone is apparently very different from encouraging someone.]

# Building Vocabulary *continued*

## Examples

Finally, context can help by giving one or more examples.

> Frank didn't have a car, so his *conveyance* was usually a bicycle.
> [*Car* and *bicycle* appear to be examples of *conveyances*, so a *conveyance* is probably a vehicle.]

> My *mishaps* included twisting my ankle, dropping my homework in the snow, and losing my keys.
> [These events are all *mishaps*, so a *mishap* is probably some sort of unlucky accident.]

> The town's *edifices* included the public library; city hall; the courthouse; and five old, stone churches.
> [The things that are listed are all buildings, so an *edifice* is probably a building—most likely a large and impressive one.]

> The *maladies* included measles and chicken pox in the children, arthritis and heart problems in the elderly, and colds and flu in all groups.
> [The things mentioned are illnesses, so a *malady* is almost certainly an illness.]

As you can see, while context clues rarely provide an exact definition of a word, they often give you a good idea about its meaning.

# Previewing

## President Cleveland, Where Are You?

by Robert Cormier

### Reading Connection

This story takes place in the 1930s in an era known as the Great Depression. After the stock market crashed in 1929, the whole economy of the United States suffered terribly. Many factories closed, and farmers who couldn't get paid for their crops fled to the cities. Soup lines formed, and homeless people begged and slept on the streets. President Franklin Roosevelt said that unemployment left "one-third of a nation ill-housed, ill-clad, ill-nourished." Anyone with a job and a home was considered fortunate. The boys in this story have to scrape for nickels and dimes, but they are still better off than a large part of the population.

### Skill Focus: Cause-and-Effect Relationships

A cause-and-effect relationship is one way writers can structure the plot of a story. Something happens that *causes* a result, or *effect*. This "something" can be an action a character takes or a decision that a character makes. These actions and decisions make a story complex and interesting to read and move the plot forward. Keep track of the cause-and-effect relationships that occur in the following story.

### Vocabulary Builder

Try using context clues for the vocabulary words in this story. Cover the definitions in the margins of the pages and see if context helps you to determine the meaning of each boldfaced word.

| | | | |
|---|---|---|---|
| allotted | splurge | dwindled | blissfully |
| indifferent | dismayed | divulge | lethargy |
| contempt | indignant | harassed | |
| disconsolately | obsessed | dejection | |

# President Cleveland, Where Are You?

Robert Cormier

Bat Boys, Lance Richbourg

That was the autumn of the cowboy cards—Buck Jones and Tom Tyler and Hoot Gibson and especially Ken Maynard.[1] The cards were available in those five-cent packages of gum: pink sticks, three together, covered with a sweet white powder. You couldn't blow bubbles with that particular gum, but it couldn't have mattered less. The cowboy cards were important—the pictures of those rock-faced men with eyes of blue steel.

On those windswept, leaf-tumbling afternoons, we gathered after school on the sidewalk in front of Lemire's Drugstore across from St. Jude's Parochial School, and we swapped and bargained and matched for the cards. Because a Ken Maynard serial[2] was playing at the Globe every Saturday afternoon, he was the most popular cowboy of all, and one of his cards was worth at least ten of any other kind. Rollie Tremaine had a treasure of thirty or so, and he guarded them jealously. He'd match you for the other cards, but he risked his Ken Maynards only when the other kids threatened to leave him out of the competition altogether.

You could almost hate Rollie Tremaine. In the first place, he was the only son of Auguste Tremaine, who operated the Uptown Dry Goods Store, and he did not live in a tenement[3] but in a big white birthday cake of a house on Laurel Street. He was too fat to be effective in the football games between the Frenchtown Tigers and the North Side Nights, and he made us constantly aware of the jingle of coins in his pockets. He was able to stroll into Lemire's and casually select a quarter's worth of cowboy cards while the rest of us watched, aching with envy.

---

1 **Buck Jones . . .Tom Tyler . . . Hoot Gibson . . . Ken Maynard**: popular western movie stars of the 1930s

2 **serial**: a film that is shown in weekly episodes

3 **tenement**: a low-rent apartment building

Once in a while I earned a nickel or dime by running errands or washing windows for blind old Mrs. Belander, or by finding pieces of copper, brass, and other valuable metals at the dump and selling them to the junkman. The coins clutched in my hand, I would race to Lemire's to buy a cowboy card or two, hoping that Ken Maynard would stare boldly out at me as I opened the pack. At one time, before a disastrous matching session with Roger Lussier (my best friend, except where the cards were involved), I owned five Ken Maynards and considered myself a millionaire of sorts.

One week I was particularly lucky; I had spent two afternoons washing floors for Mrs. Belander and received a quarter. Because my father had worked a full week at the shop, where a rush order for fancy combs had been received, he **allotted** my brothers and sisters and me an extra dime along with the usual ten cents for the Saturday-afternoon movie. Setting aside the movie fare, I found myself with a bonus of thirty-five cents, and I then planned to put Rollie Tremaine to shame the following Monday afternoon.

**allotted**
distributed to

Monday was the best day to buy the cards because the candy man stopped at Lemire's every Monday morning to deliver the new assortments. There was nothing more exciting in the world than a fresh batch of card boxes. I rushed home from school that day and hurriedly changed my clothes, eager to set off for the store. As I burst through the doorway, letting the screen door slam behind me, my brother Armand blocked my way.

He was fourteen, three years older than I, and a freshman at Monument High School. He had recently become a stranger to me in many ways— **indifferent** to such matters as cowboy cards and the Frenchtown Tigers—and he carried himself with a mysterious dignity that was fractured now and then when his voice began shooting off in all directions like some kind of vocal fireworks.

**indifferent**
uninterested

"Wait a minute, Jerry," he said. "I want to talk to you." He motioned me out of earshot of my mother, who was busy supervising the usual after-school skirmish[4] in the kitchen.

I sighed with impatience. In recent months Armand had become a figure

---

4 **skirmish:** a small battle

of authority, siding with my father and mother occasionally. As the oldest son, he sometimes took advantage of his age and experience to issue rules and regulations.

"How much money have you got?" he whispered.

"You in some kind of trouble?" I asked, excitement rising in me as I remembered the blackmail[5] plot of a movie at the Globe a month before.

He shook his head in annoyance. "Look," he said, "it's Pa's birthday tomorrow. I think we ought to chip in and buy him something . . ."

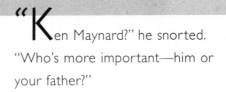

"**K**en Maynard?" he snorted. "Who's more important—him or your father?"

I reached into my pocket and caressed the coins. "Here," I said carefully, pulling out a nickel. "If we all give a nickel, we should have enough to buy him something pretty nice."

He regarded me with **contempt**. "Rita already gave me fifteen cents, and I'm throwing in a quarter. Albert handed over a dime—all that's left of his birthday money. Is that all you can do—a nickel?"

**contempt**
scorn; disgust

"Aw, come on," I protested. "I haven't got a single Ken Maynard left, and I was going to buy some cards this afternoon."

"Ken Maynard!" he snorted. "Who's more important—him or your father?"

His question was unfair because he knew that there was no possible choice—"my father" had to be the only answer. My father was a huge man who believed in the things of the spirit,[6] although my mother often maintained that the spirits he believed in came in bottles.[7] He had worked at the Monument Comb Shop since the age of fourteen; his booming laugh—or grumble—greeted us each night when he returned from the factory. A steady worker when the shop had enough work, he quickened with gaiety on Friday

---

5 **blackmail**: an attempt to get money from someone by threatening to reveal a secret

6 **spirit**: the soul

7 **spirits**: strong alcoholic beverages

nights and weekends, a bottle of beer at his elbow, and he was fond of making long speeches about the good things in life. In the middle of the Depression, for instance, he paid cash for a piano, of all things, and insisted that my twin sisters, Yolande and Yvette, take lessons once a week.

I took a dime from my pocket and handed it to Armand.

"Thanks, Jerry," he said. "I hate to take your last cent."

"That's all right," I replied, turning away and consoling myself with the thought that twenty cents was better than nothing at all.

When I arrived at Lemire's, I sensed disaster in the air. Roger Lussier was kicking **disconsolately** at a tin can in the gutter, and Rollie Tremaine sat sullenly on the steps in front of the store.

"Save your money," Roger said. He had known about my plans to **splurge** on the cards.

"What's the matter?" I asked.

"There's no more cowboy cards," Rollie Tremaine said. "The company's not making any more."

"They're going to have President cards," Roger said, his face twisting with disgust. He pointed to the store window. "Look!"

A placard in the window announced: "Attention, Boys. Watch for the New Series. Presidents of the United States. Free in Each 5-Cent Package of Caramel Chew."

"President cards?" I asked, **dismayed**.

I read on: "Collect a Complete Set and Receive an Official Imitation Major League Baseball Glove, Embossed with Lefty Grove's[8] Autograph."

Glove or no glove, who could become excited about Presidents, of all things?

Rollie Tremaine stared at the sign. "Benjamin Harrison,[9] for crying out loud," he said. "Why would I want Benjamin Harrison when I've got twenty-two Ken Maynards?"

I felt the warmth of guilt creep over me. I jingled the coins in my pocket,

disconsolately
joylessly

splurge
to spend wildly
or without care

dismayed
anxious;
fearful or full of
concern

---

8 **Lefty Grove**: a left-handed pitcher who played from 1925 to 1941

9 **Benjamin Harrison**: president of the United States from 1889 to 1893

but the sound was hollow. No more Ken Maynards to buy.

"I'm going to buy a Mr. Goodbar," Rollie Tremaine decided.

I was without appetite, indifferent even to a Baby Ruth, which was my favorite. I thought of how I had betrayed Armand and, worst of all, my father.

"I'll see you after supper," I called over my shoulder to Roger as I hurried away toward home. I took the shortcut behind the church, although it involved leaping over a tall wooden fence, and I zigzagged recklessly through Mr. Thibodeau's garden, trying to outrace my guilt. I pounded up the steps and into the house, only to learn that Armand had already taken Yolande and Yvette uptown to shop for the birthday present.

I pedaled my bike furiously through the streets, ignoring the **indignant** horns of automobiles as I sliced through the traffic. Finally I saw Armand and my sisters emerge from the Monument Men's Shop. My heart sank when I spied the long, slim package that Armand was holding.

"Did you buy the present yet?" I asked, although I knew it was too late.

"Just now. A blue tie," Armand said. "What's the matter?"

"Nothing," I replied, my chest hurting.

He looked at me for a long moment. At first his eyes were hard, but then they softened. He smiled at me, almost sadly, and touched my arm. I turned away from him because I felt naked and exposed.

"It's all right," he said gently. "Maybe you've learned something." The words were gentle, but they held a curious dignity, the dignity remaining even when his voice suddenly cracked on the last syllable.

I wondered what was happening to me, because I did not know whether to laugh or cry.

Sister Angela was amazed when, a week before Christmas vacation, everybody in the class submitted a history essay worthy of a high mark—in some cases as high as A-minus. (Sister Angela did not believe that anyone in the world ever deserved an A.) She never learned—or at least she never let on that she knew—we all had become experts on the Presidents because of the cards we purchased at Lemire's. Each card contained a picture of a President, and on the reverse side, a summary of his career. We looked at those cards so often that the

**indignant**
angry

biographies imprinted themselves on our minds without effort. Even our street-corner conversations were filled with such information as the fact that James Madison was called "The Father of the Constitution," or that John Adams had intended to become a minister.

The President cards were a roaring success and the cowboy cards were quickly forgotten. In the first place we did not receive gum with the cards but a kind of chewy caramel. The caramel could be tucked into a corner of your mouth, bulging your cheek in much the same manner as wads of tobacco bulged the mouths of baseball stars. In the second place the competition for collecting the cards was fierce and frustrating—fierce because everyone was intent on being the first to send away for a baseball glove and frustrating because although there were only thirty-two Presidents, including Franklin Delano Roosevelt, the variety at Lemire's was at a minimum. When the deliveryman left the boxes of cards at the store each Monday, we often discovered that one entire box was devoted to a single President—two weeks in a row the boxes contained nothing but Abraham Lincolns. One week Roger Lussier and I were the heroes of Frenchtown. We journeyed on our bicycles to the North Side, engaged three boys in a matching bout and returned with five new Presidents, including Chester Alan Arthur, who up to that time had been missing.

Perhaps to sharpen our desire, the card company sent a sample glove to Mr. Lemire, and it dangled, orange and sleek, in the window. I was half sick with longing, thinking of my old glove at home, which I had inherited from Armand. But Rollie Tremaine's desire for the glove outdistanced my own. He even got Mr. Lemire to agree to give the glove in the window to the first person to get a complete set of cards, so that precious time wouldn't be wasted waiting for the postman.

We were delighted at Rollie Tremaine's frustration, especially since he was only a substitute player for the Tigers. Once after spending fifty cents on cards—all of which turned out to be Calvin Coolidge—he threw them to the ground, pulled some dollar bills out of his pocket and said, "The heck with it. I'm going to buy a glove!"

"Not that glove," Roger Lussier said. "Not a glove with Lefty Grove's autograph. Look what it says at the bottom of the sign."

We all looked, although we knew the words by heart: This Glove Is Not For Sale Anywhere."

Rollie Tremaine scrambled to pick up the cards from the sidewalk, pouting more than ever. After that he was quietly **obsessed** with the Presidents, hugging the cards close to his chest and refusing to tell us how many more he needed to complete his set.

I too was obsessed with the cards, because they had become things of comfort in a world that had suddenly grown dismal. After Christmas a layoff at the shop had thrown my father out of work. He received no paycheck for four weeks, and the only income we had was from Armand's after-school job at the Blue and White Grocery store—a job he lost finally when business **dwindled** as the layoff continued.

Although we had enough food and clothing—my father's credit had always been good, a matter of pride with him—the inactivity made my father restless and irritable. He did not drink any beer at all, and laughed loudly, but not convincingly, after gulping down a glass of water and saying, "Lent[10] came early this year." The twins fell sick and went to the hospital to have their tonsils removed. My father was confident that he would return to work eventually and pay off his debts, but he seemed to age before our eyes.

When orders were received at the comb shop and he returned to work, another disaster occurred, although I was the only one aware of it. Armand fell in love.

I discovered his situation by accident, when I happened to pick up a piece of paper that had fallen to the floor in the bedroom he and I shared. I frowned at the paper, puzzled.

"Dear Sally, when I look into your eyes the world stands still . . ."

The letter was snatched from my hands before I finished reading it.

"What's the big idea, snooping around?" Armand asked, his face crimson. "Can't a guy have any privacy?"

> **obsessed**
> having one's mind completely filled with a single idea or feeling

> **dwindled**
> reduced; tapered off

---

10 **Lent**: the forty weekdays between Ash Wednesday and Easter during which many Christians fast or give up a favorite food or pastime

He had never mentioned privacy before. "It was on the floor," I said. "I didn't know it was a letter. Who's Sally?"

He flung himself across the bed. "You tell anybody and I'll muckalize you," he threatened. "Sally Knowlton."

Nobody in Frenchtown had a name like Knowlton.

"A girl from the North Side?" I asked, incredulous.

He rolled over and faced me, anger in his eyes, and a kind of despair too.

"What's the matter with that? Think she's too good for me?" he asked. "I'm warning you, Jerry, if you tell anybody . . ."

"Don't worry," I said. Love had no particular place in my life; it seemed an unnecessary waste of time. And a girl from the North Side was so remote that for all practical purposes she did not exist. But I was curious. "What are you writing her a letter for? Did she leave town, or something?"

> **L**ove had no particular place in my life; it seemed an unnecessary waste of time.

"She hasn't left town," he answered. "I wasn't going to send it. I just felt like writing to her."

I was glad that I had never become involved with love—love that brought desperation to your eyes, that caused you to write letters you did not plan to send. Shrugging with indifference, I began to search in the closet for the old baseball glove. I found it on the shelf, under some old sneakers. The webbing was torn and the padding was gone. I thought of the sting I would feel when a sharp grounder slapped into the glove, and I winced.

"You tell anybody about me and Sally and I'll—"

"I know. You'll muckalize me."

**divulge**
reveal; give away

I did not **divulge** his secret and often shared his agony, particularly when he sat at the supper table and left my mother's special butterscotch pie untouched. I had never realized before how terrible love could be. But my compassion was short-lived, because I had other things to worry about: report cards due at Eastertime; the loss of income from old Mrs. Belander, who had gone to live with a daughter in Boston; and, of course, the Presidents.

Because a stalemate[11] had been reached, the President cards were the dominant force in our lives—mine, Roger Lussier's, and Rollie Tremaine's. For three weeks as the baseball season approached, each of us had a complete set—complete except for one President, Grover Cleveland. Each time a box of cards arrived at the store, we hurriedly bought them (as hurriedly as our funds allowed) and tore off the wrappers, only to be confronted by James Monroe or Martin Van Buren or someone else. But never Grover Cleveland, never the man who had been the twenty-second *and* the twenty-fourth President of the United States. We argued about Grover Cleveland. Should he be placed between Chester Alan Arthur and Benjamin Harrison as the twenty-second President or did he belong between Benjamin Harrison and William McKinley as the twenty-fourth President? Was the card company playing fair? Roger Lussier brought up a horrifying possibility—did we need *two* Grover Clevelands to complete the set?

Indignant, we stormed Lemire's and protested to the **harassed** store owner, who had long since vowed never to stock a new series. Muttering angrily, he searched his bills and receipts for a list of rules.

**harassed**
annoyed

"All right," he announced. "Says here you only need one Grover Cleveland to finish the set. Now get out, all of you, unless you've got money to spend."

Outside the store, Rollie Tremaine picked up an empty tobacco tin and scaled[12] it across the street. "Boy," he said. "I'd give five dollars for a Grover Cleveland."

When I returned home, I found Armand sitting on the piazza[13] steps, his chin in his hands. His mood of **dejection** mirrored my own, and I sat down beside him. We did not say anything for a while.

**dejection**
gloominess;
depression

"Want to throw the ball around?" I asked.

He sighed, not bothering to answer.

"You sick?" I asked.

He stood up and hitched up his trousers, pulled at his ear and finally told

---

11 **stalemate**: a situation when no one is able to win

12 **scaled**: threw so that it moved edgewise

13 **piazza**: porch

Grover Cleveland

me what the matter was—there was a big dance next week at the high school, the Spring Promenade, and Sally had asked him to be her escort.

I shook my head at the folly[14] of love. "Well, what's so bad about that?"

"How can I take Sally to a fancy dance?" he asked desperately. "I'd have to buy her a corsage . . . And my shoes are practically falling apart. Pa's got too many worries now to buy me new shoes or give me money for flowers for a girl."

I nodded in sympathy. "Yeah," I said. "Look at me. Baseball time is almost here, and all I've got is that old glove. And no Grover Cleveland card yet . . ."

"Grover Cleveland?" he asked. "They've got some of those up on the North Side. Some kid was telling me there's a store that's got them. He says they're looking for Warren G. Harding."

"Holy Smoke!" I said. "I've got an extra Warren G. Harding!" Pure joy sang in my veins. I ran to my bicycle, swung into the seat—and found that the front tire was flat.

"I'll help you fix it," Armand said.

Within half an hour I was at the North Side Drugstore, where several boys were matching cards on the sidewalk. Silently but **blissfully** I shouted: "President Grover Cleveland, here I come!"

After Armand had left for the dance, all dressed up as if it were Sunday, the

**blissfully**
joyfully; happily

---

14 **folly**: foolishness

small green box containing the corsage under his arm, I sat on the railing of the piazza, letting my feet dangle. The neighborhood was quiet because the Frenchtown Tigers were at Daggett's Field, practicing for the first baseball game of the season.

I thought of Armand and the ridiculous expression on his face when he'd stood before the mirror in the bedroom. I'd avoided looking at his new black shoes. "Love," I muttered.

> I felt like Benedict Arnold and knew that I had to confess what I had done.

Spring had arrived in a sudden stampede of apple blossoms and fragrant breezes. Windows had been thrown open and dust mops had banged on the sills all day long as the women busied themselves with house cleaning. I was puzzled by my **lethargy**. Wasn't spring supposed to make everything bright and gay?

**lethargy**
tiredness;
exhaustion

I turned at the sound of footsteps on the stairs. Roger Lussier greeted me with a sour face.

"I thought you were practicing with the Tigers," I said.

"Rollie Tremaine," he said. "I just couldn't stand him." He slammed his fist against the railing. "Jeez, why did *he* have to be the one to get a Grover Cleveland? You should see him showing off. He won't let anybody even touch that glove . . ."

I felt like Benedict Arnold[15] and knew that I had to confess what I had done.

"Roger," I said, "I got a Grover Cleveland card up on the North Side. I sold it to Rollie Tremaine for five dollars."

"Are you crazy?" he asked.

"I needed that five dollars. It was an—an emergency."

"Boy!" he said, looking down at the ground and shaking his head. "What did you have to do a thing like that for?"

I watched him as he turned away and began walking down the stairs.

---

15 **Benedict Arnold**: (1741–1801), an American general during the Revolutionary War who became a traitor

"Hey, Roger!" I called.

He squinted up at me as if I were a stranger, someone he'd never seen before.

"What?" he asked, his voice flat.

"I had to do it," I said. "Honest."

He didn't answer. He headed toward the fence, searching for the board we had loosened to give us a secret passage.

I thought of my father and Armand and Rollie Tremaine and Grover Cleveland and wished that I could go away someplace far away. But there was no place to go.

Roger found the loose slat in the fence and slipped through. I felt betrayed; weren't you supposed to feel good when you did something fine and noble?

A moment later two hands gripped the top of the fence and Roger's face appeared. "Was it a real emergency?" he yelled.

"A real one!" I called. "Something important!"

His face dropped from sight and his voice reached me across the yard: "All right."

"See you tomorrow!" I yelled.

I swung my legs over the railing again. The gathering dusk began to soften the sharp edges of the fence, the rooftops, the distant church steeple. I sat there a long time, waiting for the good feeling to come.

# Reviewing

## President Cleveland, Where Are You?

### Discussing the Selection

1. Describe the special setting of "President Cleveland, Where Are You?"—its time and place.

2. Using a chart like the one below, write cause-and-effect incidents for each character listed. Expand the chart by adding other cause-and-effect relationships from the story,

| CHARACTER | CAUSE | EFFECT |
|-----------|-------|--------|
| Jerry | Earns an extra quarter and wants to spend it on trading cards. | Guilt, because he doesn't want to spend the quarter on his father's present. |
| Armand | | |
| Jerry's father | | |
| Rollie Tremaine | | |

3. How would you describe the narrator's relationship with his family? Explain.

4. Evaluate Jerry's decision to sell his sought-after Grover Cleveland card to Rollie. Why doesn't he feel good about it?

### Writing a Proposal

If you were an advisor to a candy company, what kind of premium (trading cards, contests, toys, and so on) would you suggest in order to attract young buyers? Write a proposal to the president of the company explaining your idea. Be specific in describing what your product would look like, and why you believe it would appeal to buyers. If you wish, include a drawing of the product.

### About Robert Cormier (1925–2000)

Born in Massachusetts, Robert Cormier began his writing career in seventh grade after one of his teachers praised his talents. His novel, *The Chocolate War*, brought him national acclaim and was made into a movie. Cormier's writing, which is often edgy and anti-authority, has been a favorite target of censors. His themes include adolescent depression, violence, bullying, drugs, vandalism, and divorce. His stories often have unexpected endings. Young people need to know, he has said, "that happy endings are not our birthright."

# Understanding Folktales

**Folktales** are stories that have been handed down over generations, mainly by word of mouth. Most folktales are simply worded and easy to understand because they were created for "the folk"—ordinary people. Often they provide a look at what a particular group of people finds important—its worldview and values.

Almost all folktales have basic elements in common. They usually have a **setting**: a real or imaginary time and place where the story occurs. The **narrator** is usually anonymous: we don't know who it is. And folktales are populated by **characters**. They can be humans, supernatural figures such as goblins and elves, or animals with human characteristics—talking wolves, bears who sleep in beds. These characters face **conflicts** that are encountered every day in nature—how to find their way home from the woods or store enough food for winter. Or problems that are comically exaggerated, like how to win the hand of the rich, beautiful princess when you're a warty toad!

Folktales include **myths**, **legends**, **tall tales**, **fables**, and **fairy tales**.

A **myth** is a traditional story that tries to explain the origins of the universe, a specific people or tribe, or things in the natural world, such as fire. The exploits of the gods who supposedly once ran the universe come down to us through myths.

A **legend** is a traditional story that may be based on real events and real persons (King Arthur) or supposedly real persons (Robin Hood) and their heroic adventures. Legends are usually rooted in a specific time and place and often told as fact.

A **tall tale** features a larger-than-life main character who solves problems in a humorous way. These greatly exaggerated tales are often associated with specific places. For example, Paul Bunyan's mighty feats as a giant lumberjack take place in the woods of Northern America during the days of westward movement.

A **fable** is usually fairly short and contains a moral or a lesson. Fables often feature nonhumans or animals with human abilities, such as speech.

A **fairy tale** is a term often used interchangeably with folktales. However, fairy tales are usually shorter than folktales. They often feature magical charms and spells, and a plot that pits good versus evil. Fairy tales often have standard beginnings ("Once upon a time") and endings ("And they lived happily ever after") and can be told with many variations. Their cast of characters makes them popular with children: wizards, giants, royalty, mermaids, dragons, elves, and, of course, fairies. Fairy tales have common themes, such as abandonment ("Hansel and Gretel"). And they have familiar characters, such as a wicked stepmother ("Cinderella") or charming prince ("Sleeping Beauty").

# Previewing

## Shrewd Todie and Lyzer the Miser
by Isaac Bashevis Singer

### Reading Connection
The trickster is a favorite character in folktales around the world. African American slave tales often employed a trickster figure, and Native-American storytelling is full of them. There is always a victim in a trickster tale, and often the victim is someone who deserves to be tricked. By outwitting someone powerful or unlikable, the trickster gets revenge. Often he is not a model of virtue himself; he may be sly, immoral, even greedy. Sometimes he is also duped, making trickster tales doubly amusing. As you read, decide how well Shrewd Todie fits the definition of a trickster.

### Skill Focus: Relevant Details
You will enjoy this folktale best if you slow down and try to catch all the humorous details that Singer supplies. Watch out for specific details that reveal what the characters are like and what they value.

### Vocabulary Builder
Which of these words do you already know? Write definitions for them.

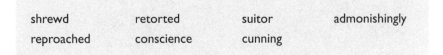

| | | | |
|---|---|---|---|
| shrewd | retorted | suitor | admonishingly |
| reproached | conscience | cunning | |

# Shrewd Todie and Lyzer the Miser

Isaac Bashevis Singer

THE SPOONFUL OF MILK, Marc Chagall, 1912

In a village somewhere in the Ukraine[1] there lived a poor man called Todie. Todie had a wife, Sheindel, and seven children, but he could never earn enough to feed them properly. He tried many trades, failing in all of them. It was said of Todie that if he decided to deal in candles the sun would never set. He was nicknamed **Shrewd** Todie because whenever he managed to make some money, it was always by trickery.

shrewd
smart; clever

This winter was an especially cold one. The snowfall was heavy and Todie had no money to buy wood for the stove. His seven children stayed in bed all day to keep warm. When the frost burns outside, hunger is stronger than ever, but Sheindel's larder[2] was empty. She **reproached** Todie bitterly, wailing, "If you can't feed your wife and children, I will go to the rabbi[3] and get a divorce."

reproached
blamed;
scolded

"And what will you do with it, eat it?" Todie **retorted**. In the same village there lived a rich man called Lyzer. Because of his stinginess he was known as Lyzer the miser. He permitted his wife to bake bread only once in four weeks because he had discovered that fresh bread is eaten up more quickly than stale.

retorted
replied
to angrily;
snapped

Todie had more than once gone to Lyzer for a loan of a few gulden,[4] but Lyzer had always replied, "I sleep better when the money lies in my strongbox rather than in your pocket."

Lyzer had a goat, but he never fed her. The goat had learned to visit the houses of the neighbors, who pitied her and gave her potato peelings. Sometimes, when there were not enough peelings, she would gnaw on the old straw of the thatched roofs. She also had a liking for tree bark. Nevertheless, each year the goat gave birth to a kid. Lyzer milked her but, miser that he was, did not drink the milk himself. Instead, he sold it to others.

Todie decided that he would take revenge on Lyzer and at the same time make some much-needed money for himself.

---

1 **Ukraine**: a region in Eastern Europe, once part of Russia

2 **larder**: pantry; place where food is kept

3 **rabbi**: a Jewish religious leader

4 **gulden**: coins

One day, as Lyzer was sitting on a box eating borscht[5] and dry bread (he used his chairs only on holidays so that the upholstery would not wear out), the door opened and Todie came in.

"Reb Lyzer," he said, "I would like to ask you a favor. My oldest daughter, Basha, is already fifteen and she's about to become engaged. A young man is coming from Janev to look her over. My cutlery[6] is tin, and my wife is ashamed to ask the young man to eat soup with a tin spoon. Would you lend me one of your silver spoons? I give you my holy word that I will return it to you tomorrow."

Lyzer knew that Todie would not dare to break a holy oath and he lent him the spoon.

No young man came to see Basha that evening. As usual, the girl walked around barefoot and in rags, and the silver spoon lay hidden under Todie's shirt. In the early years of marriage Todie had possessed a set of silver tableware himself. He had, however, long since sold it all, with the exception of three silver teaspoons that were used only on Passover.[7]

The following day, as Lyzer, his feet bare (in order to save his shoes), sat on his box eating borscht and dry bread, Todie returned.

"Here is the spoon I borrowed yesterday," he said, placing it on the table together with one of his own teaspoons.

"What is that teaspoon for?" Lyzer asked.

And Todie said, "Your tablespoon gave birth to a teaspoon. It is her child. Since I am an honest man, I'm returning both mother and child to you."

Lyzer looked at Todie in astonishment. He had never heard of a silver spoon giving birth to another. Nevertheless, his greed overcame his doubt and he happily accepted both spoons. Such an unexpected piece of good fortune! He was overjoyed that he had loaned Todie the spoon.

A few days later, as Lyzer (without his coat, to save it) was again sitting on his box eating borscht with dry bread, the door opened and Todie appeared.

"The young man from Janev did not please Basha, because he had donkey

---

5 **borscht**: beet soup

6 **cutlery**: eating utensils

7 **Passover**: important Jewish religious holiday

ears, but this evening another young man is coming to look her over. Sheindel is cooking soup for him, but she's ashamed to serve him with a tin spoon. Would you lend me . . . "

Even before Todie could finish the sentence, Lyzer interrupted. "You want to borrow a silver spoon? Take it with pleasure."

The following day Todie once more returned the spoon and with it one of his own silver teaspoons. He again explained that during the night the large spoon had given birth to a small one and in all good **conscience** he was bringing back the mother and the newborn baby. As for the young man who had come to look Basha over, she hadn't liked him either, because his nose was so long that it reached to his chin. Needless to say that Lyzer the miser was overjoyed.

> He...reported that Lyzer's silver spoon had again given birth to a baby spoon.

**conscience**
sense of honor

Exactly the same thing happened a third time. Todie related that this time his daughter had rejected her **suitor** because he stammered. He also reported that Lyzer's silver spoon had again given birth to a baby spoon.

**suitor**
one seeking
a hand in
marriage

"Does it ever happen that a spoon has twins?" Lyzer inquired.

Todie thought it over for a moment. "Why not? I've even heard of a case where a spoon had triplets."

Almost a week passed by and Todie did not go to see Lyzer. But on Friday morning, as Lyzer (in his under drawers, to save his pants) sat on his box eating borscht and dry bread, Todie came in and said, "Good day to you, Reb Lyzer."

"A good morning and many more to you," Lyzer replied in his friendliest manner. "What good fortune brings you here? Did you perhaps come to borrow a silver spoon? If so, help yourself."

"Today I have a very special favor to ask. This evening a young man from the big city of Lublin is coming to look Basha over. He is the son of a rich man, and I'm told he is clever and handsome as well. Not only do I need a silver spoon, but since he will remain with us over the Sabbath,[8] I need a pair of silver candlesticks, because mine are brass and my wife is ashamed to place them on

---

8 **Sabbath**: Saturday, the weekly day of rest and observance for religious Jews

the Sabbath table. Would you lend me your candlesticks? Immediately after the Sabbath, I will return them to you."

Silver candlesticks are of great value and Lyzer the miser hesitated, but only for a moment.

Remembering his good fortune with the spoons, he said, "I have eight silver candlesticks in my house. Take them all. I know you will return them to me just as you say. And if it should happen that any of them give birth, I have no doubt that you will be as honest as you have been in the past."

"Certainly," Todie said. "Let's hope for the best."

The silver spoon, Todie hid beneath his shirt as usual. But taking the candlesticks, he went directly to a merchant, sold them for a considerable sum, and brought the money to Sheindel. When Sheindel saw so much money, she demanded to know where he had gotten such a treasure.

"When I went out a cow flew over our roof and dropped a dozen silver eggs," Todie replied. "I sold them and here is the money."

"I have never heard of a cow flying over a roof and laying silver eggs," Sheindel said doubtingly.

"There is always a first time," Todie answered. "If you don't want the money, give it back to me."

**cunning**
sneakiness;
slyness

"There'll be no talk about giving it back," Sheindel said. She knew that her husband was full of **cunning** and tricks—but when the children are hungry and the larder is empty, it is better not to ask too many questions. Sheindel went to the market and bought meat, fish, white flour, and even some nuts and raisins for a pudding. And since a lot of money still remained, she bought shoes and clothes for the children.

It was a very gay Sabbath in Todie's house. The boys sang and the girls danced. When the children asked their father where he had gotten the money, he replied, "It is forbidden to mention money on the Sabbath."

Sunday, as Lyzer (barefoot and almost naked, to save his clothes) sat on his box finishing up a dry crust of bread with borscht, Todie arrived and, handing him his silver spoon, said, "It's too bad. This time your spoon did not give birth to a baby."

"What about the candlesticks?" Lyzer inquired anxiously.

Todie sighed deeply. "The candlesticks died."

Lyzer got up from his box so hastily that he overturned his plate of borscht.

"You fool! How can candlesticks die?"

"If spoons can give birth, candlesticks can die," he screamed.

Lyzer raised a great hue and cry[9] and had Todie called before the rabbi. When the rabbi heard both sides of the story, he burst out laughing. "It serves you right," he said to Lyzer. "If you hadn't chosen to believe that spoons give birth, now you would not be forced to believe that your candlesticks died."

"But it's all nonsense," Lyzer objected.

"Did you not expect the candlesticks to give birth to other candlesticks?" the rabbi said **admonishingly**. "If you accept nonsense when it brings you profit, you must also accept nonsense when it brings you loss." And he dismissed the case.

**admonishingly**
as a warning or reproach

The following day, when Lyzer the miser's wife brought him his borscht and dry bread, Lyzer said to her, "I will eat only the bread. Borscht is too expensive a food, even without the sour cream."

The story of the silver spoons that gave birth and the candlesticks that died spread quickly through the town. All the people enjoyed Todie's victory and Lyzer the miser's defeat. The shoemaker's and tailor's apprentices,[10] as was their custom whenever there was an important happening, made up a song about it:

> Lyzer, put your grief aside.
> What if your candlesticks have died?
> You're the richest man on earth
> with silver spoons that can give birth
> and silver eggs as living proof
> of flying cows above your roof.
> Don't sit there eating crusts of bread—
> To silver grandsons look ahead.

However, time passed and Lyzer's silver spoons never gave birth again.

9 **hue and cry**: a loud protest

10 **apprentices**: those who are learning a trade by working with experts

# Reviewing

## Shrewd Todie and Lyzer the Miser

### Discussing the Selection
1. How does Todie fit the definition of a trickster?

2. Often in fiction, characters' basic traits determine the action of the plot. What details in the story demonstrate each character's basic trait—shrewdness in Todie, and miserliness in Lyzer?

3. Why does the rabbi decide in Todie's favor? What you think of his decision?

4. Do you think the townspeople enjoy Todie's victory and Lyzer's defeat?

### Writing a Modern Folktale
Find a short folktale—perhaps one from your own family's heritage. Now rewrite it, updating it and giving it a personal touch. Start by making a list of the basic elements in the original story: its main characters, plot, and theme. Stick to these things as you write. Then change the setting, details, and perhaps the nature of the main character's quest or decision. Red Riding Hood Lost in the Suburbs? Cinderella at the Midnight Volleyball Match? Sleeping Beauty Gets a Makeover? Have fun!

### About Isaac Bashevis Singer (1904–1991)
Isaac Bashevis Singer grew up in war-torn Poland. He was encouraged to become a writer by his father, a rabbi, and his elder brother, already a published author. His first novel came out in 1935, when the Nazis were beginning to gather power in nearby Germany. Soon afterward, the author immigrated to the United States and became an American citizen. In 1957, he published his first collection of stories in English, *Gimpel the Fool*. One of Singer's favorite subjects was Polish life before the Holocaust. The author won the Nobel Prize for literature in 1978. He always spoke humbly of his vast body of work, maintaining that "a good writer is basically a story-teller, not a scholar or a redeemer of mankind."

# Previewing

## The Princess and the Tin Box
by James Thurber

### Reading Connection
Thurber's stories often have simple plot lines that remind you of fairy tales or fables. Many fairy tales include an "unsuitable" suitor—someone unattractive, poor, maybe even from a different species—who beats the odds and wins true love. "The Princess and the Frog" and *Shrek* are perfect examples of goodness triumphing over good looks. In the following tale, Thurber gives the age-old plot another playful twist.

### Skill Focus: Moral
A moral is the point or lesson of a story. For example, the moral of the fable "The Tortoise and the Hare" could be "slow and steady wins the race." Stories often have more than one meaning, and different readers may take different lessons from the same story. The moral of this story might surprise you.

### Vocabulary Builder

| | | | |
|---|---|---|---|
| disdainful | tawdry | glutted | revelry |

# The **Princess**
## and the **Tin Box**

James Thurber

THE PRINCESS AND THE TIN BOX, James Thurber

Once upon a time, in a far country, there lived a king whose daughter was the prettiest princess in the world. Her eyes were like the cornflower, her hair was sweeter than the hyacinth, and her throat made the swan look dusty.

From the time she was a year old, the princess had been showered with presents. Her nursery looked like Cartier's[1] window. Her toys were all made of gold or platinum or diamonds or emeralds. She was not permitted to have wooden blocks or china dolls or rubber dogs or linen books, because such materials were considered cheap for the daughter of a king.

When she was seven, she was allowed to attend the wedding of her brother and throw real pearls at the bride instead of rice. Only the nightingale, with his lyre[2] of gold, was permitted to sing for the princess. The common blackbird, with his boxwood flute, was kept out of the palace grounds. She walked in silver-and-samite[3] slippers to a sapphire-and-topaz bathroom and slept in an ivory bed inlaid with rubies.

On the day the princess was eighteen, the king sent a royal ambassador to the courts of five neighboring kingdoms to announce that he would give his daughter's hand in marriage to the prince who brought her the gift she liked the most.

---

1 **Cartier**: a store in New York famous for fine jewelry

2 **lyre**: a harp-like instrument played in ancient times

3 **samite**: silk woven with gold or silver thread

The first prince to arrive at the palace rode a swift white stallion and laid at the feet of the princess an enormous apple made of solid gold which he had taken from a dragon who had guarded it for a thousand years. It was placed on a long ebony table set up to hold the gifts of the princess's suitors. The second prince, who came on a gray charger,[4] brought her a nightingale made of a thousand diamonds, and it was placed beside the golden apple. The third prince, riding on a black horse, carried a great jewel box made of platinum and sapphires, and it was placed next to the diamond nightingale. The fourth prince, astride a fiery yellow horse, gave the princess a gigantic heart made of rubies and pierced by an emerald arrow. It was placed next to the platinum-and-sapphire jewel box.

Now the fifth prince was the strongest and handsomest of all the five suitors, but he was the son of a poor king whose realm had been overrun by mice and locusts and wizards and mining engineers so that there was nothing much of value left in it. He came plodding up to the palace of the princess on a plow horse and he brought her a small tin box filled with mica and feldspar and hornblende[5] which he had picked up on the way.

The other princes roared with **disdainful** laughter when they saw the **tawdry** gift the fifth prince had brought to the princess. But she examined it with great interest and squealed with delight, for all her life she had been **glutted** with precious stones and priceless metals, but she had never seen tin before or mica or feldspar or hornblende. The tin box was placed next to the ruby heart pierced with an emerald arrow.

"Now," the king said to his daughter, "you must select the gift you like best and marry the prince that brought it."

> The other princes roared with **disdainful** laughter when they saw the **tawdry** gift the fifth prince had brought . . .

**disdainful**
mocking

**tawdry**
cheap and showy

**glutted**
overfed; overstuffed

---

4 **charger**: a horse used in battle

5 **mica . . . feldspar . . . hornblende**: common minerals

The princess smiled and walked up to the table and picked up the present she liked the most. It was the platinum-and-sapphire jewel box, the gift of the third prince.

"The way I figure it," she said, "is this. It is a very large and expensive box, and when I am married, I will meet many admirers who will give me precious gems with which to fill it to the top. Therefore, it is the most valuable of all the gifts my suitors have brought me and I like it the best."

The princess married the third prince that very day in the midst of great merriment and high revelry[6]. More than a hundred thousand pearls were thrown at her and she loved it.

*Moral: All those who thought the princess was going to select the tin box filled with worthless stones instead of one of the other gifts will kindly stay after class and write one hundred times on the blackboard "I would rather have a hunk of aluminum silicate than a diamond necklace."*

---

6 **revelry**: a noisy, happy celebration

# Reviewing

## The Princess and the Tin Box

### Discussing the Selection

1. James Thurber was as famous for his cartoon-like drawings as he was for his writing. Is there anything about this story that makes it seem like a cartoon?

2. See if you can find details early in the story that suggest its tone. Can you summarize that tone in one or two words?

3. Were you surprised by the princess's decision? Explain how Thurber reverses your expectations.

4. What is the point of the moral at the story's end?

### Writing a Moral

Choose a selection from this book that you have already read. Write a moral for the story and explain why you think this moral reflects the message of the piece.

### About James Thurber (1894–1961)

Writer James Thurber was lucky to have his sight after being hit in the eye with a stray arrow as a child. He began a career as a newspaper reporter and got his big break in 1927, when *The New Yorker* hired him. Thurber became one of the magazine's most popular contributors, beloved for his witty fiction and cartoons. In "The Secret Life of Walter Mitty," Thurber created his most famous fictional character. Whenever Mitty felt stress, he retreated into a fantasy life of heroism and wild success. This form of pleasant mental escape is still referred to as the Walter Mitty Syndrome.

# Previewing

## The Curious Treasure of Captain Kidd
by Alvin Schwartz

### Reading Connection

During the Golden Age of Piracy, from about 1690 to 1730, pirates and privateers made sailing a dangerous business. Some say that anyone who robs at sea is a pirate. In fact, privateers had official permission to loot enemy ships as long as they shared their loot with the government. Pirates, on the other hand, were under license to no one. Both privateers and pirates lusted after treasure of gold and other precious metals, gems, ammunition, silk, and slaves.

Hollywood has portrayed pirates as romantic adventurers. In reality, they were brutal criminals, who obeyed few laws except their own.

### Skill Focus: Factual Accounts

A fact is something that can be proven to be true. It is usually verifiable through trusted sources, such as reference works (dictionaries, encyclopedias, government reports) and people (experts in their areas, public spokespersons). Facts can be shown numerically, as in dates, quantities, and statistics. And facts can be shown by examples. As you read the following nonfiction selection, keep your eye out for facts that help to support the case for and against Captain Kidd.

### Vocabulary Builder

Look up the definitions of these words on the pages of the selection where they occur. Using this information plus any ideas you get from the illustrations, predict what the selection will be about. Guess about as many details as you can.

| ballads | mutiny | treachery | vessel |

# The **Curious Treasure** of **Captain Kidd**

Alvin Schwartz

BURIED TREASURE, Howard Pyle, 1902

*My name is Captain Kidd.*
*What the law did forbid*
*Unluckily I did*
         *when I sailed.*

*Upon the ocean wide*
*I robbed on every side*
*With the most ambitious pride*
         *when I sailed . . .*

Captain Kidd was said to be the most famous pirate in the Western world. **Ballads** were written about him, like the one above. People still believe that he brought home a fabulous treasure from his plunderings[1] and buried it somewhere on the east coast of North America.

**ballads**
songs

Over the years, treasure hunters have dug for it on Oak Island in Nova Scotia; on Jesse Hadley's farm in Weare, New Hampshire; along the Hudson River in New York; on Clarke's Island near Northfield, Massachusetts; on Block Island, off Rhode Island; in Shark River, New Jersey; in Lewes, Delaware; and in hundreds of other places. But no one has found it.

Much of what we know of Captain Kidd has come down to us through song and story. But was he really a pirate? And did he really bury a treasure, or have tens of thousands of people searched in vain? It is a tangled tale of **mutiny**, piracy, murder, **treachery**—and gold and silver.

**mutiny**
uprising against
authority

**treachery**
betrayal

Captain William Kidd was a shipmaster in New York City in the 1690s, when New York was an English colony. He lived with his wife and children in a big house on Liberty Street.

If anyone had accused Kidd of piracy, those who knew him would have laughed.

---

1 **plunderings**: the actions of stealing goods by force

He was widely thought of as a decent, trustworthy man. In fact, he once had worked for the colonial government tracking down pirates in the waters around New York.

In those days, pirates plundered British ships wherever they found them. It was such a problem that the king of England decided to crush them once and for all, and he ordered the Royal Governor of New York, the Earl of Bellomont, to do so.

Governor Bellomont asked Kidd to take on the job. His orders were to capture as many pirates and pirate ships as he could in two years. He also was to capture any French ships he saw, because England was at war with France.

Bellomont bought Kidd a ship, the *Adventure Galley*, and armed it with thirty-four cannons. Kidd was to hire a crew. But there would be no money to pay them. Instead, they would get one-fourth of any booty[2] they took from the pirates or the French. If they took no booty, they would get no pay. Since few seamen would work under such conditions, Kidd could hire only wastrels and drifters,[3] some of whom were former pirates.

He left New York in September 1696 with one hundred and fifty-five men and sailed to the Madeira Islands off Africa. He continued south around the tip of Africa, into the Indian Ocean. Then he headed north toward the island of Madagascar, where many pirates made their headquarters. But Kidd did not find any.

In the five months since he'd left New York, he had not taken any booty, and his crew had not been paid. Frustrated and angry, they threatened to mutiny. But Kidd quieted them with talk of the dazzling riches that lay ahead. They set sail for the coast of India, where he hoped to find pirates.

**vessel**
ship

Soon they came upon a merchant ship, the *Loyal Captain*. When she turned out to be a Dutch **vessel**, Kidd decided to send her on her way. But his crew had other ideas. They grabbed the guns on board and got ready to steal whatever she had.

"Let's take her!" they yelled.

"No!" Kidd cried. "She is not our enemy."

---

2 **booty**: treasures taken from an enemy by force

3 **wastrels and drifters**: non-contributing members of society

"We'll take her anyway!"

"Desert my ship," he warned, "and I'll turn my cannons on you."

The mutiny died. But in a week or two, Kidd clashed with one of its leaders, a gunner named William Moore. Moore blamed him for not taking any ships. "You have brought us ruin," he snarled. Kidd struck him on the head with a bucket and killed him. The crew muttered and rumbled like distant thunder, but did nothing. Later, the ballad writer wrote:

> *Many long leagues[4] from shore*
> *I murdered William Moore*
> *And laid him in his gore*
> > *when I sailed.*

The *Adventure Galley* and its crew sailed on. They came to a French ship that had been wrecked. Since France and England were at war, Kidd took what gold there was and shared it with his men. But this did not satisfy them. They continued to threaten him. They wanted him to attack every ship they saw, not just French or pirate ships.

Fearing for his life, Kidd finally gave in. He and his crew plundered several small vessels. Then they took a large merchant ship, the *November*, which was loaded with cotton and sugar. Two months later, they captured the *Quedah Merchant*, with a cargo of gold, silver, jewels, silk, and other goods.

Both were owned by the Great Mogul, the emperor of India. The Mogul traded with England, but he also traded with her enemy, France. When Kidd checked the papers of the two ships, he breathed a sigh of relief. He found that France had agreed to protect them as if they were French ships. Under his orders, it seemed that he could take them as prizes of war. Kidd kept their "French papers" as proof that he had done the right thing, even if he had done so by accident.

When the *Adventure Galley* sprung a leak, he set sail for the port of St. Marie in Madagascar and took the Mogul's ships with him. What happened to their crews is not known. But on the way, some of Kidd's crew mutinied again. They stole what they could from the *November*, then sank it.

---

**4 leagues**: units of distance equal to about three miles

When Kidd and his men arrived at St. Marie, the *Adventure Galley* was leaking badly. To add to his troubles, Kidd found a pirate ship, the *Mocha Frigate*, tied up there. Kidd ordered the pirates to surrender, but they fled into the woods.

He told his crew to go after them, but most decided to join the pirates. They brought the pirates back from where they were hiding, then gave Kidd the choice of also turning pirate or losing his life.

He locked himself in his cabin on the *Adventure Galley*, loaded forty pistols, and waited for them to attack. Instead they boarded Kidd's other ship, the *Quedah Merchant*, moved part of her cargo to the *Mocha Frigate*, and sailed away. But in their haste they left behind a treasure trove of gold, silver, and jewels.

When the *Adventure Galley* began to sink where it was anchored, Kidd burned it. He then set sail for home in the *Quedah Merchant* with the seamen who had remained loyal. It was two and a half years since he had left New York.

Meanwhile, the Great Mogul had complained to England that Kidd had stolen his ships. The English quickly charged Kidd with piracy. It was a crime that carried the penalty of death, and they began to hunt him down. Only when he stopped for supplies in the West Indies did he learn that he was a hunted man.

Kidd was not sure that he could count on Governor Bellomont to help clear him. As insurance, he bought a sloop called the *San Antonio*, and with this new ship and the *Quedah Merchant*, he sailed to Hispaniola.[5] There he moved the treasure from the *Quedah Merchant* to the *San Antonio*. He hid the *Quedah Merchant* and the rest of its cargo in a small cove and left part of his crew to guard it. If he needed to, he would try to trade the ship for a pardon from the charge of piracy.

Kidd sailed north on the *San Antonio* to Delaware Bay where he stopped for supplies. Then he moved on toward New York City, anchoring nearby at Oyster Bay. He sent a note to his wife and a letter to a lawyer named James Emmot, who had defended other men charged with piracy. Would he see Governor Bellomont for him?

Emmot agreed to do so, and he and Kidd met on the *San Antonio*. Kidd

---

5 **Hispaniola**: the second-largest island in the Caribbean, home to Haiti and the Dominican Republic

told him that he was not a pirate, that he had taken the Mogul's ships as part of England's war with France. He gave him the French papers to show Bellomont as proof of this.

Since Bellomont was in Boston, Kidd sailed with Emmot to Rhode Island. There he put him ashore, and the lawyer made his way by land to see the governor. Kidd waited on the *San Antonio*.

Emmot returned in a few days. He had left the French papers with Bellomont as evidence of Kidd's innocence. And he had brought back a letter. Bellomont had written to Kidd: "If you are telling the truth, you will be safe from arrest. Come ashore and meet with me in Boston."

Kidd decided to see Bellomont, but he still did not completely trust him. He decided to leave the treasure aboard the *San Antonio* in a safe place. He sailed to Gardiner's Island, in Long Island Sound, a hundred miles from New York City. There he left Emmot to make his way home, then he talked to the owner of the island, a man named John Gardiner, into keeping part of the treasure for him. Gardiner buried it on the island. Some of Kidd's friends came aboard the *San Antonio* and took away the rest. Only then did Kidd set sail for Boston to see Bellomont.

But Bellomont had lied to him. When Kidd went ashore, he was arrested and sent to England in chains, to be tried for piracy. Bellomont told Kidd he had to arrest him. But he said he would send the French papers to England so that Kidd could use them at his trial. Whether he would keep his word this time remained to be seen.

Bellomont quickly seized the buried treasure on Gardiner's Island, as well as the treasure Kidd had given his friends to keep for him. It came to sixty-eight pounds of gold, one hundred and forty-three pounds of silver, and a pound of rubies, diamonds, and other jewels. Today the gold and silver alone would be worth half a million dollars. The governor also sent a crew to find the *Quedah Merchant* and its cargo.

At his trial in London, Kidd demanded the French papers Bellomont had promised to send. They were the only chance he had to save his life. But the government said there were no such papers, and Kidd was sentenced to hang for piracy.

It was the most famous trial of the day. As most people saw it, Kidd was a good man who had gone bad. The wildest tales were told of how wicked he had become and how much wealth he had. The ballad writer wrote of him:

*I steered from sound to sound*
*And many ships I found*
*And most of them I burned*
*    as I sailed . . .*

*I had ninety bars of gold*
*And dollars manifold[6]*
*With riches uncontrolled*
*    as I sailed.*

Captain Kidd rode to his execution, standing backward in a cart, a noose around his neck. Huge crowds jeered and pelted him with rubbish and rocks as he passed.

He was hanged three times. The first time the rope broke. So he was hanged a second time. Then his body was covered with tar and taken to the waterfront, where it was hung from another gallows[7]—a warning to seamen on passing ships not to become pirates.

There the story ends, and we return to the questions at the beginning of this account. Was Kidd really a pirate? And was there really a buried treasure?

There was a treasure, as we have seen, but it was buried for only a few weeks. Yet few knew it had been found, and people searched for it for more than two hundred years.

Whether Kidd was really a pirate is something that you must decide for yourself. Did he take the ships he captured because his crew forced him to do so? Or did he take them out of greed? Or was it both? Through song and story, Kidd became the symbol of every pirate. And his treasure, for which people searched so long, became the symbol of every treasure.

---

6 **manifold**: many

7 **gallows**: the frame used for hanging condemned people

# Reviewing

## The Curious Treasure of Captain Kidd

### Discussing the Selection

1. Why was Captain Kidd an unlikely person to become a pirate?

2. Do you think Kidd's mission was doomed from the very beginning? Explain why or why not, using facts from the selection.

3. Name some of the errors in judgment Kidd made. Be specific.

4. Would you say this piece paints a picture of Captain Kidd that is mostly positive or mostly negative? Support your answer with examples from the text.

### Writing a Biography

Captain Kidd is one of the most famous pirates in history, but there are many others, including Blackbeard and even some women. Research another of these infamous characters and write a short biography, highlighting some examples of his or her adventures.

### About Alvin Schwartz (1927–1992)

Alvin Schwartz is best known for his Scary Story books (*Scary Stories to Tell in the Dark*, *More Scary Stories to Tell in the Dark*, and *Scary Stories 3: More Tales to Chill Your Bones*), which come with creepy illustrations by his friend Stephen Gammell. According to the American Library Association, this book series is often targeted for censorship. Librarians also claim these books scoot off the shelves like "hotcakes" because young readers love a good scare. Schwartz was also deeply interested in folktales and wordplay. New generations of readers are sure to enjoy Schwartz's collections of tall tales, tongue-twisters, and silly jokes and rhymes.

# Understanding Poetry II

A poem expresses ideas and feelings in a compact form. To get to the heart of a poem's meaning, ask yourself questions like these:

- Who, What, Where, and When? (Who is writing this, and to whom? What does the **title** mean, and what is the **subject**? What is the **setting**?)
- What **word choices** does the poet make? Might some words be **symbols**?
- What **imagery**, or word pictures, does the poem contain?
- What **theme** does it all suggest—what central idea?
- What **sound devices** occur?

When you first look at a poem, notice its shape. Unlike prose, a poem's lines don't always stop or start at the margins of a standard page. Where each line ends is a clue to how it is supposed to sound. A poem is often made up of **stanzas:** rhythmical units of lines. The stanzas in a poem generally have lines with a similar rhyme pattern.

**Rhyme** refers to identical or similar sounds that are repeated (hat/cat/rat). Rhymes are the music of poetry, a source of play for the poet and delight for the reader. And while rhyme is an important feature of older verse, many modern poems do not have any rhyme at all.

**Rhythm** means a repeated pattern of beats or accents ("SHE sells SEA shells, DOWN by the SEA shore").

Comparisons are important to poetry, especially **personification, metaphors**, and **similes**. This **figurative language** allows words to mean something other than their literal definition. A rose is almost never just a rose in poetry. When in bloom, it is compared to a sweetheart's beauty. And when it is withered, poetically speaking, it refers to death.

After considering the words and meaning of any poem, you need to look at its "mechanics." **Sound devices** are techniques used to create rhythm and emphasize certain sounds in a poem. Some of the most common include:

- **Alliteration** The repetition of similar letters or sounds at the beginning of close words. **P**eter **P**iper **p**icked a **p**eck of **p**ickled **p**eppers. **W**arm, **w**et, **w**alks are **w**onderful.

- **Assonance** The repetition of vowel sounds in stressed syllables. The **time** is **ripe** for this as**sign**ment.

- **Consonance** The repetition of consonant sounds in stressed syllables. Bra**d** ha**d** a har**d** hea**d**. Sti**r** the batte**r**, mothe**r**.

- **Onomatopoeia** A word that imitates the sound it represents. Buzz, whiz, shush, kerplunk.

- **Repetition** The technique of using repeated elements in a poem to give it rhythm. A **refrain** is a repeated line or a stanza.

# Previewing

## The Highwayman
by Alfred Noyes

### Reading Connection

Narrative poetry tells a story. It is usually a little longer than other kinds of poetry because it must set up the basic elements of a story: plot, setting, and characters. It might even contain dialogue. However, it will have the shape of a poem, with rhymes and rhythm giving it the musical quality of poetry. "The Highwayman" tells a story about a type of robber who preyed on road travelers in the 1700s.

### Skill Focus: Rhythm

Rhythm refers to the pattern of stressed and unstressed syllables in the lines of a poem. This beat contributes to a poem's mood and tone. Rhythm is very important to your appreciation of "The Highwayman." Read it aloud a few times, alone or with other classmates. Pay attention to how its distinctive rhythm adds to your understanding and enjoyment of the poem.

### Vocabulary Builder

You'll find the definitions for these colorful words on the pages of the selection where they appear.

| | | | |
|---|---|---|---|
| torrent | cascade | ale | writhed |
| claret | tawny | doomed | brandished |
| breeches | | | |

# The Highwayman

Alfred Noyes

A HIGHWAYMAN, artist unknown, 18th century

## PART ONE

The wind was a **torrent** of darkness among the gusty trees,

The moon was a ghostly galleon[1] tossed upon cloudy seas,

The road was a ribbon of moonlight, over the purple moor,[2]

And the highwayman came riding—

      Riding—riding—          5

The highwayman came riding, up to the old inn-door.


He'd a French cocked-hat[3] on his forehead, a bunch of lace at his chin,

A coat of the **claret** velvet, and **breeches** of brown doe-skin;

They fitted with never a wrinkle; his boots were up to the thigh!

And he rode with a jeweled twinkle,      10

      His pistol butts a-twinkle,

His rapier hilt[4] a-twinkle, under the jeweled sky.


Over the cobbles[5] he clattered and clashed in the dark inn-yard,

And he tapped with his whip on the shutters, but all was locked and barred:

He whistled a tune to the window, and who should be waiting there      15

But the landlord's black-eyed daughter,

      Bess, the landlord's daughter,

Plaiting[6] a dark red love-knot into her long black hair.

**torrent**
a rushing
stream

**claret**
deep red

**breeches**
old-fashioned
short pants

---

1 **galleon**: a large sailing ship of the 15th to 17th centuries

2 **moor**: an area of open land too poor for farming

3 **cocked-hat**: a three-cornered hat popular during the 1700s

4 **rapier hilt**: the handle of a slender, double-edged sword

5 **cobbles**: paving stones

6 **plaiting**: braiding

And dark in the dark old inn-yard a stable-wicket[7] creaked

Where Tim the ostler[8] listened; his face was white and peaked;                    20

His eyes were hollows of madness, his hair like moldy hay,

But he loved the landlord's daughter,

        The landlord's red-lipped daughter,

Dumb as a dog he listened, and he heard the robber say—


"One kiss, my bonny sweetheart; I'm after a prize tonight,                    25

But I shall be back with the yellow gold before the morning light;

Yet, if they press[9] me sharply, and harry[10] me through the day,

Then look for me by moonlight,

        Watch for me by moonlight,

I'll come to thee by moonlight, though hell should bar the way."                    30


He rose upright in the stirrups; he scarce could reach her hand,

But she loosened her hair i' the casement![11] His face burned like a brand

**cascade**
a waterfall

As the black **cascade** of perfume came tumbling over his breast;

And he kissed its waves in the moonlight,

        (Oh, sweet black waves in the moonlight!)                    35

Then he tugged at his rein in the moonlight, and galloped away to the West.

---

7 **stable-wicket**: a small gate or door in the stable

8 **ostler**: someone who handles the horses

9 **press**: to be close

10 **harry**: to bother; harass

11 **casement**: a window that opens outwards

**Part Two**

He did not come in the dawning; he did not come at noon;
And out o' the **tawny** sunset, before the rise o' the moon,

**tawny**
golden-brown

When the road was a gypsy's ribbon, looping the purple moor,
A red-coat troop[12] came marching—
        Marching—marching—         5
King George's men came marching, up to the old inn-door.

They said no word to the landlord, they drank his **ale** instead,

**ale**
a drink similar
to beer

But they gagged his daughter and bound her to the foot of her narrow bed;
Two of them knelt at her casement, with muskets[13] at their side!
There was death at every window;          10
        And hell at one dark window;
For Bess could see, through her casement, the road that *he* would ride.

They had tied her up to attention, with many a sniggering[14] jest;
They had bound a musket beside her, with the barrel beneath her breast!
"Now keep good watch!" and they kissed her.       15
        She heard the **doomed** man say—

**doomed**
facing certain
death;
condemned

*Look for me by moonlight;*
      *Watch for me by moonlight;*
*I'll come to thee by moonlight, though hell should bar the way!*

---

12 **red-coat troop**: a group of British soldiers
13 **muskets**: heavy guns used by infantry soldiers before the modern rifle
14 **sniggering**: mocking

She twisted her hands behind her; but all the knots held good!                                        20

**writhed**
twisted

She **writhed** her hands till her fingers were wet with sweat or blood!

They stretched and strained in the darkness, and the hours crawled by like years,

Till, now, on the stroke of midnight,

       Cold, on the stroke of midnight,

The tip of one finger touched it! The trigger at least was hers!                                        25

The tip of one finger touched it; she strove[15] no more for the rest!

Up, she stood to attention, with the barrel beneath her breast,

She would not risk their hearing; she would not strive again;
For the road lay bare in the moonlight;

       Blank and bare in the moonlight;                                        30

And the blood of her veins in the moonlight throbbed to her love's refrain.

*Tlot-tlot; tlot-tlot!* Had they heard it? The horse-hoofs ringing clear;

*Tlot-tlot, tlot-tlot,* in the distance? Were they deaf that they did not hear?

Down the ribbon of moonlight, over the brow of the hill,

The highwayman came riding,                                        35

       Riding, riding!

The red-coats looked to their priming![16] She stood up straight and still!

*Tlot-tlot,* in the frosty silence! *Tlot-tlot,* in the echoing night!

Nearer he came and nearer! Her face was like a light!

Her eyes grew wide for a moment; she drew one last deep breath,                                        40

Then her finger moved in the moonlight,

       Her musket shattered the moonlight,

Shattered her breast in the moonlight and warned him—with her death.

15 **strove**: tried hard

16 **priming**: powder used to fire a musket

He turned; he spurred to the westward; he did not know who stood
Bowed, with her head o'er the musket, drenched with her own red blood! 45
Not till the dawn he heard it, his face grew grey to hear
How Bess, the landlord's daughter,
     The landlord's black-eyed daughter,
Had watched for her love in the moonlight, and died in the darkness there.

Back, he spurred like a madman, shrieking a curse to the sky, 50
With the white road smoking behind him, and his rapier **brandished** high!
Blood-red were his spurs i' the golden noon; wine-red was his velvet coat,
When they shot him down on the highway,
     Down like a dog on the highway,
And he lay in his blood on the highway, with a bunch of lace at his throat. 55

**brandished**
shook in a
threatening
manner

* * *

*And still of a winter's night, they say, when the wind is in the trees,*
*When the moon is a ghostly galleon tossed upon cloudy seas,*
*When the road is a ribbon of moonlight over the purple moor,*
*A highwayman comes riding—*
     *Riding—riding—* 60
*A highwayman comes riding, up to the old inn-door.*

*Over the cobbles he clatters and clangs in the dark inn-yard;*
*And he taps with his whip on the shutters, but all is locked and barred;*
*He whistles a tune to the window, and who should be waiting there*
*But the landlord's black-eyed daughter,* 65
     *Bess, the landlord's daughter,*
*Plaiting a dark red love-knot into her long black hair.*

# Reviewing

## The Highwayman

### Discussing the Selection

1. In your own words, tell the plot of this narrative poem.

2. Find examples of these poetic devices in "The Highwayman":
    simile
    metaphor
    onomatopoeia
    imagery (words that appeal to the senses)
    alliteration
    personification

3. Why do you think the soldiers bind and gag the landlord's daughter, Bess? Why does she eventually shoot herself?

4. There are several refrains—repeated items—in this poem. Which one do you think is the most important? Explain your answer.

### Writing About Imagery

"The Highwayman" is rich in color imagery. Reread the poem looking for words that describe color, such as *tawny* and *claret*. In an essay, discuss how much and what kind of color imagery is used and what this language adds to the poem.

### About Alfred Noyes (1880–1958)

English poet Alfred Noyes is known for two ballads, "The Highwayman" and "The Barrel Organ." He attended Oxford University and at the age of 21 published his first collection of verse, *The Loom Years*. Between 1903 and 1908, Noyes published five additional volumes of poetry. During World War I, he served the British government as a propaganda writer. In later years, he taught English literature at Princeton University in New Jersey. Noyes's worsening eyesight forced him to dictate his words. Still he managed to write over sixty books in his lifetime, including poetry, novels, and short stories. His themes are wide-ranging and include nature, scientific exploration, war, and religious faith.

# Previewing

## Ballad of Birmingham
by Dudley Randall

### Reading Connection
In 1963, four young black girls were killed by a bomb that went off during church services in Birmingham, Alabama. Their killers were members of the Ku Klux Klan, an organization based on white supremacy. According to the United Press International account, "Dozens of survivors, their faces dripping blood from the glass that flew out of the church's stained glass windows, staggered around the building in a cloud of white dust raised by the explosion. The blast crushed two nearby cars like toys and blew out windows blocks away." Riots followed. The bombings marked a turning point for the Civil Rights movement of the 1960s. After folk singer Jerry Moore read Randall's poem in a newspaper, he set it to music, and the poet granted him permission to publish the tune with the lyrics.

### Skill Focus: Irony
One type of irony that occurs in the following poem is "situational irony." This means that events turn out differently from expectations. For example, it is ironic when the shortest member of the basketball team becomes the key player. Some forms of irony are humorous, but just as often irony can be tragic. The poem you are about to read is ironic in the saddest sense possible.

# Ballad of Birmingham

Dudley Randall

Shotgun, Third Ward and #1, John T. Biggers, 1966

"Mother dear, may I go downtown
Instead of out to play,
And march the streets of Birmingham
In a Freedom March[1] today?"

---

1 **Freedom March**: Civil Rights demonstrations in the early 1960s. In Birmingham, black and white marchers were trying to eliminate racial segregation in Birmingham businesses and schools.

"No, baby, no, you may not go,                    5
For the dogs are fierce and wild,
And clubs and hoses, guns and jails[2]
Aren't good for a little child."

"But, mother, I won't be alone.
Other children will go with me,                    10
And march the streets of Birmingham
To make our country free."

"No, baby, no, you may not go,
For I fear those guns will fire.
But you may go to church instead                    15
And sing in the children's choir."

She has combed and brushed her night-dark hair,
And bathed rose petal sweet,
And drawn white gloves on her small brown hands,
And white shoes on her feet.                    20

The mother smiled to know that her child
Was in the sacred place,
But that smile was the last smile
To come upon her face.

For when she heard the explosion,                    25
Her eyes grew wet and wild.
She raced through the streets of Birmingham
Calling for her child.

She clawed through bits of glass and brick,
Then lifted out a shoe.                    30
"O, here's the shoe my baby wore,
But, baby, where are you?"

---

2 **dogs . . . jails**: Birmingham police took all of these extreme measures in order to intimidate
and punish the protesters.

# Reviewing

## Ballad of Birmingham

### Discussing the Selection

1. What is ironic in this poem?

2. In "Ballad of Birmingham," the mother tells what she does but not why she does it. Why do you think she lets her daughter go to church but not to the Freedom March?

3. The definition of a ballad is a poem that tells a story. Ballads are often used as songs and have a musical quality. Why do you think Randall chose this form for his poem?

4. What message do you think Randall intended to make with his poem?

### Writing a Comparison

An event like the church burnings in Alabama during the 1960s would have been covered by both TV and newspapers. Compare the impact of media news with a poem, song, or story about the same event. Which might be more likely to move people to action?

### About Dudley Randall (1914–2000)

Dudley Randall, an African American poet and publisher, grew up in Detroit, Michigan. His first published poem appeared in the *Detroit Free Press* when he was just thirteen years old. Randall worked at a post office while earning degrees in English and library science. In 1969, he became the librarian and poet in residence at the University of Detroit until his retirement in 1974. He founded the Broadside Press, which published some of the most important African American writers in the literary world.

# Previewing

## from **Woodsong**

by Gary Paulsen

### Reading Connection

*Woodsong* is a memoir that Gary Paulsen wrote about his life in the northern Minnesota woods and the wilds of Alaska. In Minnesota, Paulsen and his family lived in a cabin without running water or electricity while he trapped animals for fur and trained dogs for the Alaskan Iditarod. This grueling, one-of-a-kind race ranges over 1200 miles of Alaskan mountain ranges, forests, and frozen tundra. Paulsen is a lifelong outdoorsman who has written more than 150 books, many about the animals he has known.

### Skill Focus: Visual Mapping

In the essay that follows, Gary Paulsen describes an encounter with a hungry bear. Bears were regular visitors to the Paulsens' Minnesota cabin. As you read, think about what the family and bears learn about each other's habits that helps them to coexist. You might want to start by considering all that you already know about bears. Use the accompanying visual map to share your knowledge with the class.

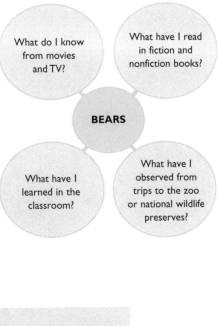

### Vocabulary Builder

Words from a particular selection often are part of a word group with connected meaning. Which of the following would fit into a group of words about animals that feed on what other animals or humans have left behind? Be prepared to explain your reasons for including each word.

| | | | |
|---|---|---|---|
| predators | evolved | novelty | menace |
| scavenging | familiarity | coherent | rummaging |

 *from* **Woodsong**

Gary Paulsen

W̶e have bear trouble. Because we feed processed meat to the dogs, there is always the smell of meat over the kennel. In the summer it can be a bit high[1] because the dogs like to "save" their food sometimes for a day or two or four—burying it to dig up later. We live on the edge of wilderness, and consequently the meat smell brings any number of visitors from the woods.

Skunks abound, and foxes and coyotes and wolves and weasels—all **predators**. We once had an eagle live over the kennel for more than a week, **scavenging** from the dogs, and a crazy group of ravens has pretty much taken over the puppy pen. Ravens are protected by the state and they seem to know it. When I walk toward the puppy pen with the buckets of meat, it's a toss-up to see who gets it—the pups or the birds. They have actually pecked the puppies away from the food pans until they have gone through and taken what they want.

**predators**
hunters; those who seek to kill

**scavenging**
picking through junk or garbage

Spring, when the bears come, is the worst. They have been in hibernation through the winter, and they are hungry beyond caution. The meat smell draws them like flies, and we frequently have two or three around the kennel at the same time. Typically they do not bother us much—although my wife had a bear chase her from the garden to the house one morning—but they do bother the dogs.

They are so big and strong that the dogs fear them, and the bears trade on this fear to get their food. It's common to see them scare a dog into his house and take his food. Twice we have had dogs killed by rough bear swats that broke their necks—and the bears took their food.

**evolved**
arrived at by a series of gradual changes

We have **evolved** an uneasy peace with them but there is the problem of **familiarity**. The first time you see a bear in the kennel it is a **novelty**, but when the same ones are there day after day, you wind up naming some of them (old Notch-Ear, Billy-Joe, etc.). There gets to be a too relaxed attitude. We started to treat them like pets.

A major mistake.

**familiarity**
a close knowledge of something

**novelty**
newness; first time

---

1 **it can be a bit high**: phrase meaning the smell can be fairly strong

There was a large male around the kennel for a week or so. He had a white streak across his head which I guessed was a wound scar from some hunter—bear hunting is allowed here. He wasn't all that bad, so we didn't mind him. He would frighten the dogs and take their hidden stashes now and then, but he didn't harm them and we became accustomed to him hanging around. We called him Scarhead and now and again we would joke about him as if he were one of the yard animals.

At this time we had three cats, forty-two dogs, fifteen or twenty chickens, eight ducks, nineteen large white geese, a few banty hens—one called Hawk—ten fryers which we'd raised from chicks and couldn't (as my wife put it) "snuff and eat," and six woods-wise goats.

The bears, strangely, didn't bother any of the yard animals. There must have been a rule, or some order to the way they lived, because they would hit the kennel and steal from the dogs but leave the chickens and goats and other yard stock completely alone—although you would have had a hard time convincing the goats of this fact. The goats spent a great deal of time with their back hair up, whuffing and blowing snot at the bears—and at the dogs who would *gladly* have eaten them. The goats never really believed in the truce.

There is not a dump or landfill to take our trash to and so we separate it—organic,[2] inorganic[3]—and deal with it ourselves. We burn the paper in a screened enclosure and it is fairly efficient, but it's impossible to get all the food particles off wrapping paper, so when it's burned the food particles burn with it.

And give off a burnt food smell.

And nothing draws bears like burning food. It must be that they have learned to understand human dumps—where they spend a great deal of time foraging.[4] And they learn amazingly fast. In Alaska, for instance, the bears already know that the sound of a moose hunter's gun means there will be a fresh gut pile when the hunter cleans the moose. They come at a run when they

---

2 **organic**: made of plant or animal material

3 **inorganic**: made of non-living things

4 **foraging**: hunting or searching

hear the shot. It's often a close race to see if the hunter will get to the moose before the bears take it away . . . .

Because we're on the south edge of the wilderness area we try to wait until there is a northerly breeze before we burn so the food smell will carry south, but it doesn't always help. Sometimes bears, wolves, and other predators are already south, working the sheep farms down where it is more settled—they take a terrible toll[5] of sheep—and we catch them on the way back through.

That's what happened one July morning.

Scarhead had been gone for two or three days and the breeze was right, so I went to burn the trash. I fired it off and went back into the house for a moment—not more than two minutes. When I came back out, Scarhead was in the burn area. His tracks (directly through the tomatoes in the garden) showed he'd come from the south.

> I have made many mistakes in my life, and will probably make many more, but I hope never to throw a stick at a bear again.

He was having a grand time. The fire didn't bother him. He was trying to reach a paw in around the edges of flame to get at whatever smelled so good. He had torn things apart quite a bit—ripped one side off the burn enclosure—and I was having a bad day and it made me mad.

I was standing across the burning fire from him, and without thinking—because I was so used to him—I picked up a stick, threw it at him, and yelled, "Get out of here."

I have made many mistakes in my life, and will probably make many more, but I hope never to throw a stick at a bear again.

In one rolling motion—the muscles seemed to move within the skin so fast that I couldn't take half a breath—he turned and came for me. Close. I could smell his breath and see the red around the sides of his eyes. Close on me he stopped and raised on his back legs and hung over me, his forelegs and paws

---

5 **take a terrible toll**: phrase meaning causing many deaths

hanging down, weaving back and forth gently as he took his time and decided whether or not to tear my head off.

I could not move, would not have time to react. I knew I had nothing to say about it. One blow would break my neck. Whether I lived or died depended on him, on his thinking, on his ideas about me—whether I was worth the bother or not.

I did not think then.

**coherent**
clear; sensible

Looking back on it, I don't remember having one **coherent** thought when it was happening. All I knew was terrible **menace**. His eyes looked very small as he studied me. He looked down on me for what seemed hours. I did not move, did not breathe, did not think or do anything.

**menace**
danger; threat

And he lowered.

Perhaps I was not worth the trouble. He lowered slowly and turned back to the trash, and I walked backward halfway to the house and then ran—anger growing now—and took the rifle from the gun rack by the door and came back out.

**rummaging**
looking or
searching

He was still there, **rummaging** through the trash. I worked the bolt and fed a cartridge in and aimed at the place where you kill bears and began to squeeze. In raw anger, I began to take up the four pounds of pull necessary to send death into him.

And stopped.

Kill him for what?

That thought crept in.

Kill him for what?

For not killing me? For letting me know it is wrong to throw sticks at four-hundred-pound bears? For not hurting me, for not killing me, I should kill him? I lowered the rifle and ejected the shell and put the gun away. I hope Scarhead is still alive. For what he taught me, I hope he lives long and is very happy because I learned then—looking up at him while he made up his mind whether or not to end me—that when it is all boiled down, I am nothing more and nothing less than any other animal in the woods.

# Reviewing

## from Woodsong

### Discussing the Selection

1. Describe what kind of person Paulsen is, based on his situation, his observations about bears, and his decision not to kill Scarhead. Use details from the story to support your answer.

2. "Whether I lived or died depended on him, on his thinking, on his ideas about me—whether I was worth the bother or not." Do you believe that bears or other animals truly think and have "ideas" about people and their worthiness? Why or why not?

3. What lesson do you think Paulsen takes away from his encounter with Scarhead the bear? Say whether or not you agree with it.

4. Of all the characters in Unit Four, who makes the most difficult decision? Why?

### Writing a Cause-Effect Essay

Wild animals have always posed problems for people living in the country. More and more frequently, however, they are becoming problems for city dwellers. The news media carry stories about deer, coyotes, mountain lions, rabbits, raccoons, skunks, and bears "trespassing" on territory where humans live. Make a guess as to what might be causing this behavior. Then suggest some possible effects of having wild animals in human habitats.

### About Gary Paulsen (1939–)

At age fourteen, Gary Paulsen ran away from an unhappy home to travel with a carnival. This spurred a lifelong sense of adventure and was the first of many odd jobs, including work as a farmer, engineer, construction worker, ranch hand, truck driver, sailor, and dog trainer for the Iditarod, an Alaskan dogsled race. Paulsen often draws from these experiences in his 175 books. As a young writer, Paulsen abruptly left an aerospace job in California and drove to northern Minnesota, where he rented a cabin on a lake and finished his first novel. His books *Hatchet*, *Dogsong*, and *The Winter Room* have all won Newbery Honor awards. What keeps the author at his desk for up to 20 hours a day? As one biographer put it, "It is Paulsen's overwhelming belief in young people that drives him to write."

## Unit Five

# TO BE A HERO

*You cannot be a hero without being a coward.*

George Bernard Shaw

Just what is heroism? And what does being a hero really mean? Yes, certainly one who is brave and fearless. But more often, the acts in everyday life are heroic. The stories, poem, and essays in Unit Five demonstrate many kinds of heroic actions. For some of the characters you will meet, taking on risks is almost second nature, something they do with a sense of relish. Others are unlikely heroes, thrust into roles that call upon all their wit, stamina, and courage.

# Building Vocabulary

## Multiple Meanings of Words

A dictionary can enlarge your vocabulary by telling you what words mean. However, many words have more than one meaning. Look at the following example:

**shock**[1] (shok) *noun* 1. a sudden, strong blow, shake, or disturbance [*The shock of the crash crushed the car.*] 2. a sudden, strong upsetting of the mind or feelings [*news that is a shock*] 3. the effect on the body of an electric current [*That wire could give you a shock.*] 4. in Medicine: a physical problem caused by serious injury, pain, or loss of blood [*suffering from shock*]

**shock**[2] (shok) *noun* a group of stalks of grain or corn, stacked together to dry [*near a shock of corn*]

**shock**[3] (shok) *noun* a bushy, thick mass, as of hair [*her shock of curls*]

Look at the following sentences and note which definition of *shock* fits each one.

A. The earthquake's second *shock* was milder than the first. (**shock**[1], definition 1)

B. The price of the new car was a *shock*. (**shock**[1], definition 2)

C. Sticking a fork in a toaster can give you a terrible *shock*. (**shock**[1], definition 3)

D. He's very pale, and his heartbeat is rapid. I think he's in *shock*. (**shock**[1], definition 4)

E. While we're in the field, if you hold each *shock* together, I'll tie it. (**shock**[2])

F. A barber could take care of that shaggy *shock* of yours. (**shock**[3])

## Choosing the Right Definition

When the dictionary gives multiple meanings, how do you decide which one you want?

1. **Think about the written context** of the word in the sentence you're reading. Which one fits the situation?

2. **Consider the grammar or structure** of the sentence in which the word appears. What part of speech—noun, verb, adjective, or adverb—are you looking for?

3. **Use the meaning that seems to fit the author's purpose and style**. Sometimes you have to use your imagination; writers like to invent new words and new meanings.

# Previewing

## Abd al-Rahman Ibrahima
by Walter Dean Myers

### Reading Connection
Beginning in the 1600s, millions of Africans were kidnapped in their own countries by both white and black slave traders. According to one writer, "With extremely tightly packed loads of human cargo that stank and carried both infectious disease and death, the ships would travel east to west across the Atlantic on a miserable voyage lasting . . . as long as three months." Tens of thousands died on the overseas trip, which is known as the "middle passage." The survivors landed in a strange place, where no one knew them or spoke their language, and were sold as slaves. After the Civil War, most freed slaves stayed in America because they had lost all ties to Africa.

### Skill Focus: Characterization
Writers know that one of their most important tasks is to create good, believable characters. This character development is called characterization and is accomplished through the use of specific details and description. Other ways to reveal characters include showing their thoughts, feelings, speech, actions, and interactions with others.

While characterization is a main element of fiction, nonfiction writers must also be aware of techniques for developing interesting characters. They must choose details, descriptions, and quotes that make their subjects interesting to their audience. As you read, note what Walter Dean Myers chooses to tell you about the life of Ibrahima.

### Vocabulary Builder
The following words are defined on the pages where they occur. Notice that the list includes *file* and *reservation*. How many meanings can you think of for these words? Now find where they are defined to see which meaning is used in this selection.

| | | | |
|---|---|---|---|
| warily | status | trek | resigned |
| privileged | venturing | hurling | resented |
| sophisticated | rout | wretched | premise |
| scholars | momentum | stifling | reservation |
| chaos | file | mockery | |

The city of Timbuktu c 1825

# Abd al-Rahman Ibrahima
## from *Now Is Your Time!*

Walter Dean Myers

The Africans came from many countries and from many cultures. Like the Native Americans, they established their territories based on centuries of tradition. Most, but not all, of the Africans who were brought to the colonies[1] came from central and West Africa. Among them was a man named Abd al-Rahman Ibrahima.

The European invaders, along with those Africans who cooperated with them, had made the times dangerous. African nations that had lived peacefully together for centuries now eyed each other **warily**. Slight insults led to major battles. Bands of outlaws roamed the countryside attacking the small villages, kidnapping those unfortunate enough to have wandered from the protection of their people. The stories that came from the coast were frightening. Those kidnapped were taken to the sea and sold to whites, put on boats, and taken across the sea. No one knew what happened then.

**warily**
cautiously;
suspiciously

---

1 **colonies**: the thirteen colonies that became the United States

Abd al-Rahman Ibrahima was born in 1762 in Fouta Djallon,[2] a district of the present country of Guinea.[3] It is a beautiful land of green mountains rising majestically from grassy plains, a land rich with minerals, especially bauxite.

Ibrahima was a member of the powerful and influential Fula people and a son of one of their chieftains. The religion of Islam had swept across Africa centuries before, and the young Ibrahima was raised in the tradition of the Moslems.[4]

The Fula were taller and lighter in complexion than the other inhabitants of Africa's west coast; they had silky hair, which they often wore long. A pastoral[5] people, the Fula had a complex system of government, with the state divided into nine provinces and each province divided again into smaller districts. Each province had its chief and its subchiefs.

As the son of a chief, Ibrahima was expected to assume a role of political leadership when he came of age.[6] He would also be expected to set a moral example and to be well versed in his religion. When he reached twelve, he was sent to Timbuktu[7] to study.

Under the Songhai dynasty[8] leader Askia the Great, Timbuktu had become a center of learning and one of the largest cities in the Songhai Empire. The young Ibrahima knew he was **privileged** to attend the best known school in West Africa. Large and **sophisticated**, with wide, tree-lined streets, the city attracted **scholars** from Africa, Europe, and Asia. Islamic law, medicine, and mathematics were taught to the young men destined to become the leaders

**privileged**
lucky;
fortunate

**sophisticated**
cultured;
advanced

**scholars**
serious
students;
intellectuals

---

2 **Fouta Djallon**: a mountainous region in West Africa

3 **Guinea**: a small nation on Africa's west coast

4 **Islam . . . Moslems**: Beginning in the 7th century, Arabs began to colonize countries in Africa, bringing with them the Moslem religion of Islam.

5 **pastoral**: refers to a rural, agricultural livelihood

6 **came of age**: entered adulthood, often with a special test or celebration

7 **Timbuktu**: a city now called Tombouactou, in what is now Mali

8 **Songhai dynasty**: a family of rulers who exercised great power and influence in the 15th and 16th centuries

of their nations. It was a good place for a young man to be. The city was well guarded, too. It had to be, to prevent the **chaos** that, more and more, dominated African life nearer the coast.

**chaos**
confusion

Ibrahima learned first to recite from the Koran, the Moslem holy book, and then to read it in Arabic. From the Koran, it was felt, came all other knowledge. After Ibrahima had finished his studies in Timbuktu, he returned to Fouta Djallon to continue to prepare himself to be a chief.

The Fula had little contact with whites, and what little contact they did have was filled with danger. So when, in 1781, a white man claiming to be a ship's surgeon stumbled into one of their villages, they were greatly surprised.

John Coates Cox hardly appeared to be a threat. A slight man, blind in one eye, he had been lost for days in the forested regions bordering the mountains. He had injured his leg, and it had become badly infected as he tried to find help. By the time he was found and brought to the Fula chiefs, he was more dead than alive.

Dr. Cox, an Irishman, told of being separated from a hunting party that had left from a ship on which he had sailed as ship's surgeon. The Fula chief decided that he would help Cox. He was taken into a hut, and a healer was assigned the task of curing his infected leg.

During the months Dr. Cox stayed with the Fula, he met Ibrahima, now a tall, brown-skinned youth who had reached manhood. His bearing reflected his **status** as the son of a major chief. Dr. Cox had learned some Fulani, the Fula language, and the two men spoke. Ibrahima was doubtless curious about the white man's world, and Dr. Cox was as impressed by Ibrahima's education as he had been by the kindness of his people.

**status**
rank; social position

When Dr. Cox was well enough to leave, he was provided with a guard; but before he left, he warned the Fula about the danger of **venturing** too near the ships that docked off the coast of Guinea. The white doctor knew that the ships were there to take captives.

**venturing**
going ahead in spite of danger

Cox and Ibrahima embraced fondly and said their goodbyes, thinking they would never meet again.

Ibrahima married and became the father of several children. He was in his mid-twenties when he found himself leading the Fula cavalry[9] in their war with the Mandingo.[10]

The first battles went well, with the enemy retreating before the advancing Fula. The foot warriors attacked first, breaking the enemy's ranks and making them easy prey for the well-trained Fula cavalry. With the enemy in full **rout**, the infantry returned to their towns while the horsemen, led by Ibrahima, chased the remaining stragglers. The Fula fought their enemies with spears, bows, slings, swords, and courage.

**rout**
retreat

The path of pursuit led along a path that narrowed sharply as the forests thickened. The fleeing warriors disappeared into the forest that covered a sharply rising mountain. Thinking the enemy had gone for good, Ibrahima felt it would be useless to chase them further.

"We could not see them," he would write later.

But against his better judgment, he decided to look for them. The horsemen dismounted at the foot of a hill and began the steep climb on foot. Halfway up the hill the Fula realized they had been lured into a trap! Ibrahima heard the rifles firing, saw the smoke from the powder and the men about him falling to the ground, screaming in agony. Some died instantly. Many horses, hit by the gunfire, thrashed about in pain and panic. The firing was coming from both sides, and Ibrahima ordered his men to the top of the hill, where they could, if time and Allah[11] permitted it, try a charge using the speed and **momentum** of their remaining horses.

**momentum**
moving force

Ibrahima was among the first to mount and urge his animal onward. The enemy warriors came out of the forests, some with bows and arrows, others with muskets that he knew they had obtained from the Europeans. The courage of the Fula could not match the fury of the guns. Ibrahima called out to his men to save themselves, to flee as they could. Many tried to escape, rushing madly past the guns. Few survived.

Those who did clustered about their young leader, determined to make one

9 **cavalry**: mounted troops

10 **Mandingo**: a West African tribe

11 **Allah**: the Muslim God

last, desperate stand. Ibrahima was hit in the back by an arrow, but the aim was not true and the arrow merely cut his broad shoulder. Then something smashed against his head from the rear.

The next thing Ibrahima knew was that he was choking. Then he felt himself being lifted from water. He tried to move his arms, but they had been fastened securely behind his back. He had been captured.

When he came to his full senses, he looked around him. Those of his noble cavalry who had not been captured were already dead. Ibrahima was unsteady on his legs as his clothes and sandals were stripped from him. The victorious Mandingo warriors now pushed him roughly into **file** with his men. They began the long **trek** that would lead them to the sea.

**file**
line

**trek**
journey; march

In Fouta Djallon, being captured by the enemy meant being forced to do someone else's bidding, sometimes for years. If you could get a message to your people, you could, perhaps, buy your freedom. Otherwise, it was only if you were well liked or if you married one of your captor's women that you would be allowed to go free or to live like a free person.

Ibrahima sensed that things would not go well for him.

The journey to the sea took weeks. Ibrahima was tied to other men, with ropes around their necks. Each day they walked from dawn to dusk. Those who were slow

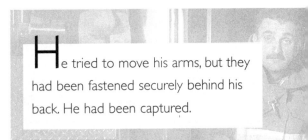

He tried to move his arms, but they had been fastened securely behind his back. He had been captured.

were knocked brutally to the ground. Some of those who could no longer walk were speared and left to die in agony. It was the lucky ones who were killed outright if they fell.

When they reached the sea, they remained bound hand and foot. There were men and women tied together. Small children clung to their mothers as they waited for the boats to come and the bargaining to begin.

Ibrahima, listening to the conversations of the men who held him captive, could understand those who spoke Arabic. These Africans were a low class of men, made powerful by the guns they had been given, made evil by the white man's goods. But it didn't matter who was evil and who was good. It only mattered who held the gun.

Abd al-Rahman Ibrahima    293

Ibrahima was inspected on the shore, then put into irons[12] and herded into a small boat that took him out to a ship that was larger than any he had ever seen.

The ship onto which Ibrahima was taken was already crowded with black captives. Some shook in fear; others, still tied, fought by **hurling** their bodies at their captors. The beating and the killing continued until the ones who were left knew that their lot was hopeless.

On board the ship there were more whites with guns, who shoved them toward the open hatch. Some of the Africans hesitated at the hatch and were clubbed down and pushed below decks.

It was dark beneath the deck and difficult to breathe. Bodies were pressed close against other bodies. In the section of the ship he was in, men prayed to various gods in various languages. It seemed that the whites would never stop pushing men into the already crowded space. Two sailors pushed the Africans into position so that each would lie in the smallest space possible. The sailors panted and sweated as they untied the men and then chained them to a railing that ran the length of the ship.

The ship rolled against its mooring[13] as the anchor was lifted, and the journey began. The boards of the ship creaked and moaned as it lifted and fell in the sea. Some of the men got sick, vomiting upon themselves in the **wretched** darkness. They lay cramped, muscles aching, irons cutting into their legs and wrists, gasping for air.

Once a day they would be brought out on deck and made to jump about for exercise. They were each given a handful of either beans or rice cooked with yams, and water from a cask. The white sailors looked hardly better than the Africans, but it was they who held the guns.

Illness and the **stifling** conditions on the ships caused many deaths. How many depended largely on how fast the ships could be loaded with Africans and how long the voyage from Africa took. It was not unusual for 10 percent of the Africans to die if the trip took longer than the usual twenty-five to thirty-five days.

---

12 **irons**: metal hand and leg cuffs

13 **mooring**: a place where a ship is tied

Ibrahima, now twenty-six years old, reached Mississippi in 1788. As the ship approached land, the Africans were brought onto the deck and fed. Some had oil put on their skins so they would look better; their sores were treated or covered with pitch.[14] Then they were given garments to wear in an obvious effort to improve their appearance.

Although Ibrahima could not speak English, he understood he was being bargained for. The white man who stood on the platform with him made him turn around, and several other white men neared him, touched his limbs, examined his teeth, looked into his eyes, and made him move about.

Although Ibrahima could not speak English, he understood he was being bargained for.

Thomas Foster, a tobacco grower and a hard-working man, had come from South Carolina with his family and had settled on the rich lands that took their minerals from the Mississippi River. He already held one captive, a young boy. In August 1788 he bought two more. One of them was named Sambo, which means "second son." The other was Ibrahima.

Foster agreed to pay $930 for the two Africans. He paid $150 down and signed an agreement to pay another $250 the following January and the remaining $530 in January of the following year.

When Ibrahima arrived at Foster's farm, he tried to find someone who could explain to the white man who he was—the son of a chief. He wanted to offer a ransom[15] for his own release, but Foster wasn't interested. He understood, perhaps from the boy whom he had purchased previously, that this new African was claiming to be an important person. Foster had probably never heard of the Fula or their culture; he had paid good money for the African and wasn't about to give him up. Foster gave Ibrahima a new name: He called him Prince.

For Ibrahima there was confusion and pain. What was he to do? A few

---

14 **pitch**: a tar-like substance

15 **ransom**: payment; payoff

months before, he had been a learned man and a leader among his people. Now he was a captive in a strange land where he neither spoke the language nor understood the customs. Was he never to see his family again? Were his sons forever lost to him?

As a Fula, Ibrahima wore his hair long; Foster insisted that it be cut. Ibrahima's clothing had been taken from him, and his sandals. Now the last remaining symbol of his people, his long hair, had been taken as well.

He was told to work in the fields. He refused, and he was tied and whipped. The sting of the whip across his naked flesh was terribly painful, but it was nothing like the pain he felt within. The whippings forced him to work.

**mockery**
bad imitation

For Ibrahima this was not life but a **mockery** of life. There was the waking in the morning and the sleeping at night; he worked, he ate, but this was not life. What was more, he could not see an end to it. It was this feeling that made him attempt to escape.

Ibrahima escaped to the backwoods regions of Natchez.[16] He hid there, eating wild berries and fruit, not daring to show his face to any man, white or black. There was no telling who could be trusted. Sometimes he saw men with dogs and knew they were searching for runaways, perhaps him.

Where was he to run? What was he to do? He didn't know the country, he didn't know how far it was from Fouta Djallon or how to get back to his homeland. He could tell that this place was ruled by white men who held him in captivity. The other blacks he had seen were from all parts of Africa. Some he recognized by their tribal markings, some he did not. None were allowed to speak their native tongues around the white men. Some already knew nothing of the languages of their people.

As time passed, Ibrahima's despair deepened. His choices were simple. He could stay in the woods and probably die, or he could submit his body back into bondage.[17] There is no place in Islamic law for a man to take his own life. Ibrahima returned to Thomas Foster.

Foster still owed money to the man from whom he had purchased Ibrahima.

16 **Natchez**: area that became Mississippi

17 **bondage**: slavery; oppression

The debt would remain whether he still possessed the African or not. Foster was undoubtedly glad to see that the African had returned. Thin, nearly starving, Ibrahima was put to work.

Ibrahima submitted himself to the will of Thomas Foster. He was a captive, held in bondage not only by Foster but by the society in which he found himself. Ibrahima maintained his beliefs in the religion of Islam and kept its rituals[18] as best he could. He was determined to be the same person he had always been: Abd al-Rahman Ibrahima of Fouta Djallon and of the proud Fula people.

By 1807 the area had become the Mississippi Territory. Ibrahima was forty-five and had been in bondage for twenty years. During those years he met and married a woman whom Foster had purchased, and they began to raise a family. Fouta Djallon was more and more distant, and he had become **resigned** to the idea that he would never see it or his family again.

**resigned**
accepting

Thomas Foster had grown wealthy and had become an important man in the territory. At forty-five Ibrahima was considered old. He was less useful to Foster, who now let the tall African grow a few vegetables on a side plot and sell them in town, since there was nowhere in the territory that the black man could go where he would not be captured by some other white man and returned.

It was during one of these visits to town that Ibrahima saw a white man who looked familiar. The smallish man walked slowly and with a limp. Ibrahima cautiously approached the man and spoke to him. The man looked closely at Ibrahima, then spoke his name. It was Dr. Cox.

The two men shook hands, and Dr. Cox, who now lived in the territory, took Ibrahima to his home. John Cox had not prospered over the years, but he was still hopeful. He listened carefully as Ibrahima told his story—the battle near Fouta Djallon, the defeat, the long journey across the Atlantic Ocean, and finally his sale to Thomas Foster and the years of labor.

Dr. Cox and Ibrahima went to the Foster plantation. Meeting with Foster, he explained how he had met the tall black man. Surely, he reasoned, knowing that Ibrahima was of royal blood, Foster would free him? The answer was a firm but polite no. No amount of pleading would make Foster change his mind. It didn't matter that Dr. Cox had supported what Ibrahima had told Foster so many

---

18 **rituals**: ceremonies

IBRAHIMA, Henry Inman, 1928

years before, that he was a prince. To Foster the man was merely his property.

Dr. Cox had to leave the man whose people had saved his life, but he told Ibrahima that he would never stop working for his freedom.

Andrew Marschalk, the son of a Dutch baker, was a printer, a pioneer in his field, and a man of great curiosity. By the time Marschalk heard about it, Cox had told a great many people in the Natchez district the story of African royalty being held in slavery in America. Marschalk was fascinated. He suggested that Ibrahima write a letter to his people, telling them of his whereabouts and asking them to ransom him. But Ibrahima had not been to his homeland in twenty years. The people there were still being captured by slave traders. He would have to send a messenger who knew the countryside and who knew the Fula. Where would he find such a man?

For a long time Ibrahima did nothing. Finally, some time after the death of Dr. Cox in 1816, Ibrahima wrote the letter that Marschalk suggested. He had little faith in the procedure but felt he had nothing to lose. Marschalk was surprised when Ibrahima appeared with the letter written neatly in Arabic. Since one place in Africa was the same as the next to Marschalk, he sent the letter not to Fouta Djallon but to Morocco.

The government of Morocco did not know Ibrahima but understood from his letter that he was a Moslem. Moroccan officials, in a letter to President James Monroe, pleaded for the release of Ibrahima. The letter reached Henry Clay, the American secretary of state.

The United States had recently ended a bitter war with Tripoli in North Africa and welcomed the idea of establishing good relations with Morocco, another North African country. Clay wrote to Foster about Ibrahima.

Foster **resented** the idea of releasing Ibrahima. The very idea that the government of Morocco had written to Clay and discussed a religion that Ibrahima shared with other Africans gave Ibrahima a past that Foster had long denied, a past as honorable as Foster's. This idea challenged a basic **premise** of slavery—a premise that Foster must have believed without **reservation**: that the Africans had been nothing but savages, with no humanity or human feelings, and therefore it was all right to enslave them. But after more letters and pressure from the State Department, Foster agreed to release Ibrahim if he could be assured that Ibrahima would leave the country and return to Fouta Djallon.

Many people who believed that slavery was wrong also believed that Africans could not live among white Americans. The American Colonization Society had been formed expressly to send freed Africans back to Africa. The society bought land, and a colony called Liberia was established on the west coast of Africa. Foster was assured that Ibrahima would be sent there.

By then Ibrahima's cause had been taken up by a number of abolitionist[19] groups in the North as well as by many free Africans. They raised money to buy his wife's freedom as well.

On February 7, 1829, Ibrahima and his wife sailed on the ship *Harriet* for Africa. The ship reached Liberia, and Ibrahima now had to find a way to reach his people again. He never found that way. Abd al-Rahman Ibrahima died in Liberia in July 1829.

Who was Ibrahima? He was one of millions of Africans taken by force from their native lands. He was the son of a chief, a warrior, and a scholar. But to Ibrahima the only thing that mattered was that he had lost his freedom. If he had been a herder in Fouta Djallon, or an artist in Benin, or a farmer along the Gambia, it would have been the same. Ibrahima was an African who loved freedom no less than other beings on earth. And he was denied that freedom.

**resented**
felt angry or annoyed

**premise**
idea; principle

**reservation**
doubt; hesitation

---

19 **abolitionist**: a person or group who is against slavery

# Reviewing

## Abd al-Rahman Ibrahima

### Discussing the Selection

1. What kind of a man is Ibrahima? Pick a passage—of dialogue, description, thought, or action—that illustrates one of his character traits.

2. How does Ibrahima deal with his situation?

3. What was your reaction to the ending of this story? Explain.

4. Do you think Ibrahima is a hero or just a victim of circumstances? Be ready to defend your answer.

### Writing a Character Sketch

Using what you have learned about how writers develop their characters, write a short profile, or character sketch, of one of your heroes. To show this person's courage, you can use description and show him or her in action or interacting with others. Remember, it's the details that make a character come alive. Write about someone you know, if possible, and remember that not all acts of heroism are headline-grabbers.

### About Walter Dean Myers (1937–)

As a young person with serious speech problems, Walter Dean Myers discovered self-expression through writing. He grew up with loving foster parents in Harlem, New York City, which was a poor but supportive community. Of his youth, Myers wrote, "Books took me, not so much to foreign lands and fanciful adventures, but to a place within myself that I have been exploring ever since. The public library was my most treasured place. I couldn't believe my luck in discovering that what I enjoyed most—reading—was free." His young adult novels *Scorpions* and *Somewhere in the Darkness* were Newbery Honor Books. Other Myers titles include *Hoops*, *Monster*, and *Harlem*, a picture book illustrated by his son and awarded a Caldecott Medal. He is a three-time recipient of the Coretta Scott King Award.

# Previewing

## The Living Kuan-yin
retold by Carol Kendall and Yao-Wen Li

## Reading Connection
Because of the influence of the philosopher and teacher Confucius, most Chinese folktales contain a strong moral message. Confucius lived from 551 to 479 B.C. He was concerned with the "ideal" in education and behavior. How should we live? How should we act toward others? What sort of society is best? In his view, order and harmony were important goals. For centuries, his sayings and beliefs have influenced people not only in China, but throughout the world.

## Skill Focus: Prediction
Predicting means using information you already have to help you guess what will happen next. As you read the following tale, pay attention to what kind of a person Po-wan, the main character, is. In literature, what a character says and does generally provide clues to how the story will end. With that in mind, try to predict what will happen to Po-wan at the completion of his journey.

## Vocabulary Builder
Although you may not know what the following words mean, see if you can tell what they do. Guess which words describe someone or something. Which ones tell how something is done? Which words express an action? Are there words that fit into more than one category? Some that don't fit any of these categories? Now find the words on the pages where they are defined. Does the context help you put them into categories?

| | | | |
|---|---|---|---|
| signify | destitute | ponder | accumulated |
| compassion | dwindled | amiable | |
| distress | seeped | cultivated | |

Kuan-Yin, Yuan Dynasty, 1271–1368 B.C.

# The **Living Kuan-yin**[1]

retold by Carol Kendall and Yao-Wen Li

Even though the family name of Chin means *gold*, it does not **signify** that everyone of that name is rich. Long ago, in the province of Chekiang, however, there was a certain wealthy Chin family of whom it was popularly said that its fortune was as great as its name. It seemed quite fitting, then, when a son was born to the family, that he should be called Po-wan, "Million," for he was certain to be worth a million pieces of gold when he came of age.

With such a happy circumstance of names, Po-wan himself never doubted that he would have a never-ending supply of money chinking through his fingers, and he spent it accordingly—not on himself, but on any unfortunate who came to his attention. He had a deep sense of **compassion** for anyone in **distress** of body or spirit: a poor man had only to hold out his hand, and Po-wan poured gold into it; if a **destitute** widow and her brood of starvlings[2] but lifted sorrowful eyes to his, he provided them with food and lodging and friendship for the rest of their days.

**signify**
mean

**compassion**
pity and understanding

**distress**
suffering; pain

**destitute**
poor; deprived

---

1 **Kuan-Yin**: the Chinese goddess of mercy
2 **brood of starvlings**: hungry group of children

In such wise did he live that even a million gold pieces were not enough to support him. His resources so **dwindled** that finally he scarcely had enough food for himself; his clothes flapped threadbare[3] on his wasted[4] frame; and the cold **seeped** into his bone marrow for lack of a fire. Still he gave away the little money that came to him.

One day, as he scraped out half of his bowl of rice for a beggar even hungrier than he, he began to **ponder** on his destitute state.

"Why am I so poor?" he wondered. "I have never spent extravagantly. I have never, from the day of my birth, done an evil deed. Why then am I, whose very name is A Million Pieces of Gold, no longer able to find even a copper to give this unfortunate creature, and have only a bowl of rice to share with him?"

He thought long about his situation and at last determined to go without delay to the South Sea. Therein, it was told, dwelt the all-merciful goddess, the Living Kuan-yin, who could tell the past and future. He would put his question to her and she would tell him the answer.

Soon he had left his home country behind and traveled for many weeks in unfamiliar lands. One day he found his way barred by a wide and furiously flowing river. As he stood first on one foot and then on the other, wondering how he could possibly get across, he heard a commanding voice calling from the top of an overhanging cliff.

"Chin Po-wan!" the voice said, "if you are going to the South Sea, please ask the Living Kuan-yin a question for me!"

"Yes, yes, of course," Po-wan agreed at once, for he had never in his life refused a request made of him. In any case, the Living Kuan-yin permitted each person who approached her three questions, and he had but one of his own to ask.

Craning[5] his head toward the voice coming from above, he suddenly began to tremble, for the speaker was a gigantic snake with a body as large as a temple column. Po-wan was glad he had agreed so readily to the request.

"Ask her, then," said the snake, "why I am not yet a dragon even though I

---

3 **threadbare**: completely worn down

4 **wasted**: thin

5 **craning**: stretching the neck while looking

have practiced self-denial[6] for more than one thousand years."

"That I will do, and gl-gladly," stammered Po-wan, hoping that the snake would continue to practice self-denial just a bit longer. "But, your . . . your Snakery . . . or your Serpentry, perhaps I should say . . . that is . . . you see, don't you . . . first I must cross this raging river, and I know not how."

"That is no problem at all," said the snake. "I shall carry you across, of course."

"Of course," Po-wan echoed weakly. Overcoming his fear and his reluctance to touch the slippery-slithery scales, Chin Po-wan climbed onto the snake's back and rode across quite safely. Politely, and just a bit hurriedly, he thanked the self-denying serpent and bade him goodbye. Then he continued on his way to the South Sea.

By noon he was very hungry. Fortunately a nearby inn offered meals at a price he could afford. While waiting for his bowl of rice, he chatted with the innkeeper and told him of the Snake of the Cliff, which the innkeeper knew well and respected, for the serpent always denied bandits the crossing of the river. Inadvertently,[7] during the exchange of stories, Po-wan revealed the purpose of his journey.

"Why then," cried the innkeeper, "let me prevail[8] upon your generosity to ask a word for me." He laid an appealing hand on Po-wan's ragged sleeve. "I have a beautiful daughter," he said, "wonderfully **amiable** and pleasing of disposition.[9] But although she is in her twentieth year, she has never in all her life uttered a single word. I should be very much obliged if you would ask the Living Kuan-yin why she is unable to speak."

**amiable**
friendly; good-natured

Po-wan, much moved by the innkeeper's plea for his mute daughter, of course promised to do so. For after all, the Living Kuan-yin allowed each person three questions, and he had but one of his own to ask.

Nightfall found him far from any inn, but there were houses in the

---

6 **self-denial**: doing without the things one wants and desires

7 **inadvertently**: accidentally or by mistake

8 **prevail upon**: take advantage of

9 **disposition**: personality; temperament

neighborhood, and he asked for lodging at the largest. The owner, a man obviously of great wealth, was pleased to offer him a bed in a fine chamber, but first begged him to partake of a hot meal and good drink. Po-wan ate well, slept soundly, and, much refreshed, was about to depart the following morning when his good host, having learned that Po-wan was journeying to the South Sea, asked if he would be kind enough to put a question for him to the Living Kuan-yin.

**cultivated**
labored in;
attended

"For twenty years," he said, "from the time this house was built, my garden has been **cultivated** with the utmost care; yet in all those years, not one tree, not one small plant, has bloomed or borne fruit, and because of this, no bird comes to sing, nor bee to gather nectar. I don't like to put you to a bother, Chin Po-wan, but as you are going to the South Sea anyway, perhaps you would not mind seeking out the Living Kuan-yin and asking her why the plants in my garden don't bloom?"

"I shall be delighted to put the question to her," said Po-wan. For after all, the Living Kuan-yin allowed each person three questions, and he had but . . .

**accumulated**
collected;
gathered

Traveling onward, Po-wan examined the quandary[10] in which he found himself. The Living Kuan-yin allowed but three questions, and he had somehow, without quite knowing how, **accumulated** four questions. One of them would have to go unasked, but which? If he left out his own question, his whole journey would have been in vain.[11] If, on the other hand, he left out the question of the snake or the innkeeper or the kind host, he would break his promise and betray their faith in him.

"A promise should never be made if it cannot be kept," he told himself. "I made the promises and therefore I must keep them. Besides, the journey will not be in vain, for at least some of these problems will be solved by the Living Kuan-yin. Furthermore, assisting others must certainly be counted as a good deed, and the more good deeds abroad in the land, the better for everyone, including me."

At last he came into the presence of the Living Kuan-yin.

---

10 **quandary**: a perplexing or confusing situation

11 **in vain**: a waste of time

First, he asked the serpent's question: "Why is the Snake of the Cliff not yet a dragon, although he has practiced self-denial for more than one thousand years?"

And the Living Kuan-yin answered: "On his head are seven bright pearls. If he removes six of them, he can become a dragon."

Next, Po-wan asked the innkeeper's question: "Why is the innkeeper's daughter unable to speak, although she is in the twentieth year of her life?"

And the Living Kuan-yin answered: "It is her fate to remain mute until she sees the man destined[12] to be her husband."

Last, Po-wan asked the kind host's question: "Why are there never blossoms in the rich man's garden, although it has been carefully cultivated for twenty years?"

And the Living Kuan-yin answered: "Buried in the garden are seven big jars filled with silver and gold. The flowers will bloom if the owner will rid himself of half the treasure."

Then Chin Po-wan thanked the Living Kuan-yin and bade her goodbye.

On his return journey, he stopped first at the rich man's house to give him the Living Kuan-yin's answer. In gratitude the rich man gave him half the buried treasure.

Next Po-wan went to the inn. As he approached, the innkeeper's daughter saw him from the window and called out, "Chin Po-wan! Back already! What did the Living Kuan-yin say?"

Upon hearing his daughter speak at long last, the joyful innkeeper gave her in marriage to Chin Po-wan.

Lastly, Po-wan went to the cliffs by the furiously flowing river to tell the snake what the Living Kuan-yin had said. The grateful snake immediately gave him six of the bright pearls and promptly turned into a magnificent dragon, the remaining pearl in his forehead lighting the headland like a great beacon.[13]

And so it was that Chin Po-wan, that generous and good man, was once more worth a million pieces of gold.

---

12 **destined**: meant to be

13 **beacon**: guiding light

# Reviewing

## The Living Kuan-yin

### Discussing the Selection

1. Did you predict that Po-wan would leave out one of the others' questions in order to include his own? Why or why not?

2. What do you think Po-wan did with his new riches of buried treasure and pearls?

3. What elements in this selection make it a folktale? Review the elements on page 240 if necessary.

4. Compare the character of Po-wan to that of Ibrahima. How are they alike? How are they different?

### Writing an Analysis

Confucius's philosophy about life is captured in many of his famous sayings. For example, "To know what is right and not to do it is the worst cowardice." In a short essay, explain what you think this means. Then tell how it connects to the characters and events in "The Living Kuan-yin."

### About Carol Kendall and Yao-Wen Li
### Carol Kendall (1917–)

Carol Kendall is best known for her fantasy series about the Minnipins, a race of tiny people who live in a floating slipper. In the Newbery award-winning novel *The Gammage Cup*, their ideal world is challenged by outsiders. The other books in the series include *The Whisper of Glocken*, *The Firelings*, and *Fantasy 4*. Regarding Kendall's reputation with young readers, one publisher said, "There were the Hobbits of the Hill, the Borrowers, and now the Minnipins of Slipper-on-the-Water. Such tales are golden events in the publication of children's stories."

### Yao-wen Li

Yao-wen Li co-authored with Carol Kendall the acclaimed folktale collection, *Sweet and Sour: Tales from China*. Like her co-writer, Yao-wen Li writes for both children and adults. She has a special interest in folktales and their influences.

# Previewing

## Where the Girl Rescued Her Brother

retold by Joseph Bruchac

### Reading Connection

Long ago, Native-American storytellers sat in the middle of a circle formed by their listeners. Often the occasion began with singing and drumming. According to writer and scholar Joseph Bruchac, Native-American stories almost always have lessons. The finest ones "tell people how they should act toward the earth and toward each other." He believes they share "knowledge that, like an elder's voice, can help guide a young person along a trail on which his or her feet have never been."

### Skill Focus: Imagery

Imagery refers to the word pictures created through the use of sensory details—that is, words that appeal to a reader's sight, sound, touch, taste, and smell. Writers and storytellers know the value of using such colorful images. As you read, watch for any details that Bruchac includes that make the story more vivid.

### Vocabulary Builder

Look for these words as you read. Are there any others in the story that are not familiar to you?

| allies | confronted | ferocity | vaulted |

LITTLE BIG HORN, Amos Bad Heart Bull

# Where the Girl Rescued Her Brother

Retold by Joseph Bruchac

It was the moon when the chokecherries were ripe. A young woman rode out of a Cheyenne camp with her husband and her brother. The young woman's name was Buffalo Calf Road Woman.

Her husband, Black Coyote, was one of the chiefs of the Cheyenne, the people of the plains who call themselves Tsis-tsis-tas, meaning simply "The People." Buffalo Calf Road Woman's brother, Comes-in-Sight, was also one of the Cheyenne chiefs, and it was well-known how close he was to his sister.

Like many of the other young women of the Cheyenne, Buffalo Calf Road Woman was respected for her honorable nature. Although it was the men who most often went to war to defend the people—as they were doing on this day—women would accompany their husbands when they went to battle. If a man held an important position among the Cheyenne, such as the keeper of the Sacred Arrows, then his wife, too, would have to be of the highest moral character, for she shared the weight of his responsibility.

Buffalo Calf Road Woman was well aware of this, and as she rode by her husband she did so with pride. She knew that today they were on their way to meet their old **allies**, the Lakota.[1] They were going out to try to drive back the *veho*, the spider people who were trying to claim all the lands of the Native peoples.

The Cheyenne had been worried about the *veho*, the white people, for a long time. They had given them that name because, like the black widow spider, they were very beautiful but it was dangerous to get close to them. And unlike the Cheyenne, they seemed to follow a practice of making promises and not keeping them. Although their soldier chief Custer had promised to be friendly with the Cheyenne, now he and the others had come into their lands to make war upon them.

Buffalo Calf Road Woman wore a robe embroidered with porcupine quills. The clothing of her brother and her husband, Black Coyote, was also beautifully decorated with those quills, which had been flattened, dyed in different colors, folded, and sewed on in patterns. Buffalo Calf Road Woman was proud that she belonged to the Society of Quilters. As with the men's societies, only a few women—those of the best character—could join. Like the men, the women had to be strong, honorable, and brave. Buffalo Calf Road Woman had grown up hearing stories of how Cheyenne women would defend their families when the men were away. The women of the Cheyenne were brave, and those in the Society of Quilters were the bravest of all.

Buffalo Calf Road Woman smiled as she remembered one day when the women of the Society of Quilters showed such bravery. It was during the Moon of Falling Leaves. A big hunt had been planned. The men who acted as scouts had gone out and located the great buffalo herd. They had seen, too, that there were no human enemies anywhere near their camp. So almost none of the men remained behind.

On that day, when all the men were away, a great grizzly bear came into the camp. Such things seldom happened, but this bear was one that had been wounded in the leg by a white fur-trapper's bullet. It could no longer hunt as

---

1 **Lakota**: a Native American tribe belonging to the Teton branch of the Dakota Indians

it had before, and hunger brought it to the Cheyenne camp, where it smelled the food cooking.

When the huge bear came walking into the camp, almost everyone scattered. Some women grabbed their little children. Old people shut the door flaps of their tepees, and the boys ran to find their bows and arrows. Only a group of seven women who had been working on the embroidery of an elk-skin robe did not run. They were members of the Society of Quilters, and Buffalo Calf Road Woman was among them. The seven women put down their work, picked up the weapons they had close to hand, and stood to face the grizzly bear.

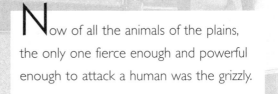

Now of all the animals of the plains, the only one fierce enough and powerful enough to attack a human was the grizzly.

Now of all the animals of the plains, the only one fierce enough and powerful enough to attack a human was the grizzly. But **confronted** by that determined group of women, the grizzly bear stopped in its tracks. It had come to steal food, not fight. The head of the Society of Quilters stepped forward a pace and spoke to the bear.

**confronted**
faced

"Grandfather," she said, her voice low and firm, "we do not wish to harm you, but we will protect our camp. Go back to your own home."

The grizzly shook its head and then turned and walked out of the camp. The women stood and watched it as it went down through the cottonwoods and was lost from sight along the bend of the stream.

Buffalo Calf Road Woman turned her mind away from her memories. They were close to Rosebud Creek. The scouts had told them that a great number of the *veho* soldiers would be there and that the Gray Fox, General George Crook, was in command. The Cheyenne had joined up now with the Oglala,[2] led by Crazy Horse. The Lakota people were always friends to the Cheyenne, but this man, Crazy Horse, was the best friend of all. Some even said that he was one of their chiefs, too, as well as being a war leader of his Oglala.

There were Crow and Shoshone scouts with Crook, and the *veho* had many

---

2 **Oglala**: a Native American tribe, also of the Teton branch of the Dakotas

cannons. The Lakota and the Cheyenne were outnumbered by the two thousand men in Crook's command. But they were prepared to fight. They had put on their finest clothes, for no man should risk his life without being dressed well enough so that if he died, the enemy would know a great warrior had fallen. Some of the men raised their headdresses three times, calling out their names and the deeds they had done. Those headdresses of eagle feathers were thought to give magical protection to a warrior. Other men busied themselves painting designs on their war ponies.

Now they could hear Crook's army approaching. The rumble of the horses' hooves echoed down the valley, and there was the sound of trumpets. War ponies reared up and stomped their feet. Many of the Cheyenne men found it hard to put on the last of their paint as their hands shook from the excitement of the coming battle.

Crazy Horse vaulted onto his horse and held up one arm, *"Hoka Hey,"* he cried. "It is a good day to die."

Buffalo Calf Road Woman watched from a hill as the two lines of men—the blue soldiers to one side, and the Lakota and Cheyenne to the other—raced toward each other. The battle began. It was not a quick fight or an easy one. There were brave men on both sides. Two Moons, Little Hawk, Yellow Eagle, Sitting Bull, and Crazy Horse were only a few of the great warriors who fought for the Cheyenne and the Lakota. And Crook, the Gray Fox general of the whites, was known to be a tough fighter and a worthy enemy.

Buffalo Calf Road Woman's husband, Black Coyote, and her brother, Comes-in-Sight, were in the thick of the fight. The odds in the battle were almost even. Although the whites had more soldiers and guns, the Lakota and the Cheyenne were better shots and better horsemen. Had it not been for the Crow and Shoshone scouts helping Crook, the white soldiers might have broken quickly from the **ferocity** of the attack.

From one side to the other, groups of men attacked and retreated as the guns cracked, cannons boomed, and smoke filled the air. The war shouts of the Lakota and the Cheyenne were almost as loud as the rumble of the guns. The sun moved across the sky as the fight went on, hour after hour, while the confusion of battle swirled below.

Then Buffalo Calf Road Woman saw something that horrified her. Her

**ferocity**
extreme violence or rage

brother had been drawn off to one side, surrounded by Crow scouts. He tried to ride free of them, but his pony went down, struck by a rifle bullet and killed. Now he was on foot, still fighting. The Crow warriors were trying to get close, to count coup[3] on him. It was more of an honor to touch a living enemy, so they were not firing their rifles at him. And he was able to keep them away with his bow and arrows. But it was clear that soon he would be out of ammunition and would fall to the enemy.

Buffalo Calf Road Woman waited no longer. She dug her heels into her pony's sides and galloped down the hill. Her head low, her braids streaming behind her, she rode into the heart of the fight. Some men moved aside as they saw her coming, for there was a determined look in her eyes. She made the long howling cry that Cheyenne women used to urge on the warriors. This time, however, she was the one going into the fight. Her voice was as strong as an eagle's. Her horse scattered the ponies of the Crow scouts who were closing in on her brother, Comes-in-Sight. She held out a hand; her brother grabbed it and **vaulted** onto the pony behind her. Then she wheeled, ducking the arrows of the Crow scouts, and heading back up the hill.

**vaulted**
to jump or leap up

That was when it happened. For a moment, it seemed as if all the shooting stopped. The Cheyenne and the Lakota, and even the *veho* soldiers, lowered their guns to watch this act of great bravery. A shout went up, not from one side but from both, as Buffalo Calf Road Woman reached the safety of the hilltop again, her brother safe behind her on her horse. White men and Indians cheered her.

So it was that Buffalo Calf Road Woman performed the act for which the people would always remember her. Inspired by her courage, the Cheyenne and Lakota drove back the Gray Fox—Crook made a strategic withdrawal.

"Even the *veho* general was impressed," said the Cheyenne people. "He saw that if our women were that brave, he would stand no chance against us in battle."

So it is that to this day, the Cheyenne and the Lakota people do not refer to the fight as the Battle of the Rosebud. Instead, they honor Buffalo Calf Road Woman by calling the fight Where the Girl Rescued Her Brother.

---

3 **count coup**: to touch an enemy in battle with a rod, called a coup stick, while he is still alive

# Reviewing

## Where the Girl Rescued Her Brother

### Discussing the Selection
1. Point out some of the sensory images the writer uses. What do they contribute to this story?

2. What is the Cheyenne attitude about the role of women?

3. How does the incident with the Society of Quilters predict what will happen later in the story?

4. How much of this tale do you think is true? What kind of research could you do to find out?

### Writing a Comparison
The theme of heroism runs through all of the writing in Unit Five. Compare the heroism in "Where the Girl Rescued Her Brother" with the heroism of any other selection in this book. Explain any new ideas you have about heroes or heroism.

### About Joseph Bruchac (1942–)
Joseph Bruchac's ethnic heritage includes American Indian, Slovak, and English ancestors, but he identifies most strongly with his Abenaki Indian lineage. Working from a rich oral tradition, Bruchac creates memorable characters who teach as well as entertain. He says, "The central themes in my work are simple ones—that we have to listen to each other and to the earth, that we have to respect each other and the earth, that we never know anyone until we know what they have in their heart." Bruchac has won numerous awards, including the Lifetime Achievement Award from the Native Writers Circle of the Americas. In addition to writing and telling stories, he is dedicated to preserving Abenaki culture and language, including traditional and contemporary Abenaki music.

# Previewing

## Paul Revere's Ride

by Henry Wadsworth Longfellow

### Reading Connection

Poet Henry Wadsworth Longfellow's huge popularity during the 19th century gave him the power to shape the way Americans saw their nation. According to U.S. Poet Laureate Dana Gioa, Longfellow's poems gave his fellow citizens "the words, images, myths, and heroes by which they explained America to one another and themselves." Longfellow's most famous poem, "Paul Revere's Ride," was published right before the Civil War began. Longfellow wanted to remind Americans going into that war of the ideals upon which the country had been founded. He also wanted to arouse their patriotic courage. Gioa claims the actions in the poem are amazingly close to what actually happened that night in April 1775, on the very brink of the Revolutionary War.

### Skill Focus: Previewing

With your classmates, brainstorm what you already know about Paul Revere and his famous ride. As you read the poem, note all of the dates, names, and other historical references that Longfellow includes in the poem to give it the feel of reality.

### Vocabulary Builder

Can you match up these definitions with the following words: horse, horrified, watchman, step, golden, resistance?

| | | | |
|---|---|---|---|
| tread | steed | aghast | defiance |
| sentinel | gilded | | |

# Paul Revere's Ride

Henry Wadsworth Longfellow

PAUL REVERE, N. C. Wyeth, 1922

Listen my children, and you shall hear
Of the midnight ride of Paul Revere,
On the eighteenth of April, in seventy-five;
Hardly a man is now alive
Who remembers that famous day and year.          5

He said to his friend, "If the British march
By land or sea from the town tonight,
Hang a lantern aloft in the belfry[1] arch
Of the North Church tower as a signal light,—
One, if by land, and two, if by sea;          10
And I on the opposite shore will be,
Ready to ride and spread the alarm
Through every Middlesex[2] village and farm,
For the country folk to be up and to arm."

Then he said "Good-night!" and with muffled oar      15
Silently rowed to the Charlestown[3] shore,
Just as the moon rose over the bay,
Where swinging wide at her moorings lay
The *Somerset*, British man-of-war;[4]
A phantom ship, with each mast and spar      20
Across the moon like a prison bar,
And a huge black hulk, that was magnified
By its own reflection in the tide.

Meanwhile, his friend, through alley and street,
Wanders and watches, with eager ears,      25
Till in the silence around him he hears
The muster of men at the barrack door,[5]
The sound of arms, and the tramp of feet,
And the measured **tread** of the grenadiers,[6]       **tread**
Marching down to their boats on the shore.      30    footstep

---

1 **belfry**: a church's bell tower

2 **Middlesex**: a Massachusetts county where the first Revolutionary War battle was fought

3 **Charlestown**: an area now in northeast Boston

4 **man-of-war**: battleship

5 **muster . . . barrack door**: assembly of soldiers at their lodging quarters

6 **grenadiers**: selected foot soldiers

Then he climbed the tower of the Old North Church,
By the wooden stairs, with stealthy tread,
To the belfry chamber overhead,
And startled the pigeons from their perch
On the sombre rafters, that round him made        35
Masses and moving shapes of shade—
By the trembling ladder, steep and tall,
To the highest window in the wall,
Where he paused to listen and look down
A moment on the roofs of the town,               40
And the moonlight flowing over all.

Beneath, in the churchyard, lay the dead,
In their night-encampment on the hill,
Wrapped in silence so deep and still

**sentinel**
person who
stands watch;
guard

That he could hear, like a **sentinel**'s tread,   45
The watchful night-wind, as it went
Creeping along from tent to tent,
And seeming to whisper, "All is well!"
A moment only he feels the spell
Of the place and the hour, and the secret dread  50
Of the lonely belfry and the dead;
For suddenly all his thoughts are bent
On a shadowy something far away,
Where the river widens to meet the bay, —
A line of black that bends and floats           55
On the rising tide, like a bridge of boats.

Meanwhile, impatient to mount and ride,
Booted and spurred, with a heavy stride
On the opposite shore walked Paul Revere.
Now he patted his horse's side,                          60
Now he gazed at the landscape far and near,
Then, impetuous, stamped the earth,
And turned and tightened his saddle-girth;
But mostly he watched with eager search
The belfry-tower of the Old North Church,                65
As it rose above the graves on the hill,
Lonely and spectral[7] and sombre and still.
And lo! as he looks, on the belfry's height
A glimmer, and then a gleam of light!
He springs to the saddle, the bridle he turns,           70
But lingers and gazes, till full on his sight
A second lamp in the belfry burns!

A hurry of hoofs in a village street,
A shape in the moonlight, a bulk in the dark,
And beneath, from the pebbles, in passing, a spark       75
Struck out by a **steed** flying fearless and fleet;
That was all! And yet, through the gloom and the light,
The fate of a nation was riding that night;
And the spark struck out by that steed, in his flight,
Kindled[8] the land into flame with its heat.            80

**steed**
a powerful
horse

---

7 **spectral**: ghostly
8 **kindled**: lighted

He has left the village and mounted the steep,
And beneath him, tranquil and broad and deep,
Is the Mystic,[9] meeting the ocean tides;
And under the alders that skirt its edge,
Now soft on the sand, now loud on the ledge,          85
Is heard the tramp of his steed as he rides.

It was twelve by the village clock,
When he crossed the bridge into Medford town.
He heard the crowing of the cock,
And the barking of the farmer's dog,                  90
And felt the damp of the river fog,
That rises after the sun goes down.

It was one by the village clock,
When he galloped into Lexington.

**gilded**
covered with
gold

He saw the **gilded** weathercock                     95
Swim in the moonlight as he passed.
And the meeting-house windows, black and bare,
Gaze at him with a spectral glare,

**aghast**
shocked;
amazed

As if they already stood **aghast**
At the bloody work they would look upon.              100

It was two by the village clock,
When he came to the bridge in Concord town.
He heard the bleating of the flock,
And the twitter of birds among the trees,
And felt the breath of the morning breeze             105

---

9 **Mystic**: a river that flows through New England

Blowing over the meadow brown.
And one was safe and asleep in his bed
Who at the bridge would be first to fall,
Who that day would be lying dead,
Pierced by a British musket-ball.                                     110

You know the rest. In the books you have read
How the British Regulars fired and fled,—
How the farmers gave them ball for ball,
From behind each fence and farmyard wall,
Chasing the red-coats down the lane,                                  115
Then crossing the fields to emerge again
Under the trees at the turn of the road,
And only pausing to fire and load.

So through the night rode Paul Revere;
And so through the night went his cry of alarm                        120
To every Middlesex village and farm,—
A cry of **defiance** and not of fear,                                **defiance**
A voice in the darkness, a knock at the door,                         resistance
And a word that shall echo for evermore!

For, borne[10] on the night-wind of the Past,                        125
Through all our history, to the last,
In the hour of darkness and peril and need,
The people will waken and listen to hear
The hurrying hoof-beats of that steed,
And the midnight message of Paul Revere.                              130

---

10 **borne**: carried

# Reviewing

## Paul Revere's Ride

### Discussing the Selection
1. Why do you think Longfellow addresses his poem to children ("Listen my children, and you shall hear . . .")?

2. Narrative poetry such as "Paul Revere's Ride" tells a story. How does Longfellow build suspense and add conflict to the plot?

3. Although there is much factual information in this poem, there is also much that Longfellow could only have imagined. List some of the facts. Then list some details that come from the poet's imagination.

4. Read the poem aloud. Explain how its rhyme and rhythm aid in telling the story of this famous "midnight ride."

### Writing a Timeline
Now that you have read Longfellow's poem, find an account of the actual events on April 17, 1775. Create two timelines that run parallel to each other. Write capsule descriptions of what really happened on one timeline and what took place only in the poem on the other. How accurate is Longfellow's description?

### About Henry Wadsworth Longfellow (1807–1882)
Almost every biography of Longfellow begins with the words "He was the most popular American poet of the 19th century." He is especially well-known for "The Song of Hiawatha," a long narrative poem about Native Americans and, of course, "Paul Revere's Ride." In fact, so much of his own writing was translated into other languages that he may truly have been the most famous American of his day. Even those who did not care for his sing-songy verse or myth-making did not find fault with him.

# Previewing

## Sally Ann Thunder Ann Whirlwind
by Mary Pope Osborne

### Reading Connection

What exactly are the makings of a good tall tale? First, there is usually a larger-than-life character. The story's details are comically exaggerated, and the language is simple but colorful. Tall tales were good entertainment for the pioneers, who otherwise endured difficult physical conditions. Many stories were about real people, such as Davy Crockett, though the tales were greatly "embroidered" by storytellers. Mary Pope Osborne discovered Crockett's fictional wife, Sally Ann Thunder Ann Whirlwind, in the Davy Crockett Almanacks. Knowing that few tall tales celebrated women, she made up a rough and ready heroine of her own.

### Skill Focus: Hyperbole

Hyperbole is a kind of comic exaggeration. Examples are "I'm as dry as a bone" and "I'm so hungry I could eat a horse." Tall tales rely on such exaggeration for much of their entertainment value. As you read, look for examples of this kind of language.

### Vocabulary Builder

This tall tale should not present any vocabulary challenges for you, but here are three interesting words for you to learn.

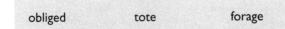

| obliged | tote | forage |

Illustrations by Michael McCurdy, 1991

# Sally Ann Thunder Ann Whirlwind

Mary Pope Osborne

One early spring day, when the leaves of the white oaks were about as big as a mouse's ear, Davy Crockett set out alone through the forest to do some bear hunting. Suddenly it started raining real hard, and he felt **obliged** to stop for shelter under a tree. As he shook the rain out of his coonskin cap,[1] he got sleepy, so he laid back into the crotch of the tree,[2] and pretty soon he was snoring.

Davy slept so hard, he didn't wake up until nearly sundown. And when he did, he discovered that somehow or another in all that sleeping his head had gotten stuck in the crotch of the tree, and he couldn't get it out.

Well, Davy roared loud enough to make the tree lose all its little mouse-ear leaves. He twisted and turned and carried on for over an hour, but still that tree wouldn't let go. Just as he was about to give himself up for a goner, he heard a girl say, "What's the matter, stranger?"

**obliged**
forced

---

1 **coonskin cap**: Davy Crockett is often pictured wearing a hat made of raccoon fur
2 **crotch of the tree**: the V created where the branches meet the trunk

Even from his awkward position, he could see that she was extraordinary—tall as a hickory sapling,[3] with arms as big as a keelboat tiller's.[4]

"My head's stuck, sweetie," he said, "And if you help me get it free, I'll give you a pretty little comb."

"Don't call me sweetie," she said. "And don't worry about giving me no pretty little comb, neither. I'll free your old coconut, but just because I want to."

Then this extraordinary girl did something that made Davy's hair stand on end. She reached in a bag and took out a bunch of rattlesnakes. She tied all the wriggly critters together to make a long rope, and as she tied, she kept talking. "I'm not a shy little colt," she said. "And I'm not a little singing nightingale, neither. I can **tote** a steamboat on my back, outscream a panther, and jump over my own shadow. I can double up crocodiles any day, and I like to wear a hornets' nest for my Sunday bonnet."

**tote**
carry; haul

As the girl looped the ends of her snake rope to the top of the branch that was trapping Davy, she kept bragging: "I'm a streak of lightning set up edgeways and buttered with quicksilver. I can outgrin, outsnort, outrun, outlift, outsneeze, outsleep, outlie any varmint[5] from Maine to Louisiana. Furthermore, *sweetie*, I can blow out the moonlight and sing a wolf to sleep." Then she pulled on the other end of the snake rope so hard, it seemed as if she might tear the world apart.

The right-hand fork of that big tree bent just about double. Then Davy slid his head out as easy as you please. For a minute he was so dizzy, he couldn't tell up from down. But when he got everything going straight again, he took a good look at that girl. "What's your name, ma'am?"

"Sally Ann Thunder Ann Whirlwind," she said. "But if you mind your manners, you can call me Sally."

From then on Davy Crockett was crazy in love with Sally Ann Thunder Ann Whirlwind. He asked everyone he knew about her, and everything he heard

---

3 **hickory sapling**: a young hickory tree

4 **keelboat tiller**: an oar used to steer a roughly built freight boat

5 **varmint**: animal

caused another one of cupid's arrows to jab him in the gizzard.[6]

"Oh, I know Sally!" the preacher said. "She can dance a rock to pieces and ride a panther bareback!"

"Sally's a good ole friend of mine," the blacksmith said. "Once I seen her crack a walnut with her front teeth."

"Sally's so very special," said the schoolmarm. "She likes to whip across the Salt River, using her apron for a sail and her left leg for a rudder!"

Sally Ann Thunder Ann Whirlwind had a reputation for being funny, too. Her best friend, Lucy, told Davy, "Sally can laugh the bark off a pine tree. She likes to whistle out one side of her mouth while she eats with the other side and grins with the middle!"

> **B**ut just as the King Bear blew his hot breath in her face, she gathered the courage to say, "Would you like to dance?"

According to her friends, Sally could tame about anything in the world, too. They all told Davy about the time she was churning butter and heard something scratching outside. Suddenly the door swung open, and in walked the Great King Bear of the Mud Forest. He'd come to steal one of her smoked hams. Well, before the King Bear could say boo, Sally grabbed a warm dumpling from the pot and stuffed it in his mouth.

The dumpling tasted so good, the King Bear's eyes winked with tears. But then he started to think that Sally might taste pretty good, too. So opening and closing his big old mouth, he backed her right into a corner.

Sally was plenty scared, with her knees a-knocking and her heart a-hammering. But just as the King Bear blew his hot breath in her face, she gathered the courage to say, "Would you like to dance?"

As everybody knows, no bear can resist an invitation to a square dance, so of course the old fellow forgot all about eating Sally and said, "Love to."

Then he bowed real pretty, and the two got to kicking and whooping and swinging each other through the air, as Sally sang:

---

6 **gizzard**: a tough muscle that helps birds digest food

*We are on our way to Baltimore,*
*With two behind, and two before:*
*Around, around, around we go,*
*Where oats, peas, beans, and barley grow!*

And while she was singing, Sally tied a string from the bear's ankle to her butter churn, so that all the time the old feller was kicking up his legs and dancing around the room, he was also churning her butter!

And folks loved to tell the story about Sally's encounter with another stinky varmint—only this one was a *human* varmint. It seems that Mike Fink, the riverboat man, decided to scare the toenails off Sally because he was sick and tired of hearing Davy Crockett talk about how great she was.

**forage**
search

One evening Mike crept into an old alligator skin and met Sally just as she was taking off to **forage** in the woods for berries. He spread open his gigantic mouth and made such a howl that he nearly scared himself to death. But Sally paid no more attention to that fool than she would have to a barking puppy dog.

However, when Mike put out his claws to embrace her, her anger rose higher than a Mississippi flood. She threw a flash of eye lightning at him, turning the dark to daylight. Then she pulled out a little toothpick and with a single swing sent the alligator head flying fifty feet! And then to finish him off good, she rolled up her sleeves and knocked Mike Fink clear across the woods and into a muddy swamp.

When the fool came to, Davy Crockett was standing over him. "What in the world happened to you, Mikey?" he asked.

"Well, I—I think I must-a been hit by some kind of wild alligator!" Mike stammered, rubbing his sore head.

Davy smiled, knowing full well it was Sally Ann Thunder Ann Whirlwind just finished giving Mike Fink the only punishment he'd ever known.

That incident caused Cupid's final arrow to jab Davy's gizzard. "Sally's the whole steamboat," he said, meaning she was something great. The next day he put on his best raccoon hat and sallied forth[7] to see her.

---

7 **sallied forth**: strode briskly forward

When he got within three miles of her cabin, he began to holler her name. His voice was so loud, it whirled through the woods like a hurricane.

Sally looked out and saw the wind a-blowing and the trees a-bending. She heard her name a-thundering through the woods, and her heart began to thump. By now she'd begun to feel that Davy Crockett was the whole steamboat, too. So she put on her best hat—an eagle's nest with a wildcat's tail for a feather—and ran outside.

Just as she stepped out the door, Davy Crockett burst from the woods and jumped onto her porch as fast as a frog. "Sally, darlin'!" he cried. "I think my heart is bustin'! Want to be my wife?"

"Oh, my stars and possum dogs, why not?" she said.

From that day on, Davy Crockett had a hard time acting tough around Sally Ann Thunder Ann Whirlwind. His fightin' and hollerin' had no more effect on her than dropping feathers on a barn floor. At least that's what *she'd* tell you. *He* might say something else.

# Reviewing

## Sally Ann Thunder Ann Whirlwind

### Discussing the Selection

1. Why doesn't Sally want to be called "sweetie"?

2. Name some examples of hyperbole, or comic exaggeration, that you especially liked.

3. Dialect is the nonstandard use of English. It can include unusual or regional pronunciation, word choices, and even grammar. Point out some examples of dialect in the story.

4. "Sally Ann Thunder Ann Whirlwind" has many examples of figurative language, such as metaphors and similes. Find some examples and share them with your class.

### Writing an "Autobiographical" Tall Tale

Try this twist on writing tall tales: Write one about yourself! Be sure to stretch the truth of each detail to absurd lengths. Or, start off with an ordinary event and gradually build up to a tale that is outrageously exaggerated. You might ease into the story by starting off like this: "It was just a typical day . . ."

### About Mary Pope Osborne (1949–)

As a child from a military family, Mary Pope Osborne lived all over the world. In college, she majored in religion because of her interest in mythology and other cultures. After graduation, she backpacked around Europe, surviving earthquakes and riots. Now she is the author of the hugely popular series for early readers, *The Magic Tree House*, which encourages children to take on adventures of their own. She has published everything from picture books to young adult novels. In an interview, she once said, "The best part of being a writer is being transported to other places and living other experiences. By surrounding myself with the smells, weather, animals, and people of imaginary landscapes, I feel as if I'm living an extraordinary life."

# Previewing

## The Mysterious Mr. Lincoln
by Russell Freedman

### Reading Connection

Abraham Lincoln has become a larger-than-life figure in American history. He is especially celebrated for his leadership during the Civil War, which freed the slaves and kept the Union intact. It is easy to forget that Lincoln was a flesh-and-blood person, not just the Honest Abe of legend. In this selection, writer Russell Freedman takes special pains to uncover the human being behind the myths created by countless writers, teachers, and politicians. He said, "The Lincoln I grew up with was a cardboard figure, too good to believe." Freedman's goal is to show how even such a revered figure as our 16th president was funnier, more flawed, and definitely more complex than we have been led to believe.

### Skill Focus: Biography

A biography is the story of a person's life told by someone else. While a biographer is obliged to present factual information, he or she will choose which facts to include and which to leave out. Also, those facts will be interpreted in different ways. As you read the next selection, think about Freedman's attitude toward Lincoln and what his purpose in writing might be.

### Vocabulary Builder

| | | | |
|---|---|---|---|
| gawky | reticent | melancholy | bungling |
| listless | eloquent | denounced | magnitude |
| animation | rollicking | | |

# The Mysterious
## Mr. Lincoln

Russell Freedman

Abraham Lincoln wasn't the sort of man who could lose himself in a crowd. After all, he stood six feet four inches tall, and to top it off, he wore a high silk hat.

His height was mostly in his long, bony legs. When he sat in a chair, he seemed no taller than anyone else. It was only when he stood up that he towered above other men.

At first glance most people thought he was homely. Lincoln thought so too, referring once to his "poor, lean, lank face." As a young man he was sensitive about his **gawky** looks, but in time, he learned to laugh at himself. When a rival called him "two-faced" during a political debate, Lincoln replied: "I leave it to my audience. If I had another face, do you think I'd wear this one?"

**gawky**
awkward;
clumsy

Cartoon of Abraham Lincoln
from *Harper's Weekly*, 1864

According to those who knew him, Lincoln was a man of many faces. In repose[1] he often seemed sad and gloomy. But when he began to speak, his expression changed. "The dull, **listless** features dropped like a mask," said a Chicago newspaperman. "The eyes began to sparkle, the mouth to smile; the whole countenance[2] was wreathed[3] in **animation**, so that a stranger would have said, "Why, this man, so angular[4] and solemn a moment ago, is really handsome!"

Lincoln was the most photographed man of his time, but his friends insisted that no photo ever did him justice. It's no wonder. Back then, cameras required long exposures. The person being photographed had to "freeze" as the seconds ticked by. If he blinked an eye the picture would be blurred. That's why Lincoln looks so stiff and formal in his photos. We never see him laughing or joking.

Artists and writers tried to capture the "real" Lincoln that the camera missed, but something about the man always escaped them. His changeable features, his tones, gestures, and expressions, seemed to defy description.

Today it's hard to imagine Lincoln as he really was. And he never cared to reveal much about himself. In company he was witty and talkative, but he rarely betrayed his inner feelings. According to William Herndon, his law partner, he was "the most secretive—**reticent**—shut-mouthed man that ever lived."

In his own time, Lincoln was never fully understood even by his closest friends. Since then, his life story has been told and retold so many times that he has become as much legend as flesh-and-blood human being. While the legend is based on truth, it is only partly true. And it hides the man behind it like a disguise.

The legendary Lincoln is known as Honest Abe, a humble man of the people who rose from a log cabin to the White House. There's no doubt that Lincoln was a poor boy who made good. And it's true that he carried his

**listless**
spiritless; indifferent

**animation**
liveliness; energy

**reticent**
quiet; reserved

---

1 **in repose**: at rest

2 **countenance**: face; expression

3 **wreathed**: covered; encircled

4 **angular**: lean and bony

folksy manners and homespun[5] speech to the White House with him. He said "howdy" to visitors and invited them to "stay a spell." He greeted diplomats while wearing carpet slippers, called his wife "mother" at receptions, and told bawdy[6] jokes at cabinet meetings.

Lincoln may have seemed like a common man, but he wasn't. His friends agreed that he was one of the most ambitious people they had ever known. Lincoln struggled hard to rise about his log-cabin origins, and he was proud of his achievements. By the time he ran for president he was a wealthy man, earning a large income from his law practice and his many investments.

As for the nickname Abe, he hated it. No one who knew him well ever called him Abe to his face. They addressed him as Lincoln or Mr. Lincoln.

Lincoln is often described as a sloppy dresser, careless about his appearance. In fact, he patronized[7] the best tailor in Springfield, Illinois, buying two suits a year. That was at a time when many lived, died, and were buried in the same suit.

It's true that Lincoln had little formal "eddication," as he would have pronounced it. Almost everything he "larned" he taught himself. All his life he said "thar" for *there*, "git" for *get*, "kin" for *can*. Even so, he became an **eloquent** speaker who could hold a vast audience spellbound and a great writer whose finest phrases still ring in our ears. He was known to sit up late into the night, discussing Shakespeare's plays with White House visitors.

**eloquent**
powerful;
expressive

He was certainly a humorous man, famous for his **rollicking** stories. But he was also moody and **melancholy**, tormented by long and frequent bouts of depression. Humor was his therapy. He relied on his yarns,[8] a friend observed, to "whistle down sadness."

**rollicking**
jolly;
boisterous

He had a cool, logical mind, trained in the courtroom, and a practical, commonsense approach to problems. Yet he was deeply superstitious, a believer in dreams, omens, and visions.

**melancholy**
depressed;
gloomy

---

5 **homespun**: simple; not fancy

6 **bawdy**: slightly indecent

7 **patronized**: was a regular customer of

8 **yarns**: stories

We admire Lincoln today as an American folk hero. During the Civil War, however, he was the most unpopular president the nation had ever known. His critics called him a tyrant, a hick, a stupid baboon who was unfit for his office. As commander in chief of the armed forces, he was **denounced** as a **bungling** amateur who meddled in military affairs he knew nothing about. But he also had his supporters. They praised him as a farsighted statesman, a military mastermind who engineered the Union victory.

**denounced**
accused

**bungling**
clumsy;
performing
poorly

Lincoln is best known as the Great Emancipator, the man who freed the slaves. Yet he did not enter the war with that idea in mind. "My paramount[9] object in this struggle *is* to save the Union," he said in 1862, "and is *not* either to save or destroy slavery." As the war continued, Lincoln's attitude changed. Eventually he came to regard the conflict as a moral crusade to wipe out the sin of slavery.

During the Civil War . . . he was the most unpopular president the nation had ever known.

No black leader was more critical of Lincoln than the fiery abolitionist writer and editor Frederick Douglass. Douglass had grown up as a slave. He had won his freedom by escaping to the North. Early in the war, impatient with Lincoln's cautious leadership, Douglass called him "preeminently[10] the white man's president, entirely devoted to the welfare of white men." Later, Douglass changed his mind and came to admire Lincoln. Several years after the war, he said this about the sixteenth president: "His greatest mission was to accomplish two things: first, to save his country from dismemberment[11] and ruin; and second, to free his country from the great crime of slavery . . . . Taking him for all in all, measuring the tremendous **magnitude** of the work before him, considering the necessary means to ends, and surveying the end from the beginning, infinite wisdom has seldom sent any man into the world better fitted for his mission than Abraham Lincoln."

**magnitude**
size; scale

---

9 **paramount**: most important; supreme

10 **preeminently**: most prominently or outstandingly

11 **dismemberment**: being taken apart

# Reviewing

## The Mysterious Mr. Lincoln

### Discussing the Selection

1. How does this portrait of Lincoln compare to other accounts you have read or heard about him?

2. What did you learn about Lincoln that surprised you?

3. Why was the "real" Lincoln so difficult to capture in a photograph, according to Freedman?

4. What did the abolitionist Frederick Douglass say were Lincoln's two greatest accomplishments? Do you think these required heroism on Lincoln's part? Explain.

### Writing a Photo Essay

For each book that Russell Freedman writes, he finds as many as 1000 photographs even though he will use only a fraction of them. Freedman believes that photographs make his subjects seem more real to readers. Choose an historical figure that has always interested you. At the library or on the Internet, select some interesting photographs from this person's life. Then write a short biographical sketch, attaching any photographs that convey things that are hard to put into words.

### About Russell Freedman (1929–)

Russell Freedman is a nonfiction writer who prefers to call himself a "factual writer." Freedman has written close to fifty books on subjects such as animal behavior and important people in history. He has written about Eleanor Roosevelt, Crazy Horse, and the Wright brothers, and was awarded a Newbery Medal for his book *Lincoln: A Photobiography*. The people Freedman writes about are distinguished by some outstanding mark of character, such as the spirit and inventiveness of the Wright brothers. One of his goals is to write biographies that breathe life into historical subjects and events.

# Previewing

## Casey at the Bat
by Ernest Lawrence Thayer

### Reading Connection

For its author, "Casey the Bat" was almost a curse. For the actor De Wolf Hopper, however, the poem was a career-booster. He performed it over ten thousand times, in baseball stadiums, parks, and onstage, almost always to rousing applause and cheers. "Casey . . ." is still beloved by baseball fans, not to mention comedians, politicians, and schoolchildren. Because it was first published with Thayer's pen name, for years no one knew who had written it. Eventually its authorship came out. Ironically, Thayer was not a huge fan of his own poem, and recited it reluctantly and not very well.

### Skill Focus: Suspense

Suspense is the feeling of excitement that grows when a reader wants to know how a plot will turn out. Of course the pacing, or timing, of events is important to stirring a reader's anticipation. But character and plot are equally important. A character has to be capable of surprising us. And a plot must have conflict and tension.

### Vocabulary Builder

These are the only words that might be troublesome as you read the following humorous poem.

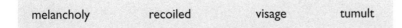

| melancholy | recoiled | visage | tumult |

STRIKE, Lawrence Jacobs, 1949

# Casey at the **Bat**

Ernest Lawrence Thayer

The outlook wasn't brilliant for the Mudville nine that day;
The score stood four to two, with but one inning more to play;
And so, when Cooney died[1] at first, and Barrows did the same,
A sickly silence fell upon the patrons of the game.

A straggling few got up to go in deep despair. The rest                      5
Clung to the hope which springs eternal in the human breast;
They thought, if only Casey could but get a whack; at that,
They'd put up even money now, with Casey at the bat.

But Flynn preceded Casey, as did also Jimmy Blake;
And the former was a pudding,[2] and the latter was a fake;                   10
So upon that stricken multitude grim **melancholy** sat,
For there seemed but little chance of Casey's getting to the bat.            **melancholy**
But Flynn let drive a single, to the wonderment of all,                       sadness
And Blake, the much despiséd, tore the cover off the ball;
And when the dust had lifted, and they saw what had occurred,                15
There was Jimmy safe on second, and Flynn a-hugging third.

---

1 **died**: was called out
2 **pudding**: a term for a stupid person

Then from the gladdened multitude went up a joyous yell;
It bounded from the mountaintop and rattled in the dell;[3]

**recoiled**
bounced back
from

It struck upon the hillside and **recoiled** upon the flat,
For Casey, mighty Casey, was advancing to the bat.                    20

There was ease in Casey's manner as he stepped into his place;
There was pride in Casey's bearing and a smile on Casey's face;
And when, responding to the cheers, he lightly doffed[4] his hat,
No stranger in the crowd could doubt 'twas Casey at the bat.

Ten thousand eyes were on him as he rubbed his hands with dirt;       25
Five thousand tongues applauded when he wiped them on his shirt;
Then, while the writhing pitcher ground the ball into his hip,
Defiance gleamed in Casey's eye, a sneer curled Casey's lip.

And now the leather-covered sphere came hurtling through the air,
And Casey stood a-watching it in haughty grandeur there;             30
Close by the sturdy batsman the ball unheeded sped.
"That ain't my style," said Casey. "Strike one," the umpire said.

From the benches, black with people, there went up a muffled roar,
Like the beating of the storm waves on a stern and distant shore;
"Kill him! Kill the umpire!" shouted someone in the stand.           35
And it's likely they'd have killed him had not Casey raised his hand.

3 **dell**: valley
4 **doffed**: tipped

With a smile of Christian charity great Casey's **visage** shone;

He stilled the rising **tumult**; he bade[5] the game go on;

He signaled to the pitcher, and once more the spheroid[6] flew;

But Casey still ignored it, and the umpire said, "Strike two."          40

"Fraud!" cried the maddened thousands, and the echo answered, "Fraud!"

But one scornful look from Casey, and the audience was awed;

They saw his face grow stern and cold; they saw his muscles strain;

And they knew that Casey wouldn't let that ball go by again.

The sneer is gone from Casey's lips; his teeth are clenched in hate;          45

He pounds with cruel violence his bat upon the plate;

And now the pitcher holds the ball, and now he lets it go,

And now the air is shattered by the force of Casey's blow.

Oh, somewhere in this favored land the sun is shining bright;

The band is playing somewhere, and somewhere hearts are light,          50

And somewhere men are laughing, and somewhere children shout;

But there is no joy in Mudville—mighty Casey has struck out!

**visage**
face or
expression

**tumult**
very loud
noise

---

5 **bade**: asked for

6 **spheroid**: like a sphere, or a round object

# Reviewing

## Casey at the Bat

### Discussing the Selection

1. What kind of a man is Casey? Explain why the crowd has such faith in him.

2. Find two examples of hyperbole—comic exaggeration—in this poem. Translate a few examples into more realistic language and compare the effect. What is lost?

3. How does Thayer build suspense as he moves from verse to verse?

4. This is one of the most popular poems in American history. Name some of the things that have probably made it such a favorite.

### Writing a Parody

Write a parody, or comic imitation, of "Casey at the Bat." You don't have to write as many verses as there are in the original poem, but you should try to imitate its basic rhythm and word choices. Make it a narrative poem on a subject that has built-in suspense, such as a sporting event or contest.

### About Ernest Lawrence Thayer (1863–1940)

Ernest Lawrence Thayer, a mild-mannered Harvard graduate, wrote the most famous poem ever written about baseball. In college Thayer edited the *Harvard Lampoon*, a popular humor magazine. After he graduated, he began writing a newspaper column under the pen name "Phin." "Casey at the Bat" was published in the *San Francisco Examiner* in 1888 under this name, which kept the public from knowing its true author for years. Thayer never accepted any royalty payments for the poem's use. But over a hundred years later, it is still winning awards. A richly illustrated version of "Casey at the Bat" was named a Caldecott Honor book in 2001.

# Previewing

## Rikki-tikki-tavi
Rudyard Kipling

### Reading Connection
This story takes place in India during the time it was a British colony. Much literature has been written about the British officials and families who lived there, including this famous tale about a heroic mongoose who does battle in the family garden.

### Skill Focus: Setting
Setting refers to the time and place in which a story occurs. Usually the setting is very important to a plot, adding to its mood and meaning. As you read the Kipling story, notice how many details contribute to its distinctive setting.

### Vocabulary Builder
These words are defined on the pages where they occur. Are there any that you already know?

| | | | |
|---|---|---|---|
| revived | scuttled | gait | consolation |
| motto | cowered | scornfully | cunningly |

Banded Mongooses

Unit Five    To Be a Hero

# Rikki-tikki-tavi ████████

Rudyard Kipling

This is the story of the great war that Rikki-tikki-tavi fought single-handed, through the bathrooms of the big bungalow[1] in Segowlee cantonment.[2] Darzee, the tailorbird, helped him, and Chuchundra, the muskrat, who never comes out into the middle of the floor, but always creeps round by the wall, gave him advice; but Rikki-tikki did the real fighting. He was a mongoose, rather like a little cat in his fur and his tail, but quite like a weasel in his head and his habits. His eyes and the end of his restless nose were pink; he could scratch himself anywhere he pleased, with any leg, front or back, that he chose to use; he could fluff up his tail till it looked like a bottle-brush, and his war-cry, as he scuttled through the long grass, was: *"Rikk-tikk-tikki-tikki-tchk!"*

One day, a high summer flood washed him out of the burrow where he lived with his father and mother, and carried him, kicking and clucking, down a roadside ditch. He found a little wisp of grass floating there, and clung to it till he lost his senses. When he **revived**, he was lying in the hot sun on the middle of a garden path, very draggled indeed, and a small boy was saying: "Here's a dead mongoose. Let's have a funeral."

**revived**
returned to consciousness

---

1 **bungalow**: a one-story house
2 **Segowlee cantonment**: a British army post in Segowlee, India, during the colonial era

"No," said his mother; "let's take him in and dry him. Perhaps he isn't really dead."

They took him into the house, and a big man picked him up between his finger and thumb, and said he was not dead but half choked; so they wrapped him in cotton-wool, and warmed him, and he opened his eyes and sneezed.

"Now," said the big man (he was an Englishman who had just moved into the bungalow); "don't frighten him, and we'll see what he'll do."

It is the hardest thing in the world to frighten a mongoose, because he is eaten up from nose to tail with curiosity. The **motto** of all the mongoose family is "Run and find out"; and Rikki-tikki was a true mongoose. He looked at the cotton-wool, decided that it was not good to eat, ran all around the table, sat up and put his fur in order, scratched himself, and jumped on the small boy's shoulder.

**motto**
slogan; saying

"Don't be frightened, Teddy," said his father. "That's his way of making friends."

"Ouch! He's tickling under my chin," said Teddy.

Rikki-tikki looked down between the boy's collar and neck, snuffed at his ear, and climbed down to the floor, where he sat rubbing his nose.

"Good gracious," said Teddy's mother, "and that's a wild creature! I suppose he's so tame because we've been kind to him."

"All mongooses are like that," said her husband. "If Teddy doesn't pick him up by the tail, or try to put him in a cage, he'll run in and out of the house all day long. Let's give him something to eat."

They gave him a little piece of raw meat. Rikki-tikki liked it immensely, and when it was finished he went out into the veranda[3] and sat in the sunshine and fluffed up his fur to make it dry to the roots. Then he felt better.

"There are more things to find out about in this house," he said to himself, "than all my family could find out in all their lives. I shall certainly stay and find out."

He spent all that day roaming over the house. He nearly drowned himself in the bathtubs, put his nose into the ink on a writing table, and burned it on

---

3 **veranda**: outdoor living area, such as a patio or terrace

the end of the big man's cigar, for he climbed up in the big man's lap to see how writing was done. At nightfall he ran into Teddy's nursery to watch how kerosene lamps were lighted, and when Teddy went to bed Rikki-tikki climbed up too; but he was a restless companion, because he had to get up and attend to every noise all through the night, and find out what made it. Teddy's mother and father came in, the last thing, to look at their boy, and Rikki-tikki was awake on the pillow. "I don't like that," said Teddy's mother; "he may bite the child." "He'll do no such thing," said the father. "Teddy's safer with that little beast than if he had a bloodhound to watch him. If a snake came into the nursery now—"

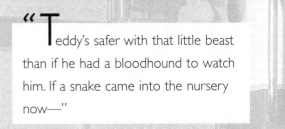

"Teddy's safer with that little beast than if he had a bloodhound to watch him. If a snake came into the nursery now—"

But Teddy's mother wouldn't think of anything so awful.

Early in the morning Rikki-tikki came to early breakfast in the veranda riding on Teddy's shoulder, and they gave him banana and some boiled egg; and he sat on all their laps one after the other, because every well-brought-up mongoose always hopes to be a house-mongoose some day and have rooms to run about in, and Rikki-tikki's mother (she used to live in the General's house at Segowlee) had carefully told Rikki what to do if ever he came across white men.

Then Rikki-tikki went out into the garden to see what was to be seen. It was a large garden, only half cultivated, with bushes as big as summer-houses of Marshal Niel roses, lime and orange trees, clumps of bamboos, and thickets of high grass. Rikki-tikki licked his lips. "This is a splendid hunting-ground," he said, and his tail grew bottle-brushy at the thought of it, and he **scuttled** up and down the garden, snuffing here and there till he heard very sorrowful voices in a thornbush.

**scuttled**
scurried;
moved quickly

It was Darzee, the tailorbird, and his wife. They had made a beautiful nest by pulling two big leaves together and stitching them up the edges with fibers, and had filled the hollow with cotton and downy fluff. The nest swayed to and fro, as they sat on the rim and cried.

"What is the matter?" asked Rikki-tikki.

"We are very miserable," said Darzee. "One of our babies fell out of the nest yesterday, and Nag ate him."

"H'm!" said Rikki-tikki, "that is very sad—but I am a stranger here. Who is Nag?"

**cowered**
crouched;
shrank in fear

Darzee and his wife only **cowered** down in the nest without answering, for from the thick grass at the foot of the bush there came a low hiss—a horrid cold sound that made Rikki-tikki jump back two clear feet. Then inch by inch out of the grass rose up the head and spread hood of Nag, the big black cobra, and he was five feet long from tongue to tail. When he had lifted one-third of himself clear of the ground, he stayed balancing to and fro exactly as a dandelion-tuft balances in the wind, and he looked at Rikki-tikki with the wicked snake's eyes that never change their expression, whatever the snake may be thinking of.

Then inch by inch out of the grass rose up the head and spread hood of Nag, the big black cobra.

"Who is Nag?" said he. "*I* am Nag. The great god Brahm[4] put his mark upon all our people when the first cobra spread his hood to keep the sun off Brahm as he slept. Look, and be afraid!"

He spread out his hood more than ever, and Rikki-tikki saw the spectacle-mark on the back of it that looks exactly like the eye part of a hook-and-eye fastening. He was afraid for the minute; but it is impossible for a mongoose to stay frightened for any length of time, and though Rikki-tikki had never met a live cobra before, his mother had fed him on dead ones, and he knew that all a grown mongoose's business in life was to fight and eat snakes. Nag knew that too, and at the bottom of his cold heart he was afraid.

"Well," said Rikki-tikki, and his tail began to fluff up again, "marks or no marks, do you think it is right for you to eat fledglings[5] out of a nest?"

Nag was thinking to himself, and watching the least little movement in the

---

4 **Brahm**: the supreme god of the Hindu religion

5 **fledglings**: young birds

grass behind Rikki-tikki. He knew that mongooses in the garden meant death sooner or later for him and his family, but he wanted to get Rikki-tikki off his guard. So he dropped his head a little, and put it on one side.

"Let us talk," he said. "You eat eggs. Why should not I eat birds?"

"Behind you! Look behind you!" sang Darzee.

Rikki-tikki knew better than to waste time in staring. He jumped up in the air as high as he could go, and just under him whizzed by the head of Nagaina, Nag's wicked wife. She had crept up behind him as he was talking, to make an end of him; and he heard her savage hiss as the stroke missed. He came down almost across her back, and if he had been an old mongoose he would have know that then was the time to break her back with one bite; but he was afraid of the terrible lashing return-stroke of the cobra. He bit, indeed, but did not bite long enough, and he jumped clear of the whisking tail, leaving Nagaina torn and angry.

"Wicked, wicked Darzee!" said Nag, lashing up as high as he could reach toward the nest in the thornbush; but Darzee had built it out of reach of snakes, and it only swayed to and fro.

Rikki-tikki felt his eyes growing red and hot (when a mongoose's eyes grow red, he is angry), and he sat back on his tail and hind legs like a little kangaroo, and looked all round him, and chattered with rage. But Nag and Nagaina had disappeared into the grass. When a snake misses its stroke, it never says anything or gives any sign of what it means to do next. Rikki-tikki did not care to follow them, for he did not feel sure that he could manage two snakes at once. So he trotted off to the gravel path near the house, and sat down to think. It was a serious matter for him.

If you read the old books of natural history, you will find they say that when the mongoose fights the snake and happens to get bitten, he runs off and eats some herb that cures him. That is not true. The victory is only a matter of quickness of eye and quickness of foot,—snake's blow against mongoose's jump,—and as no eye can follow the motion of a snake's head when it strikes, that makes things much more wonderful than any magic herb. Rikki-tikki knew he was a young mongoose, and it made him all the more pleased to think that he had managed to escape a blow from behind. It gave him confidence in himself, and when Teddy came running down the path, Rikki-tikki was ready to be petted. But just as Teddy was stooping, something wriggled a little in the dust, and a tiny voice said: "Be careful. I am death!" It was Karait, the dusty brown snakeling that lies for choice on the dusty earth; and his bite is as dangerous as the cobra's. But he is so small that nobody thinks of him, and so he does the more harm to people.

Rikki-tikki's eyes grew red again, and he danced up to Karait with the peculiar rocking, swaying motion that he had inherited from his family. It looks very funny, but it is so perfectly balanced a **gait** that you can fly off from it at any angle you please; and in dealing with snakes this is an advantage. If Rikki-tikki had only known, he was doing a much more dangerous thing than fighting Nag, for Karait is so small, and can turn so quickly, that unless Rikki bit him close to the back of the head, he would get the return-stroke in his eye or his lip. But Rikki did not know: his eyes were all red, and he rocked back and forth, looking for a good place to hold. Karait struck out. Rikki jumped sideways and tried to run in, but the wicked little dusty gray head lashed within a fraction of his shoulder, and he had to jump over the body, and the head followed his heels close.

Teddy shouted to the house: "Oh, look here! Our mongoose is killing a snake"; and Rikki-tikki heard a scream from Teddy's mother. His father ran out with a stick, but by the time he came up, Karait had lunged out once too far, and Rikki-tikki had sprung, jumped on the snake's back, dropped his head far between his fore-legs, bitten as high up the back as he could get hold, and rolled away. That bite paralyzed Karait, and Rikki-tikki was just going to eat him up from the tail, after the custom of his family at dinner, when he remembered that a full meal makes a slow mongoose, and if wanted all his strength and quickness ready, he must keep himself thin. He went away for a dust-bath under the castor-oil bushes, while Teddy's father beat the dead Karait. "What is the use of that?" thought Rikki-tikki. "I have settled it all"; and then Teddy's mother picked him up from the dust and hugged him, crying that he had saved

Teddy from death, and Teddy's father said that he was a providence,[6] and Teddy looked on with big scared eyes. Rikki-tikki was rather amused at all the fuss, which, of course, he did not understand. Teddy's mother might just as well have petted Teddy for playing in the dust. Rikki was thoroughly enjoying himself.

That night at dinner, walking to and fro among the wine-glasses on the table, he might have stuffed himself three times over with nice things; but he remembered Nag and Nagaina, and though it was very pleasant to be patted and petted by Teddy's mother, and to sit on Teddy's shoulder, his eyes would get red from time to time, and he would go off into his long war-cry of "*Rikk-tikk-tikki-tikki-tchk!*"

Teddy carried him off to bed, and insisted on Rikki-tikki sleeping under his chin. Rikki-tikki was too well bred to bite or scratch, but as soon as Teddy was asleep he went off for his nightly walk round the house, and in the dark he ran up against Chuchundra, the muskrat, creeping round by the wall. Chuchundra is a broken-hearted little beast. He whimpers and cheeps all night, trying to make up his mind to run into the middle of the room; but he never gets there.

"Don't kill me," said Chuchundra, almost weeping. "Rikki-tikki, don't kill me."

"Do you think a snake-killer kills muskrats?" said Rikki-tikki **scornfully**.

> **scornfully**
> with disgust or anger

"Those who kill snakes get killed by snakes," said Chuchundra, more sorrowfully than ever. "And how am I to be sure that Nag won't mistake me for you some dark night?"

"There's not the least danger," said Rikki-tikki; "but Nag is in the garden, and I know you don't go there."

"My cousin Chua, the rat, told me—" said Chuchundra, and then he stopped.

"Told you what?"

"H'sh! Nag is everywhere, Rikki-tikki. You should have talked to Chua in the garden."

"I didn't—so you must tell me. Quick, Chuchundra, or I'll bite you!"

---

6 **a providence**: a gift of fate or God

Chuchundra sat down and cried till the tears rolled off his whiskers. "I am a very poor man," he sobbed. "I never had spirit enough to run out into the middle of the room. H'sh! I musn't tell you anything. Can't you *hear*, Rikki-tikki?"

Rikki-tikki listened. The house was as still as still, but he thought he could just catch the faintest *scratch-scratch* in the world,—a noise as faint as that of a wasp walking on a windowpane,—the dry scratch of a snake's scales on brickwork.

"That's Nag or Nagaina," he said to himself; "and he is crawling into the bathroom sluice.[7] You're right Chuchundra; I should have talked to Chua."

He stole off to Teddy's bathroom, but there was nothing there, and then to Teddy's mother's bathroom. At the bottom of the smooth plaster wall there was a brick pulled out to make a sluice for the bathwater, and as Rikki-tikki stole in by the masonry curb where the bath is put, he heard Nag and Nagaina whispering together outside in the moonlight.

"When the house is emptied of people," said Nagaina to her husband, "*he* will have to go away, and then the garden will be our own again. Go in quietly, and remember that the big man who killed Karait is the first one to bite. Then come out and tell me, and we will hunt for Rikki-tikki together."

"But are you sure that there is anything to be gained by killing the people?" said Nag.

"Everything. When there were no people in the bungalow, did we have any mongoose in the garden? So long as the bungalow is empty, we are king and queen of the garden; and remember that as soon as our eggs in the melon-bed hatch (as they may tomorrow), our children will need room and quiet."

"I had not thought of that," said Nag. "I will go, but there is no need that we should hunt for Rikki-tikki afterward. I will kill the big man and his wife, and the child if I can, and come away quietly. Then the bungalow will be empty, and Rikki-tikki will go."

Rikki-tikki tingled all over with rage and hatred at this, and then Nag's head came through the sluice, and his five feet of cold body followed it. Angry

---

7 **sluice**: drain

as he was, Rikki-tikki was very frightened as he saw the size of the big cobra. Nag coiled himself up, raised his head, and looked into the bathroom in the dark, and Rikki could see his eyes glitter.

"Now, if I kill him here, Nagaina will know; and if I fight him on the open floor, the odds are in his favor. What am I to do?" said Rikki-tikki-tavi.

Nag waved to and fro, and then Rikki-tikki heard him drinking from the biggest water-jar that was used to fill the bath. "That is good," said the snake. "Now, when Karait was killed, the big man had a stick. He may have that stick still, but when he comes in to bathe in the morning he will not have a stick. I shall wait here till he comes. Nagaina—do you hear me? —I shall wait here in the cool till daytime."

There was no answer from outside, so Rikki-tikki knew Nagaina had gone away. Nag coiled himself down, coil by coil, round the bulge at the bottom of the water-jar, and Rikki-tikki stayed still as death. After an hour he began to move, muscle by muscle, toward the jar. Nag was asleep, and Rikki-tikki looked at his big back, wondering which would be the best place for a good hold. "If I don't break his back at the first jump," said Rikki, "he can still fight; and if he fights—O Rikki!" He looked at the thickness of the neck below the hood, but that was too much for him; and a bite near the tail would only make Nag savage.

Nag coiled himself down, coil by coil, round the bulge at the bottom of the water-jar, and Rikki-tikki stayed still as death.

"It must be the head," he said at last; "the head above the hood; and, when I am once there, I must not let go."

Then he jumped. The head was lying a little clear of the water-jar, under the curve of it; and, as his teeth met, Rikki braced his back against the bulge of the red earthenware to hold down the head. This gave him just one second's purchase,[8] and he made the most of it. Then he was battered to and fro as a rat is shaken by a dog—to and fro on the floor, up and down, and round in great circles; but his eyes were red, and he held on as the body cart-whipped over

---

8 **purchase**: an effective hold; leverage

the floor, upsetting the tin dipper and the soap-dish and the flesh-brush, and banged against the tin side of the bath. As he held he closed his jaws tighter and tighter, for he made sure he would be banged to death, and, for the honor of his family, he preferred to be found with his teeth locked. He was dizzy, aching, and felt shaken to pieces when something went off like a thunderclap just behind him; a hot wind knocked him senseless, and red fire singed his fur. The big man had been wakened by the noise, and had fired both barrels of a shotgun into Nag just behind the hood.

Rikki-tikki held on with his eyes shut, for now he was quite sure he was dead; but the head did not move, and the big man picked him up and said: "It's the mongoose again, Alice; the little chap has saved *our* lives now." Then Teddy's mother came in with a very white face, and saw what was left of Nag, and Rikki-tikki dragged himself to Teddy's bedroom and spent half the rest of the night shaking himself tenderly to find out whether he was really broken into forty pieces, as he fancied.[9]

When morning came he was very stiff, but well pleased with his doings. "Now I have Nagaina to settle with, and she will be worse than five Nags, and there's no knowing when the eggs she spoke of will hatch. Goodness! I must go and see Darzee," he said.

Without waiting for breakfast, Rikki-tikki ran to the thornbush where Darzee was singing a song of triumph at the top of his voice. The news of Nag's death was all over the garden, for the sweeper had thrown the body on the rubbish-heap.

"Oh, you stupid tuft of feathers!" said Rikki-tikki angrily. "Is this the time to sing?"

"Nag is dead—is dead—is dead!" sang Darzee. "The valiant Rikki-tikki caught him by the head and held fast. The big man brought the bang-stick, and Nag fell in two pieces! He will never eat my babies again."

"All that's true enough; but where's Nagaina?" said Rikki-tikki, looking carefully round him.

---

9 **fancied**: imagined

"Nagaina came to the bathroom sluice and called for Nag," Darzee went on; "and Nag came out on the end of a stick—the sweeper picked him up on the end of a stick and threw him upon the rubbish-heap. Let us sing about the great, the red-eyed Rikki-tikki!" and Darzee filled his throat and sang.

"If I could get up to your nest, I'd roll all your babies out!" said Rikki-tikki. "You don't know when to do the right thing at the right time. You're safe enough in your nest there, but it's war for me down here. Stop singing a minute, Darzee."

"For the great, beautiful Rikki-tikki's sake I will stop," said Darzee. "What is it, O Killer of the terrible Nag?"

"Where is Nagaina, for the third time?"

"On the rubbish-heap by the stables, mourning for Nag. Great is Rikki-tikki with the white teeth."

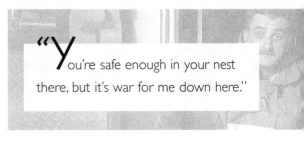

"You're safe enough in your nest there, but it's war for me down here."

"Bother my white teeth! Have you ever heard where she keeps her eggs?"

"In the melon-bed, on the end nearest the wall, where the sun strikes nearly all day. She hid them there weeks ago."

"And you never thought it worth while to tell me? The end nearest the wall, you said?"

"Rikki-tikki, you are not going to eat her eggs?"

"Not eat exactly; no. Darzee, if you have a grain of sense you will fly off to the stables and pretend that your wing is broken, and let Nagaina chase you away to this bush. I must get to the melon-bed, and if I went there now she'd see me."

Darzee was a feather-brained little fellow who could never hold more than one idea at a time in his head; and just because he knew that Nagaina's children were born in eggs like his own, he didn't think at first that it was fair to kill them. But his wife was a sensible bird, and she knew that cobra's eggs meant young cobras later on; so she flew off from the nest, and left Darzee to keep the babies warm, and continue his song about the death of Nag. Darzee was very like a man in some ways.

Egyptian Cobra, artist unknown, 1869

She fluttered in front of Nagaina by the rubbish heap, and cried out, "Oh, my wing is broken! The boy in the house threw a stone at me and broke it." Then she fluttered more desperately than ever.

Nagaina lifted up her head and hissed, "You warned Rikki-tikki when I would have killed him. Indeed and truly, you've chosen a bad place to be lame in." And she moved toward Darzee's wife, slipping along over the dust.

"The boy broke it with a stone!" shrieked Darzee's wife.

**consolation**
comfort; relief

"Well! It may be some **consolation** to you when you're dead to know that I shall settle accounts with the boy. My husband lies on the rubbish-heap this morning, but before the night the boy in the house will lie very still. What is the use of running away? I am sure to catch you. Little fool, look at me!"

Darzee's wife knew better than to do *that*, for a bird who looks at a snake's eyes gets so frightened that she cannot move. Darzee's wife fluttered on, piping sorrowfully, and never leaving the ground, and Nagaina quickened her pace.

Rikki-tikki heard them going up the path from the stables, and he raced for the end of the melon-patch near the wall. There, in the warm litter about the melons, very **cunningly** hidden, he found twenty-five eggs, about the size of a bantam's[10] eggs, but with whitish skin instead of shell.

**cunningly**
cleverly

"I was not a day too soon," he said; for he could see the baby cobras curled up inside the skin, and he knew that the minute they were hatched they could each kill a man or a mongoose. He bit off the tops of the eggs as fast as he could, taking care to crush the young cobras, and turned over the litter from time to time to see whether he had missed any. At last there were only three eggs left, and Rikki-tikki began to chuckle to himself, when he heard Darzee's wife screaming:

"Rikki-tikki, I led Nagaina toward the house, and she has gone into the veranda, and—oh, come quickly—she means killing!"

Rikki-tikki smashed two eggs, and tumbled backward down the melon-bed with the third egg in his mouth, and scuttled to the verandah as hard as he could put foot to the ground. Teddy and his mother and father were there at early breakfast; but Rikki-tikki saw that they were not eating anything. They sat stone-still, and their faces were white. Nagaina was coiled up on the matting by Teddy's chair, within easy striking-distance of Teddy's bare leg, and she was swaying to and fro singing a song of triumph.

"Son of the big man that killed Nag," she hissed, "stay still. I am not ready yet. Wait a little. Keep very still, all you three. If you move I strike, and if you do not move I strike. Oh, foolish people, who killed my Nag!"

Teddy's eyes were fixed on his father, and all his father could do was to whisper, "Sit still, Teddy. You mustn't move. Teddy, keep still."

Then Rikki-tikki came up and cried: "Turn round Nagaina; turn and fight!"

"All in good time," said she, without moving her eyes. "I will settle my account with *you* presently. Look at your friends, Rikki-tikki. They are still and

---

10 **bantam:** a miniature chicken

white; they are afraid. They dare not move, and if you come a step nearer I strike."

"Look at your eggs," said Rikki-tikki, "in the melon-bed near the wall. Go and look, Nagaina."

The big snake turned half round, and saw the egg on the veranda.

"Ah-h! Give it to me," she said.

Rikki-tikki put his paws one on each side of the egg, and his eyes were blood-red. "What price for a snake's egg? For a young cobra? For a young king-cobra? For the last—the very last of the brood? The ants are eating all the others down by the melon-bed."

Nagaina spun clear round, forgetting everything for the sake of the one egg; and Rikki-tikki saw Teddy's father shoot out a big hand, catch Teddy by the shoulder, and drag him across the little table with the teacups, safe and out of reach of Nagaina.

"Tricked! Tricked! Tricked! *Rikk-tck-tck!*" chuckled Rikki-tikki. "The boy is safe, and it was I—I—I that caught Nag by the hood last night in the bathroom." Then he began to jump up and down, all four feet together, his head close to the floor. "He threw me to and fro, but he could not shake me off. He was dead before the big man blew him in two. I did it! *Rikki-tikki-tck-tck!* Come then, Nagaina, Come and fight with me. You shall not be a widow long."

Nagaina saw that she had lost her chance of killing Teddy, and the egg lay between Rikki-tikki's paws. "Give me the egg, Rikki-tikki. Give me the last of my eggs, and I will go away and never come back," she said, lowering her hood.

"Yes, you will go away, and you will never come back; for you will go to the rubbish-heap with Nag. Fight, widow! The big man has gone for his gun! Fight!"

Rikki-tikki was bounding all round Nagaina, keeping just out of reach of her stroke, his little eyes like hot coals. Nagaina gathered herself together, and flung out at him. Rikki-tikki jumped up and backward. Again and again and again she struck, and each time her head came with a whack on the matting of the veranda, and she gathered herself together like a watch-spring. Then Rikki-tikki danced in a circle to get behind her, and Nagaina spun round to keep her head to his head, so that the rustle of her tail on the matting sounded like dry leaves blown along by the wind.

He had forgotten the egg. It still lay on the veranda, and Nagaina came nearer and nearer to it, till at last, while Rikki-tikki was drawing breath, she caught it in her mouth, turned to the veranda steps, and flew like an arrow down the path, with Rikki-tikki behind her. When the cobra runs for her life, she goes like a whip-lash flicked across a horse's neck.

Rikki-tikki knew that he must catch her, or all the trouble would begin again. She headed straight for the long grass by the thornbush, and as he was running, Rikki-tikki heard Darzee still singing his foolish little song of triumph. But Darzee's wife was wiser. She flew off her nest as Nagaina came along, and flapped her wings about Nagaina's head. If Darzee had helped they might have turned her; but Nagaina only lowered her hood and went on. Still, the instant's delay brought Rikki-tikki up to her, and as she plunged into the rat-hole where she and Nag used to live, his little white teeth were clenched on her tail, and he went down with her—and very few mongooses, however wise and old they may be, care to follow a cobra into its hole. It was dark in the hole; and Rikki-tikki never knew when it might open out and give Nagaina room to turn and strike at him. He held on savagely, and stuck out his feet to act as brakes on the dark slope of the hot, moist earth. Then the grass by the mouth of the hole stopped waving, and Darzee said: "It is all over with Rikki-tikki! We must sing his death song. Valiant Rikki-tikki is dead! For Nagaina will surely kill him underground."

So he sang a very mournful song that he made up on the spur of the minute, and just as he got to the most touching part the grass quivered again, and Rikki-tikki, covered with dirt, dragged himself out of the hole leg by leg, licking his whiskers. Darzee stopped with a little shout. Rikki-tikki shook some of the dust out of his fur and sneezed. "It is all over," he said. "The widow will never come

> Very few mongooses, however wise and old they may be, care to follow a cobra into its hole.

out again." And the red ants that live between the grass stems heard him, and began to troop down one after another to see if he had spoken the truth.

Rikki-tikki curled himself up in the grass and slept where he was—slept and slept till it was late in the afternoon, for he had done a hard day's work.

"Now," he said, when he awoke, "I will go back to the house. Tell the Coppersmith, Darzee, and he will tell the garden that Nagaina is dead."

The Coppersmith is a bird who makes a noise exactly like the beating of a little hammer on a copper pot; and the reason he is always making it is because he is the town-crier to every Indian garden, and tells all the news to everybody who cares to listen. As Rikki-tikki went up the path, he heard his "attention" notes like a tiny dinner-gong; and then the steady "*Ding-dong-tock!* Nag is dead—*dong!* Nagaina is dead! *Ding-dong-tock!*" That set all the birds in the garden singing, and the frogs croaking; for Nag and Nagaina used to eat frogs as well as little birds.

When Rikki got to the house, Teddy and Teddy's mother (she looked very white still, for she had been fainting) and Teddy's father came out and almost cried over him; and that night he ate all that was given him till he could eat no more, and went to bed on Teddy's shoulder, where Teddy's mother saw him when she came to look late at night.

"He saved our lives and Teddy's life," she said to her husband. "Just think, he saved all our lives!"

Rikki-tikki woke up with a jump, for the mongooses are light sleepers.

"Oh, it's you," said he. "What are you bothering for? All the cobras are dead; and if they weren't, I'm here."

Rikki-tikki had a right to be proud of himself; but he did not grow too proud, and he kept that garden as a mongoose should keep it, with tooth and jump and spring and bite, till never a cobra dared show its head inside the walls.

# Reviewing

## Rikki-tikki-tavi

### Discussing the Selection

1. Kipling was beloved for his romantic stories about the English in "strange and distant parts of the world." How do the details of the setting make this story special?

2. All the animals in this story are given human characteristics. List each animal by name and write one adjective that best describes him or her.

3. Do you feel any sympathy for Nag and Nagaina? Why or why not?

4. You have read about many kinds of heroes in this unit. Make a "hero-meter" graphic by drawing a vertical line down your paper. On the top, write "Most Heroic" and on the bottom, "Least Heroic." Now, mark and label the position for each main character in this unit. For example, the character you thought most heroic would be closest to the top of your graphic.

### Writing a Children's Story

Try your hand at writing an animal tale for young children. Give your animal special powers and a distinct personality like Rikki-tikki-tavi. As you write, keep your audience in mind by using simple vocabulary and situations that young children will understand and enjoy. When you have finished writing, add appropriate illustrations or photos.

### About Rudyard Kipling (1865–1936)

The British writer Rudyard Kipling was born in India when it was still a colony of Great Britain. Later Kipling became a newspaper correspondent, traveling around the world and writing about different cultures. Though he has written many works of nonfiction and fiction, he is probably most famous for his children's stories: *The Jungle Book* and *Just So Stories for Little Children*. He is also known for his poems "Gunga Din" and "If—," which at one time was voted Britain's favorite work of poetry. In 1907 Kipling was awarded the Nobel Prize for literature. Despite this high honor, Kipling's popularity waned because of his association with British colonialism. In recent decades his reputation has returned, a tribute to his ability to create lively and entertaining stories.

# On the Edge

*Hunger, love, pain, and fear are some of those inner forces which rule the individual's instinct for self-preservation.*

Albert Einstein

The selections in Unit Six focus on the many ways in which human beings are tested or set out to stretch their own abilities or imagination. To some people life "on the edge" might mean hang gliding over a jungle or skiing down an icy canyon. But for most people, life's edges are not so sharp and threatening. You may have to go outside your comfort zone to deal with personal and social issues, but usually these challenges are manageable. In the selections that follow, the characters show a variety of responses to mysterious goings on, disappointment, and even disaster. Some of the pieces are lighthearted. Others take you to darker places, where there may not be any happy endings.

# Building Vocabulary

### Analogies
One way to build a more impressive vocabulary and stretch your word skills is to look at groups of related words. By studying related words, you can deepen your understanding of new vocabulary as well as your knowledge of word relationships.

An **analogy** is a way of comparing things that have similar relationships. Here's an example:

A <u>kitten</u> is a baby <u>cat</u>, just as a <u>puppy</u> is a baby <u>dog</u>. You can say it like this: "A kitten *is to* a baby cat as a puppy *is to* a baby dog." You can write it like this:

> *kitten : baby cat :: puppy : baby dog*

Analogies show how pairs of things go together. They explain the relationship. Analogies on worksheets and tests look like this:

> *swamp : wet :: desert : ?*

To complete the analogy, you have to figure out how the first two words go together. Make up a sentence that describes the relationship. "A <u>swamp</u> is a place that is <u>wet</u>." Then think about how to finish the analogy. "A <u>desert</u> is a place that is . . . <u>dry</u>."

Here are some easy examples that show how to make up a sentence that explains the relationship between the first two words.

| | |
|---|---|
| *mitten : hand* | A <u>mitten</u> is worn on a <u>hand</u>. |
| *sad : happy* | <u>Sad</u> is the opposite of <u>happy</u>. |
| *cow : grass* | A <u>cow</u> eats <u>grass</u>. |
| *oven : bake* | An <u>oven</u> is used to <u>bake</u> things. |
| *noisy : loud* | <u>Noisy</u> means something similar to <u>loud</u>. |
| *bee : hive* | A <u>bee</u> lives in a <u>hive.</u> |

Figuring out the relationship between the first two words is the first step. Then you must find another pair of words that go together the same way. You can do this by putting the new words in the sentence you made up and seeing which ones make sense.

# Building Vocabulary *continued*

**Example**      *chapter : book :: day :*
                      A. night        C. week
                      B. diary        D. sunrise

**Step 1**      A <u>chapter</u> is part of a <u>book</u>.

**Step 2**      A. A <u>day</u> is part of a <u>night</u>.
                      B. A <u>day</u> is part of a <u>diary</u>.
                      C. A <u>day</u> is part of a <u>week</u>.
                      D. A <u>day</u> is part of a <u>sunrise</u>.

**Step 3**      Answer C is the only one that makes a logical sentence.

There are many kinds of relationships that are used in analogies.
Here are some common ones:

| Type of Analogy | Examples |
| --- | --- |
| A. Synonyms | *harm : damage :: guard : protect* |
| B. Antonyms | *love : hate :: soothe : upset* |
| C. Part to Whole | *violin : orchestra :: singer : choir* |
| D. Worker and Tool | *carpenter : hammer :: painter : brush* |
| E. Characteristic | *fire : hot :: ice : cold* |
| F. Object and Purpose | *saw : cut :: shovel : dig* |
| G. Example | *trout : fish :: collie : dog* |
| H. Manner | *nibble : eat :: sip : drink* |
| I. Degree or Intensity | *warm : hot :: cool : cold* |
| J. Place | *horse : stable :: chicken : coop* |
| K. Grammatical | *I : me :: he : him* |

# Building Vocabulary *continued*

Sometimes the first two words in an analogy can go together in several ways. You may have to guess about the right way to explain their relationship. You know your guess is right if only one answer choice works. What should you do if more than one answer works?

| **Example 1** | *attractive : beautiful :: afraid :* |
| | A. sorry      C. fearless |
| | B. scared    D. terrified |

| **Sentence** | Attractive is a synonym for beautiful. |
| **Result** | Two answers are correct: |
| | Afraid is a synonym for scared. |
| | Afraid is a synonym for terrified. |

Only one answer can be the correct one. So what should you do? The solution is to explain the relationship between the first two words more exactly.

| **Sentence** | Someone who is extremely attractive is beautiful. |
| **Result** | Now, only one answer is correct. |
| | Someone who is extremely afraid is terrified. |
| | The correct answer is D. |

| **Example 2** | *inch : foot :: month :* |
| | A. year     C. century |
| | B. week    D. calendar |

| **Sentence** | An inch is shorter than a foot. |
| **Result** | Two answers are correct: |
| | A month is shorter than a year. |
| | A month is shorter than a century. |

Since only one answer can be the correct one, you need to describe the relationship between the first two words more precisely.

| **Sentence** | An inch is one-twelfth of a foot. |
| | Now only one answer is correct—*year.* |
| | A month is one-twelfth of a year. |

# Previewing

## On Being Seventeen, Bright, and Unable to Read
by David Raymond

### Reading Connection

Perhaps one out of ten people has dyslexia, a difficulty with language that used to be called "word blindness." People affected have problems with speech and grammar—skills that depend on ordering processes in the mind. For example, a dyslexic may confuse "b" and "d" when reading, or "won" and "now." A wide range of symptoms go with dyslexia. Some people may not have trouble learning other things, but struggle with symbols such as letters. Despite huge challenges, many dyslexics find ways to overcome their disorder. Famous dyslexic people include Alexander Graham Bell, F. Scott Fitzgerald, President John F. Kennedy, and Steven Spielberg.

### Skill Focus: Writer's Purpose

Most writers write for a specific purpose, such as to persuade, offer an opinion, inform, or entertain. They may write to explore their own feelings and ideas or to dazzle readers with their wit and imagination. Writers can have more than one purpose for writing, though one usually dominates. As you read the following essay, try to determine the writer's main purpose for writing it.

# On **Being Seventeen, Bright,** and **Unable** to **Read**

David Raymond

SKATEBOARD SET, Margie Livingston Campbell, 1995

One day a substitute teacher picked me to read aloud from the textbook. When I told her, "No thank you," she came unhinged.[1] She thought I was acting smart and told me so. I kept calm, and that got her madder and madder. We must have spent 10 minutes trying to solve the problem, and finally she got so red in the face I thought she'd blow up. She told me she'd see me after class.

Maybe someone like me was a new thing for that teacher. But she wasn't new to me. I've been through scenes like that all my life. You see, even though I'm 17 and a junior in high school, I can't read because I have dyslexia.[2] I'm told I read "at a fourth-grade level," but from where I sit, that's not reading. You can't know what that means unless you've been there. It's not easy to tell how it feels when you can't read your homework assignments or the newspaper or a menu in a restaurant or even notes from your own friends.

My family began to suspect I was having problems from the first day I started school. My father says my early years in school were the worst years of his life. They weren't so good for me, either. As I look back on it now, I can't find the words to express how bad it really was. I wanted to die. I'd come home from school screaming, "I'm dumb. I'm dumb—I wish I were dead!"

I guess I couldn't read anything at all then—not even my own name—and they tell me I didn't talk as good as other kids. But what I remember about those days is that I couldn't throw a ball where it was supposed to go, I couldn't learn to swim, and I wouldn't learn to ride a bike, because no matter what anyone told me, I knew I'd fail.

Sometimes my teachers would try to be encouraging. When I couldn't read the words on the board, they'd say, "Come on, David, you know that word." Only I didn't. And it was embarrassing. I just felt dumb. And dumb was how the kids treated me. They'd make fun of me every chance they got, asking me to spell *cat* or something like that. Even if I knew how to spell it, I wouldn't; they'd only give me another word. Anyway, it was awful, because more than anything I wanted friends. On my birthday when I blew out the candles I didn't wish I could learn to read; what I wished for was that the kids would like me.

---

1 **came unhinged**: grew disturbed or upset

2 **dyslexia**: a learning disability

With all the bad reports coming from school, and with me moaning about wanting to die and how everybody hated me, my parents began looking for help. That's when the testing started. The school tested me, the child-guidance center tested me, private psychiatrists tested me. Everybody knew something was wrong—especially me.

It didn't help much when they stuck a fancy name onto it. I couldn't pronounce it then—I was only in second grade—and I was ashamed to talk about it. Now it rolls off my tongue, because I've been living with it for a lot of years—dyslexia.

### Elementary School

All through elementary school it wasn't easy. I was always having to do things that were "different," things the other kids didn't have to do. I had to go to a child psychiatrist, for instance.

One summer my family forced me to go to a camp for children with reading problems. I hated the idea, but the camp turned out pretty good, and I had a good time. I met a lot of kids who couldn't read and somehow that helped. The director of the camp said I had a higher IQ than 90 percent of the population. I didn't believe him.

About the worst thing I had to do in fifth and sixth grade was go to a special education class in another school in our town. A bus picked me up, and I didn't like that at all. The bus also picked up emotionally disturbed kids and retarded kids. It was like going to a school for the retarded. I always worried that someone I knew would see me on that bus. It was a relief to go to the regular junior high school.

### Junior High School

Life began to change a little for me, then, because I began to feel better about myself. I found the teachers cared; they had meetings abut me and I worked harder for them for a while. I began to work on the potter's wheel, making vases and pots that the teachers said were pretty good. Also, I got a letter for being on the track team. I could always run pretty fast.

## High School

At high school the teachers are good and everyone is trying to help me. I've gotten honors some marking periods, and I've won a letter on the cross-country team. Next quarter I think the school might hold a show of my pottery. I've got some friends. But there are still some embarrassing times. For instance, every time there is writing in the class, I get up and go to the special education room. Kids ask me where I go all the time. Sometimes I say, "to Mars."

Homework is a real problem. During free periods in school I go into the special ed room, and staff members read assignments to me. When I get home, my mother reads to me. Sometimes she reads an assignment into a tape recorder, and then I go into my room and listen to it. If we have a novel or something like that to read, she reads it out loud to me. Then I sit down with her and we do the assignment. She'll write, while I talk my answers to her. Lately I've taken to dictating into a tape recorder, and then someone—my father, a private tutor, or my mother—types up what I've dictated. Whatever homework I do takes someone else's time, too. That makes me feel bad.

We had a big meeting in school the other day—eight of us, four from the guidance department, my private tutor, my parents and me. The subject was me. I said I wanted to go to college, and they told me about colleges that have facilities and staff to handle people like me. That's nice to hear.

As for what happens after college, I don't know and I'm worried about that. How can I make a living if I can't read? Who will hire me? How will I fill out the application form? The only thing that gives me any courage is the fact that I've learned about well-known people who couldn't read or had other problems and still made it. Like Albert Einstein, who didn't talk until he was 4 and flunked math. Like Leonardo da Vinci, who everyone seems to think had dyslexia.

I've told this story because maybe some teacher will read it and go easy on a kid in the classroom who has what I've got. Or, maybe some parent will stop nagging his kid and stop calling him lazy. Maybe he's not lazy or dumb. Maybe he just can't read and doesn't know what's wrong. Maybe he's scared, like I was.

## Reviewing

# On Being Seventeen, Bright, and Unable to Read

### Discussing the Selection

1. There's a saying that applies to elementary school education: "First you learn to read. Then you read to learn." What do you think this means? Explain how it relates to David Raymond's experience.

2. What affected you most when you were reading this piece? Point out any specific images or details that you think will stay in your memory.

3. Why do you think the author wrote this essay? Is his purpose implied (suggested) or does he come right out and state it?

4. What questions remain for you after finishing this selection?

### Writing About Reading

Many people have vivid memories of their first experiences with reading. Do you remember picking out your first words? Did you feel passionate about any of your books? Imagine how different things might have been for you if you did not learn to read "on track" with your classmates. Write about your experiences with reading.

### About David Raymond

David Raymond graduated from college with honors, a feat that seemed unlikely for a severely dyslexic youth. He managed to get through high school with the help of a learning "team." The leader of this team was his mother. Sally Raymond, who also has a brother with dyslexia, became a dyslexia activist because of her family's experience with this condition. She has written books that help parents cope with their dyslexic children and travels around the country giving lectures and workshops on the subject.

# Previewing

## The Tell-Tale Heart
by Edgar Allan Poe

### Reading Connection

Edgar Allan Poe is a master of horror fiction, sometimes referred to as gothic fiction. Gothic writers aim for a mood of suspense and terror. Anything bad can happen, and probably will. The more gruesome, mysterious, or violent the details, the better. A good horror story is often set in a dark, confined place, where there seems to be no way out. Many times the main characters are all alone. The popularity of gothic writing over the ages seems to show that many readers enjoy being shocked or frightened.

### Skill Focus: Mood

Mood refers to the overall feeling or atmosphere created by a piece of writing. Mood is developed through the details, imagery, and language used to tell the story. Horror writers strive to create a mood that is drenched in doom and filled with suspense.

### Vocabulary Builder

Vocabulary in the 1800s—the time when this story was written—was very different from that of today. Don't let that stop you from enjoying this classic horror story. Readers of all ages, including yours, have been thrilled by its gory details.

| | | | |
|---|---|---|---|
| acute | profound | mournful | stimulates |
| conceived | stifled | crevice | refrained |
| cunningly | awe | stealthily | audacity |
| vexed | | | |

"Under the floorboards"; a latex installation for a theatrical performance of "The Tell-Tale Heart," Craig Denston, 1999

# The **Tell-Tale Heart**

### Edgar Allan Poe

True!—nervous—very, very dreadfully nervous I have been and am; but why *will* you say that I am mad? The disease had sharpened my senses—not destroyed—not dulled them. Above all was the sense of hearing **acute**. I heard all things in the heaven and in the earth. I heard many things in hell. How then, am I mad? Hearken![1] and observe how healthily—how calmly I can tell you the whole story.

It is impossible to say how first the idea entered my brain; but once **conceived**, it haunted me day and night. Object there was none. Passion there was none. I loved the old man. He had never wronged me. He had never given me insult. For his gold I had no desire. I think it was his eye! Yes, it was this! He had the eye of a vulture—a pale blue eye, with a film over it. Whenever it fell upon me, my blood ran cold; and so by degrees—very gradually—I made up my mind to take the life of the old man, and thus rid myself of the eye forever.

**acute**
sharp; sensitive

**conceived**
pictured;
imagined

---

1 **hearken!**: Old English for *listen, heed,* or *pay attention*

Now this is the point. You fancy me mad. Madmen know nothing. But you should have seen *me*. You should have seen how wisely I proceeded—with what caution—with what foresight—with what dissimulation[2] I went to work! I was never kinder to the old man than during the whole week before I killed him. And every night, about midnight, I turned the latch of his door and opened it—oh so gently! And then, when I had made an opening sufficient for my head, I put in a dark lantern, all closed, closed, so that no light shone out, and then I thrust in my head. Oh, you would have laughed to see how **cunningly** I thrust it in! I moved it slowly—very, very slowly, so that I might not disturb the old man's sleep. It took me an hour to place my whole head within the opening so far that I could see him as he lay upon his bed. Ha!—would a madman have been so wise as this? And then, when my head was well in the room, I undid the lantern cautiously—oh, so cautiously—cautiously (for the hinges creaked)—I undid it just so much that a single thin ray fell upon the vulture eye. And this I did for seven long nights—every night just at midnight—but I found the eye always closed; and so it was impossible to do the work; for it was not the old man who **vexed** me, but his Evil Eye. And every morning, when the day broke, I went boldly into the chamber, and spoke courageously to him, calling him by name in a hearty tone, and inquiring how he had passed the night. So you see he would have been a very **profound** old man, indeed, to suspect that every night, just at twelve, I looked in upon him while he slept.

Upon the eighth night I was more than usually cautious in opening the door. A watch's minute hand moves more quickly than did mine. Never before that night, had I *felt* the extent of my own powers—of my sagacity.[3] I could scarcely contain my feelings of triumph. To think that there I was,

**cunningly**
sneakily;
cleverly

> I was never kinder to the old man than during the whole week before I killed him.

**vexed**
annoyed;
bothered

**profound**
sharp; smart

---

2 **dissimulation**: hiding one's feelings or plans

3 **sagacity**: wisdom and good sense

opening the door, little by little, and he not even to dream of my secret deeds or thoughts. I fairly chuckled at the idea; and perhaps he heard me; for he moved on the bed suddenly, as if startled. Now you may think that I drew back—but no. His room was as black as pitch with the thick darkness (for the shutters were close fastened, through fear of robbers), and so I knew that he could not see the opening of the door, and I kept pushing it on steadily, steadily.

I had my head in, and was about to open the lantern, when my thumb slipped upon the tin fastening, and the old man sprang up in bed, crying out—"Who's there?"

> Presently I heard a slight groan, and I knew it was the groan of mortal terror.

I kept quite still and said nothing. For a whole hour I did not move a muscle, and in the meantime I did not hear him lie down. He was still sitting up in the bed listening;—just as I have done night after night, hearkening to the deathwatches[4] in the wall.

Presently I heard a slight groan, and I knew it was the groan of mortal terror. It was not a groan of pain or of grief—oh, no!—it was the low, **stifled** sound that arises from the bottom of the soul when over-charged with **awe**. I knew the sound well. Many a night, just at midnight, when all the world slept, it has welled up from my own bosom,[5] deepening, with its dreadful echo, the terrors that distracted me. I say I knew it well. I knew what the old man felt, and pitied him, although I chuckled at heart. I knew that he had been lying awake ever since the first slight noise, when he had turned in the bed. His fears had been ever since growing upon him. He had been trying to fancy them causeless, but could not. He had been saying to himself—"It is nothing but the wind in the chimney—it is only a mouse crossing the floor," or "it is merely a cricket which has made a single chirp."

**stifled**
smothered; muffled

**awe**
a feeling of wonder

---

4 **deathwatches**: beetles that burrow into wood and make a tapping sound

5 **bosom**: chest

Yes, he had been trying to comfort himself with these suppositions:[6] but he had found all in vain. *All in vain*; because Death, in approaching him had stalked with his black shadow before him, and enveloped the victim. And it was the **mournful** influence of the unperceived[7] shadow that caused him to feel—although he neither saw nor heard—to *feel* the presence of my head within the room.

**mournful**
full of sorrow

**crevice**
crack; gap

When I had waited a long time, very patiently, without hearing him lie down, I resolved to open a little—a very, very little **crevice** in the lantern. So I opened it—you cannot imagine how **stealthily**, stealthily—until at length a single dim ray, like the thread of the spider, shot from out the crevice and fell full upon the vulture eye.

**stealthily**
sneakily;
cautiously

It was open—wide, wide open—and I grew furious as I gazed upon it. I saw it with perfect distinctness—all a dull blue, with a hideous veil over it that chilled the very marrow in my bones; but I could see nothing else of the old man's face or person: for I had directed the ray, as if by instinct, precisely upon the damned spot.

*M*eantime the hellish tattoo of the heart increased. It grew quicker and quicker, and louder and louder every instant.

And have I not told you that what you mistake for madness is but over acuteness of the senses?—now, I say, there came to my ears a low, dull, quick sound, such as a watch makes when enveloped in cotton. I knew *that* sound well, too. It was the beating of the old man's heart. It increased my fury, as the beating of a drum **stimulates** the soldier into courage.

**stimulates**
arouses; makes active

**refrained**
held back

But even yet I **refrained** and kept still. I scarcely breathed. I held the lantern motionless. I tried how steadily I could maintain the ray upon the eye. Meantime the hellish tattoo[8] of the heart increased. It grew quicker and quicker, and louder and louder every instant. The old man's terror *must* have

6 **suppositions**: guesses

7 **unperceived**: not seen or heard

8 **tattoo**: a beating sound

been extreme! It grew louder, I say, louder every moment!—do you mark me well? I have told you that I am nervous: so I am. And now at the dead hour of the night, amid the dreadful silence of that old house, so strange a noise as this excited me to uncontrollable terror. Yet, for some minutes longer I refrained and stood still. But the beating grew louder, louder! I thought the heart must burst. And now a new anxiety seized me—the sound would be heard by a neighbor! The old man's hour had come! With a loud yell, I threw open the lantern and leaped into the room. He shrieked

The old man's hour had come! With a loud yell, I threw open the lantern and leaped into the room.

once—once only. In an instant I dragged him to the floor, and pulled the heavy bed over him. I then smiled gaily, to find the deed so far done. But, for many minutes, the heart beat on with a muffled sound. This however, did not vex me; it would not be heard through the wall. At length it ceased. The old man was dead. I removed the bed and examined the corpse. Yes, he was stone, stone dead. I placed my hand upon the heart and held it there many minutes. There was no pulsation.[9] He was stone dead. His eye would trouble me no more.

If still you think me mad, you will think so no longer when I describe the wise precautions I took for the concealment of the body. The night waned,[10] and I worked hastily, but in silence. First of all I dismembered the corpse. I cut off the head and the arms and the legs.

I then took up three planks from the flooring of the chamber, and deposited all between the scantlings.[11] I then replaced the boards so cleverly, so cunningly, that no human eye—not even *his*—could have detected anything wrong. There was nothing to wash out—no stain of any

9 **pulsation**: beating; throbbing

10 **waned**: faded; became less

11 **scantlings**: small pieces of lumber

kind—no blood-spot whatever. I had been too wary for that. A tub had caught all—ha! ha!

When I had made an end of these labors, it was four o'clock—still dark as midnight. As the bell sounded the hour, there came a knocking at the street door. I went down to open it with a light heart,—for what had I *now* to fear? There entered three men, who introduced themselves, with perfect suavity,[12] as officers of the police. A shriek had been heard by a neighbor during the night; suspicion of foul play had been aroused; information had been lodged at the police office, and they (the officers) had been deputed[13] to search the premises.

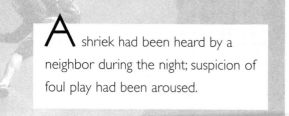

A shriek had been heard by a neighbor during the night; suspicion of foul play had been aroused.

I smiled,—for *what* had I to fear? I bade[14] the gentlemen welcome. The shriek, I said, was my own in a dream. The old man, I mentioned, was absent in the country. I took my visitors all over the house. I bade them search—search *well*. I led them, at length, to *his* chamber. I showed them his treasures, secure, undisturbed. In the enthusiasm of my confidence, I brought chairs into the room, and desired them *here* to rest from their fatigues, while I myself, in the wild **audacity** of my perfect triumph, placed my own seat upon the very spot beneath which reposed the corpse of the victim.

**audacity**
daring;
boldness

The officers were satisfied. My *manner* had convinced them. I was singularly at ease. They sat, and while I answered cheerily, they chatted of familiar things. But, ere long, I felt myself getting pale and wished them gone. My head ached, and I fancied[15] a ringing in my ears: but still they sat and still chatted. The ringing became more distinct:—it continued and became more distinct: I talked more freely to get rid of the feeling: but it

---

12 **suavity**: politeness; smoothness

13 **deputed**: sent; delegated

14 **bade**: invited; wished

15 **fancied**: imagined

continued and gained definiteness—until, at length, I found that the noise was *not* within my ears.

No doubt I now grew *very* pale;—but I talked more fluently, and with a heightened voice. Yet the sound increased—and what could I do? It was *a low, dull, quick sound—much such a sound as a watch makes when enveloped in cotton*. I gasped for breath—and yet the officers heard it not. I talked more quickly—more vehemently;[16] but the noise steadily increased. I arose and argued about trifles, in a high key and with violent gesticulations;[17] but the noise steadily increased. Why *would* they not be gone? I paced the floor to and fro with heavy strides, as if excited to fury by the observations of the men—but the noise steadily increased. Oh God! what *could* I do? I foamed—I raved—I swore! I swung the chair upon which I had been sitting, and grated it upon the boards, but the noise arose over all and continually increased. It grew louder—louder—*louder!* And still the men chatted pleasantly, and smiled. Was it possible they heard not? Almighty God!—no, no! They heard!—they suspected!—they *knew!*—they were making a mockery of my horror!—this I thought, and this I think. But anything was better than this agony! Anything was more tolerable than this derision![18] I could bear those hypocritical[19] smiles no longer! I felt that I must scream or die! and now—again!—hark! louder! louder! louder! *louder!*

"Villians!" I shrieked, "dissemble[20] no more! I admit the deed!—tear up the planks! here, here!—it is the beating of his hideous heart!"

---

16 **vehemently**: strongly; passionately

17 **gesticulations**: movements or gestures of the hands and arms

18 **derision**: ridicule or mockery

19 **hypocritical**: saying one thing but doing another

20 **dissemble**: tell lies; evade the truth

# Reviewing

## The Tell-Tale Heart

### Discussing the Selection

1. "The Tell-Tale Heart" makes a powerful impression on most readers. What effect does it have on you? Point out some of the details or imagery that add to its distinct mood.

2. What words would you use to describe the narrator?

3. Analyze how Poe builds suspense. What is the climax, or most emotional point, of the story?

4. "The Tell-Tale Heart" is one of Poe's most popular short stories. What is the main source of its appeal in your opinion?

### Writing About Atmosphere/Mood

Write a description of the most terrible place you can think of, whether it exists in reality or is simply the product of your imagination. Make sure every detail is specific and that it contributes to the horrifying nature of this place. Remember, good descriptive writing uses sensory details—ones that appeal to the five senses (hearing, sight, touch, taste, and smell).

### About Edgar Allan Poe (1809–1849)

In his short life, Edgar Allan Poe was a fearless and extremely productive writer. Although he is widely considered a master of terror, he also pioneered the modern detective and science fiction story. After being orphaned from his actor-parents, Poe went to live with wealthy adoptive parents. When that relationship failed, he moved in with an aunt. Money troubles and personal problems hounded Poe, but he continued to write groundbreaking fiction, poetry, and essays. His classic tales include "Murder in the Rue Morgue" and "The Pit and the Pendulum." "The Raven" is still one of the most widely read poems in literature. One critic called him "perhaps the most original writer that ever existed in America."

# Previewing

## Southbound on the Freeway
by May Swenson

### Reading Connection
In 1963, when this poem was written, the space age was just beginning. The media encouraged the public's enthusiasm with constant reports on the manned and unmanned spacecraft being launched into orbit. Writers such as May Swenson were fascinated by the possible effects of technology on human beings.

### Skill Focus: Speaker
A poem is written by an author, but is spoken by an invented speaker. Even when the words in a poem sound like the author's own voice, it is important to remember that in a poem you are hearing a particular speaker in a particular situation. When you talk about the voice you hear in a poem, you refer to it as the speaker, voice, mask, or persona. The first question you ask yourself when reading a poem is: Who is speaking?

# Southbound on the Freeway

May Swenson

A tourist came in from Orbitville,
parked in the air, and said:

The creatures of this star
are made of metal and glass.

Through the transparent parts            5
you can see their guts.

Their feet are round and roll
on diagrams or long

measuring tapes, dark
with white lines.                        10

They have four eyes.
The two in back are red.

Sometimes you can see a five-eyed
one, with a red eye turning

on the top of his head.                  15
He must be special—

the others respect him
and go slow

when he passes, winding
among them from behind.                                    20

They all hiss as they glide,
like inches, down the marked

tapes. Those soft shapes,
shadowy inside

the hard bodies—are they                                   25
their guts or their brains?

MAGNETICALLY DISTORTED CITY, Robert F. Kauffman, 1994

# Reviewing

## Southbound on the Freeway

### Discussing the Selection

1. Identify the speaker of the poem. Who do you think is speaking, and to whom?

2. When "Southbound on the Freeway" was written, our nation's interstate highway system was being constructed. What might the writer be suggesting about technological progress?

3. What meaning do you take from the last lines: "Those soft shapes,/shadowy inside/the hard bodies—are they/their guts or their brains?"

4. What does a car represent to you? To the speaker? To the poet?

### Writing a Pro/Con Essay

Describe your favorite piece of hi-tech gear. The one you think you couldn't live without. Then list its advantages (pros)—those that are promised in advertisements and those that you have experienced. What is gained by using this piece of equipment? Is it helpful? Entertaining? Efficient? How is your life better because of it? Now think seriously about the negative aspects (cons) as experienced by you or claimed by others. What are its drawbacks? What does it cost you in time, money, safety, friendships, family life, and so on? Finally, state your opinion on whether or not this invention has actually been a positive development.

### About May Swenson (1919–1989)

Despite the fact that Swedish was her first language, May Swenson became one of America's most inventive poets. Born in Utah, Swenson earned her degree from Utah State University in 1939 and went on to teach poetry at several colleges, including Bryn Mawr and the University of North Carolina. She served as an editor at the New Directions Press, while placing her own work in *Atlantic Monthly*, *The Nation*, and *The New Yorker*. The author of more than ten poetry collections, including *Another Animal* and *In Other Words*, Swenson's writing often delights in the natural world. She was especially interested in exploring the nature of scientific inquiries, in particular, space research.

# Previewing

## All Summer in a Day
by Ray Bradbury

### Reading Connection

According to Ray Bradbury, "Science fiction is really sociological studies of the future, things that the writer believes are going to happen by putting two and two together." Usually science fiction takes place in the future in a setting made possible by some technological advance. It concerns itself with human problems and the human condition, which distinguishes it from fantasy. As the writer John W. Campbell, Jr., puts it, "Fantasy makes its rules as it goes along. . . . The basic nature of fantasy is 'The only rule is, make up a new rule any time you need one!' "

### Skill Focus: Conflict

The plot of a story is usually built around a problem or conflict involving the main character. Without "trouble" there is no story. This trouble can come from outside forces, such as nature, or from other people. It can also come from within, as when a character wrestles with difficult ideas or emotions. Look for the conflict in the story you are about to read.

### Vocabulary Builder

Review the information on analogies on pages 366–368. Then try making a few of your own using the words below. Start with some of the easier relationships such as synonyms or antonyms. For example, *cold : frozen :: wet : _____*. (The answer is *drenched*.) Challenge your classmates to solve the analogies you create.

| | | | |
|---|---|---|---|
| slackening | consequence | apparatus | resilient |
| drenched | surged | tremor | savored |
| vital | | | |

March Wind, Robert Vickrey

# All **Summer** in a **Day**

Ray Bradbury

"Ready?"

"Ready."

"Now?"

"Soon."

"Do the scientists really know? Will it happen today, will it?"

"Look, look; see for yourself!"

The children pressed to each other like so many roses, so many weeds, intermixed, peering out for a look at the hidden sun.

It rained.

It had been raining for seven years; thousands upon thousands of days compounded and filled from one end to the other with rain, with the drum and gush of water, with the sweet crystal fall of showers and the concussion[1] of storms so heavy they were tidal waves come over the islands. A thousand forests had been crushed under the rain and grown up a thousand times to be crushed again. And this was the way life was forever on the planet Venus, and this was the schoolroom of the children of the rocket men and women who had come to a raining world to set up civilization and live out their lives.

---

1 **concussion:** pounding

"It's stopping, it's stopping!"

"Yes, yes!"

Margot stood apart from them, from these children who could never remember a time when there wasn't rain and rain and rain. They were all nine years old, and if there had been a day, seven years ago, when the sun came out for an hour and showed its face to the stunned world, they could not recall. Sometimes, at night, she heard them stir, in remembrance, and she knew they were dreaming and remembering gold or a yellow crayon or a coin large enough to buy the world with. She knew that they thought they remembered warmness, like a blushing in the face, in the body, in the arms and legs and trembling hands. But then they always awoke to the tatting drum, the endless shaking down of clear bead necklaces upon the roof, the walk, the gardens, the forest; and their dreams were gone.

All day yesterday they had read in class about the sun, and about how like a lemon it was and how hot. And they had written small stories or essays or poems about it:

> I think the sun is a flower,
> That blooms for just one hour.

That was Margot's poem, read in a quiet voice in the still classroom while the rain was falling outside.

"Aw, you didn't write that!" protested one of the boys.

"I did," said Margot. "I *did.*"

"William!" said the teacher.

**slackening**
letting up;
lessening

But that was yesterday. Now, the rain was **slackening**, and the children were crushed to the great thick windows.

"Where's teacher?"

"She'll be back."

"She'd better hurry, we'll miss it!"

They turned on themselves, like a feverish wheel, all tumbling spokes.

Margot stood alone. She was a very frail girl who looked as if she had been lost in the rain for years and the rain had washed out the blue from her eyes and the red from her mouth and the yellow from her hair. She was an old photograph dusted from an album, whitened away, and if she spoke at all, her voice would be a ghost. Now she stood, separate, staring at the rain and the loud wet world beyond the huge glass.

"What're *you* looking at?" said William.

Margot said nothing.

"Speak when you're spoken to." He gave her a shove. But she did not move; rather, she let herself be moved only by him and nothing else.

They edged away from her, they would not look at her. She felt them go away. And this was because she would play no games with them in the echoing tunnels of the underground city. If they tagged her and ran, she stood blinking after them and did not follow. When the class sang songs about happiness and life and games, her lips barely moved. Only when they sang about the sun and the summer did her lips move, as she watched the **drenched** windows.

> ...**t**he biggest crime of all was that she had come here only five years ago from Earth, and she remembered the sun ...

**drenched**
soaked;
sopping wet

And then, of course, the biggest crime of all was that she had come here only five years ago from Earth, and she remembered the sun and the way the sun was and the sky was, when she was four, in Ohio. And they, they had been on Venus all their lives, and they had been only two years old when last the sun came out, and had long since forgotten the color and heat of it and the way that it really was. But Margot remembered.

"It's like a penny," she said once, eyes closed.

"No, it's not!" the children cried.

"It's like a fire," she said, "in the stove."

"You're lying, you don't remember!" cried the children.

But she remembered and stood quietly apart from all of them and watched the patterning windows. And once, a month ago, she had refused to shower in the school shower rooms, had clutched her hands to her ears and over her head, screaming the water mustn't touch her head. So after that, dimly, dimly, she sensed it, she was different, and they knew her difference and kept away.

There was talk that her father and mother were taking her back to Earth next year; it seemed **vital** to her that they do so, though it would mean the loss of thousands of dollars to her family. And so, the children hated her for all these reasons, of big and little **consequence**. They hated her pale snow face, her waiting silence, her thinness, and her possible future.

"Get away!" The boy gave her another push. "What're you waiting for?"

Then, for the first time, she turned and looked at him. And what she was waiting for was in her eyes.

"Well, don't wait around here!" cried the boy, savagely. "You won't see nothing!"

Her lips moved.

"Nothing!" he cried. "It was all a joke, wasn't it?" He turned to the other children. "Nothing's happening today. *Is* it?"

They all blinked at him and then, understanding, laughed and shook their heads. "Nothing, nothing!"

"Oh, but," Margot whispered, her eyes helpless. "But, this is the day, the scientists predict, they say, they *know*, the sun . . ."

"All a joke!" said the boy and seized her roughly. "Hey, everyone, let's put her in a closet before the teacher comes!"

"No," said Margot, falling back.

They **surged** about her, caught her up, and bore her, protesting and then pleading and then crying, back into a tunnel, a room, a closet, where they slammed and locked the door. They stood looking at the door and saw it tremble from her beating and throwing herself against it. They heard her muffled cries. Then, smiling, they turned and went out and back down the tunnel, just as the teacher arrived.

"Ready, children?" She glanced at her watch.

"Yes!" said everyone.

"Are we all here?"

"Yes!"

The rain slackened still more.

They crowded to the huge door.

The rain stopped.

It was as if, in the midst of a film concerning an avalanche, a tornado, a hurricane, a volcanic eruption, something had, first, gone wrong with the sound **apparatus**, thus muffling and finally cutting off all noise, all of the blasts and repercussions and thunders, and then, secondly, ripped the film from the projector and inserted in its place a peaceful tropical slide which did not move or **tremor**. The world ground to a standstill. The silence was so immense and unbelievable that you felt that your ears had been stuffed or you had lost your hearing altogether. The children put their hands to their ears. They stood apart. The door slid back and the smell of the silent, waiting world came in to them.

**apparatus** equipment; machinery

**tremor** tremble; shake

The sun came out.

It was the color of flaming bronze and it was very large. And the sky around it was a blazing blue tile color. And the jungle burned with sunlight as the children, released from their spell, rushed out, yelling, into the summertime.

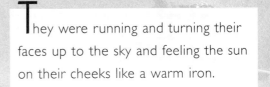

They were running and turning their faces up to the sky and feeling the sun on their cheeks like a warm iron.

"Now, don't go too far," called the teacher after them. "You've only one hour, you know. You wouldn't want to get caught out!"

But they were running and turning their faces up to the sky and feeling the sun on their cheeks like a warm iron; they were taking off their jackets and letting the sun burn their arms.

"Oh, it's better than the sun lamps, isn't it?"

"Much, much better!"

They stopped running and stood in the great jungle that covered Venus, that grew and never stopped growing, tumultuously,[2] even as you watched it. It was a nest of octopuses, clustering up great arms of flesh-like weed, wavering, flowering in this brief spring. It was the color of rubber and ash, this jungle, from the many years without sun. It was the color of stones and white cheeses and ink.

---

2 **tumultuously**: wildly; recklessly

The children lay out, laughing, on the jungle mattress, and heard it sigh and squeak under them, **resilient** and alive. They ran among the trees, they slipped and fell, they pushed each other, they played hide-and-seek and tag; but most of all they squinted at the sun until tears ran down their faces, they put their hands up at that yellowness and that amazing blueness, and they breathed of the fresh air and listened and listened to the silence which suspended them in a blessed sea of no sound and no motion. They looked at

everything and **savored** everything. Then, wildly, like animals escaped from their caves, they ran and ran in shouting circles. They ran for an hour and did not stop running.

And then—

In the midst of their running, one of the girls wailed.

Everyone stopped.

The girl, standing in the open, held out her hand.

"Oh, look, look," she said, trembling.

They came slowly to look at her opened palm.

In the center of it, cupped and huge, was a single raindrop.

She began to cry, looking at it.

They glanced quickly at the sky.

"Oh. Oh."

A few cold drops fell on their noses and their cheeks and their mouths. The sun faded behind a stir of mist. A wind blew cool around them. They turned and started to walk back toward the underground house, their hands at their sides, their smiles vanishing away.

A boom of thunder startled them, and like leaves before a new hurricane, they tumbled upon each other and ran. Lightning struck ten miles away, five miles away, a mile, a half-mile. The sky darkened into midnight in a flash.

They stood in the doorway of the underground for a moment until it was raining hard. Then they closed the door and heard the gigantic sound of the rain falling in tons and avalanches everywhere and forever.

"Will it be seven more years?"

"Yes. Seven."

Then one of them gave a little cry.

"Margot!"

"What?"

"She's still in the closet where we locked her."

"Margot."

They stood as if someone had driven them, like so many stakes, into the floor. They looked at each other and then looked away. They glanced out at the world that was raining now and raining and raining steadily. They could not meet each other's glances. Their faces were solemn and pale. They looked at their hands and feet, their faces down.

"Margot."

One of the girls said, "Well . . . ?"

No one moved.

"Go on," whispered the girl.

They walked slowly down the hall in the sound of cold rain. They turned through the doorway to the room, in the sound of the storm and thunder, lightning on their faces, blue and terrible. They walked over to the closet door slowly and stood by it.

Behind the closet door was only silence.

They unlocked the door, even more slowly, and let Margot out.

# Reviewing

## All Summer in a Day

### Discussing the Selection

1. Why do you think that the other children bully Margot?

2. Make a list of some similes and metaphors in this story. Do they have anything in common?

3. How does the tone of this science fiction story differ from that about the aliens in "Southbound on the Freeway"? Are the authors' attitudes about the future similar or different?

4. How long do you think you will remember this story? Point out any images or phrases that will stick with you.

### Writing a Prediction

In the story you just read, the future doesn't seem to be a particularly happy place. What is your own vision of the future? Will the population still be living on Earth or will they have migrated to nearby planets, where the conditions may be severe and challenging? Write a prediction about the future, either based on what you already know—or created from pure fantasy.

### About Ray Bradbury (1920–)

Ray Bradbury once described the act of writing as "a fever—something I must do." He wrote his first story at age eleven on butcher paper. Since then, this genius of science fiction and fantasy has published more than 500 short stories, novels, plays, screenplays, television scripts, and poems. Many of his books are classic bestsellers, such as *The Martian Chronicles*, *The Illustrated Man*, *Fahrenheit 451*, and *Something Wicked This Way Comes*. He has been awarded the Grand Master Award from the Science Fiction Writers of America and the National Book Foundation Medal for his distinguished contribution to American letters.

# Previewing

## The Cremation of Sam McGee
by Robert Service

### Reading Connection

Robert Service's popular ballads were inspired by the characters he met as an adventurous young man in Canada's Yukon Territory. The miners who took part in the Alaskan gold rush of the 1890s were notoriously rugged characters. To survive they had to put up with astonishing extremes of cold and snow. Many did not make it. Service once said, "The only society I like is that which is rough and tough—and the tougher the better. That's where you get down to bedrock and meet human people."

### Skill Focus: Diction

Diction simply means "word choice." A poet's diction is very important to the mood and meaning of a poem as well as its rhythm and rhyme. As you read, notice what special diction the poet uses. Is the language down-to-earth, sophisticated, or old-fashioned in its vocabulary? What mood does the poet create for the reader by using certain words and phrases?

# The **Cremation**
## of **Sam McGee**

Robert Service

DAWN OVER THE YUKON, Ted Harrison

*There are strange things done in the midnight sun*
*    By the men who moil[1] for gold;*
*The Arctic trails have their secret tales*
*    That would make your blood run cold;*
*The Northern Lights[2] have seen queer sights,*                    5
*    But the queerest they ever did see*
*Was that night on the marge[3] of Lake Lebarge*
*    I cremated[4] Sam McGee.*

Now Sam McGee was from Tennessee,
    Where the cotton blooms and blows.                              10
Why he left his home in the South to roam
    'Round the Pole, God only knows.
He was always cold, but the land of gold
    Seemed to hold him like a spell;
Though he'd often say in his homely way                             15
    That he'd "sooner live in hell."

On a Christmas Day we were mushing[5] our way
    Over the Dawson trail.[6]
Talk of your cold! through the parka's fold
    It stabbed like a driven nail.                                  20
If our eyes we'd close, then the lashes froze
    Till sometimes we couldn't see;
It wasn't much fun, but the only one
    To whimper was Sam McGee.

---

1 **moil**: toil; work very hard

2 **Northern Lights**: the aurora borealis, a light show that occurs in the upper atmosphere
of the north

3 **marge**: edge; margin

4 **cremated**: disposed of a dead body by burning it to ashes

5 **mushing**: traveling by dog sled

6 **Dawson trail**: a route in Canada's Yukon Territory

And that very night, as we lay packed tight                25
    In our robes beneath the snow,
And the dogs were fed, and the stars o'erhead
    Were dancing heel and toe,
He turned to me, and "Cap," says he,
    "I'll cash in this trip, I guess;                30
And if I do, I'm asking that you
    Won't refuse my last request."

Well, he seemed so low that I couldn't say no;
    Then he says with a sort of moan:
"It's the cursed cold, and it's got right hold            35
    Till I'm chilled clean through to the bone.
Yet 'tain't being dead—it's my awful dread
    Of the icy grave that pains;
So I want you to swear that, foul or fair,
    You'll cremate my last remains."[7]               40

A pal's last need is a thing to heed,
    So I swore I would not fail;
And we started on at the streak of dawn;
    But God! he looked ghastly pale.
He crouched on the sleigh, and he raved all day          45
    Of his home in Tennessee;
And before nightfall a corpse was all
    That was left of Sam McGee.

---

7 **last remains**: dead body

There wasn't a breath in that land of death,
    And I hurried, horror-driven,                        50
With a corpse half hid that I couldn't get rid,
    Because of a promise given;
It was lashed[8] to the sleigh, and it seemed to say:
    "You may tax your brawn[9] and brains,
But you promised true, and it's up to you              55
    To cremate those last remains."

Now a promise made is a debt unpaid,
    And the trail has its own stern code.
In the days to come, though my lips were dumb,
    In my heart how I cursed that load.             60
In the long, long night, by the lone firelight,
    While the huskies, round in a ring,
Howled out their woes to the homeless snows—
    O God! how I loathed the thing.

And every day that quiet clay                      65
    Seemed to heavy and heavier grow;
And on I went, though the dogs were spent
    And the grub was getting low;
The trail was bad, and I felt half mad,
    But I swore I would not give in;           70
And I'd often sing to the hateful thing,
    And it hearkened with a grin.

---

8 **lashed**: tied

9 **tax your brawn**: strain your muscles

Till I came to the marge of Lake Lebarge,
    And a derelict[10] there lay;
It was jammed in the ice, but I saw in a trice        75
    It was called the *Alice May.*
And I looked at it, and I thought a bit,
    And I looked at my frozen chum;
Then "Here," said I, with a sudden cry,
    "Is my cre-ma-tor-eum."        80

Some planks I tore from the cabin floor,
    And I lit the boiler fire;
Some coal I found that was lying around,
    And I heaped the fuel higher;
The flames just soared, and the furnace roared—        85
    Such a blaze you seldom see;
And I burrowed a hole in the glowing coal,
    And I stuffed in Sam McGee.

Then I made a hike, for I didn't like
    To hear him sizzle so;        90
And the heavens scowled, and the huskies howled,
    And the wind began to blow.
It was icy cold, but the hot sweat rolled
    Down my cheeks, and I don't know why;
And the greasy smoke in an inky cloak        95
    Went streaking down the sky.

---

10 **derelict**: a ship that had been abandoned

I do not know how long in the snow
    I wrestled with grisly[11] fear;
But the stars came out and they danced about
    Ere again I ventured near;                      100
I was sick with dread, but I bravely said:
    "I'll just take a peep inside.
I guess he's cooked, and it's time I looked;" . . .
    Then the door I opened wide.

And there sat Sam, looking cool and calm,          105
    In the heart of the furnace roar;
And he wore a smile you could see a mile,
    And he said: "Please close that door.
It's fine in here, but I greatly fear
    You'll let in the cold and storm—             110
Since I left Plumtree, down in Tennessee,
It's the first time I've been warm."

*There are strange things done in the midnight sun*
    *By the men who moil for gold;*
*The Arctic trails have their secret tales*        115
    *That would make your blood run cold;*
*The Northern Lights have seen queer sights,*
    *But the queerest they ever did see*
*Was that night on the marge of Lake Lebarge*
    *I cremated Sam McGee.*               120

---

11 **grisly**: shocking; gruesome

# Reviewing

## The Cremation of Sam McGee

### Discussing the Selection

1. Narrative poems tell a story and have many of the same elements. Describe the plot, characters, and setting of "The Cremation of Sam McGee."

2. Analyze the poet's choice of words, or diction. What words in particular help you see, hear, and feel the event?

3. The first and last stanzas of this poem are the same. How does the mood differ between the two?

4. One critic claimed that a Service poem was "a lilting thing, clear, clean and power-packed, beating out a story with a dramatic intensity that made the nerves tingle." Do you agree with this opinion? Why or why not?

### Writing a Literary Opinion

Besides "The Cremation of Sam McGee," there are several other narrative poems in this book including "The Highwayman" (p. 266), "Casey at the Bat" (p. 341), and "Paul Revere's Ride" (p. 318). Assume that you are an editor at a literary magazine for young people. You must choose which of these poems to publish in the next edition. Review the poems, listing pros and cons for each one. Make your choice and write a memo to the editor-in-chief giving detailed reasons for your choice AND the reasons for rejecting the others.

### About Robert Service (1874–1958)

Robert Service's obituary claimed "He was not a poet's poet. He was a people's poet." Perhaps for that reason, "his stuff made money hand over fist." His poem "Dan McGrew" was recited and reprinted so often it earned him half a million dollars. Service did not lead a poet's quiet life, either, employed at one time or another as a banker, war reporter, ranch hand, and ambulance driver. In later years, his success as a writer allowed him to live the high life in Monte Carlo, France, in the company of the rich and famous.

# Previewing

## from *Frozen Man*
by David Getz

### Reading Connection

There are two kinds of mummies: intentional and unintentional. Intentional mummies are the types you see in natural history museums—shrouded in cloth, often buried in distinctively decorated coffins, perhaps even accompanied by a favorite mummified animal, such as a cat. Unintentional mummies are created when natural elements maintain their bodies without any human intervention. Some of these mummies have been found in deserts or icy mountain areas—climates that helped to preserve the bodies for thousands of years.

### Skill Focus: KWL

Before you read about something that might be unfamiliar, it can be helpful to consider what you may already know about the topic (K) as well as what you would like to know (W). When you finish the story, you record what you learned (L). You can record your thoughts in a chart like the one below.

| WHAT I KNOW ABOUT MUMMIES | WHAT I WANT TO LEARN | WHAT I LEARNED |
|---|---|---|
|  |  |  |
|  |  |  |

### Vocabulary Builder

How many of the words below do you already know? Make a guess at the meaning of each one, then check yourself by looking at the definitions on the selection pages where the words occur.

| mutilated | treacherous | contemporaries | scavengers |

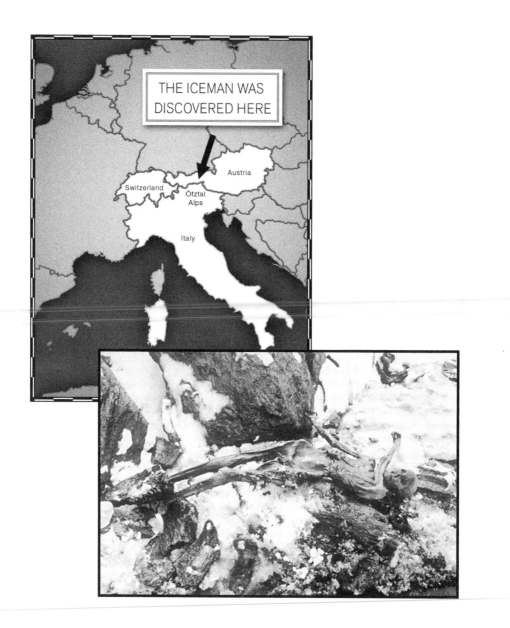

THE ICEMAN WAS
DISCOVERED HERE

Austria

Switzerland

Ötztal
Alps

Italy

# from *Frozen Man*

David Getz

N obody knew what stories the body could tell.

### Frozen in Time

On September 19, 1991, German tourists Erika and Helmut Simon had just climbed Finail Peak, the second-highest summit in the Ötztal Alps.[1] Deciding to try something new, they took an unmarked path back down across the Similaun Glacier to their lodge. They spotted the body at an altitude of about 10,500 feet, nearly two miles above sea level. It lay near the border of Italy and Austria.

At first glance they thought they had come upon an abandoned doll. Getting closer, they both realized that the body was an adult man. Still frozen to the glacier, the dead man seemed to have risen from the ice, as if he was getting out of a pool. He appeared to be naked. His face was pressed down into the snow.

The Simons discovered a small hole in the back of the victim's head. Suspicious that the man had been murdered,

---

1 **Ötztal Alps**: a mountain range near the border of Austria and Italy, close to Switzerland

they rushed to a hiker's shelter to report the crime.

Markus Pirpomer, the owner of the shelter, called both the Italian and the Austrian police. The Italian authorities showed no interest. They assumed the body was simply another victim of a mountaineering accident. The Austrian authorities agreed to send over an officer. That summer they had already retrieved the bodies of eight accident victims from the snow and ice of the Alps.

When Markus Pirpomer reached the body, it struck him as remarkably different from other bodies that had emerged from the glacier.

A glacier is a river of ice. As snow on mountains gets deeper and heavier, it gradually turns into ice that can be hundreds of feet thick. Sometimes glaciers flow slowly down mountains.

Pirpomer knew that it wasn't unusual for a hiker to die in the Alps, get covered by falling snow, and be trapped in a glacier. He knew that as a glacier moves down a mountain, it occasionally reveals a body it captured higher up. These bodies are usually horribly crushed and mangled from being dragged by the massive glacier over rocks and boulders.

Pirpomer noticed that the body the Simons had discovered was remarkably intact. It was in the position of someone who had stretched out to take a nap. How could a man dragged down a mountain under tons of ice appear nearly undamaged?

Just as puzzling to Pirpomer was the body's skin. Being trapped in a glacier prevents oxygen from reaching a body's soft tissues. This turns the skin, muscles, and fat into adipocere, or "grave wax," a creamy or waxy substance that makes these victims appear to be made of soap or plaster.

This man was brown and leathery, as dried out as an Egyptian mummy. How could this happen to a man surrounded by ice and snow? Pirpomer suspected that there was something remarkable about this victim. He guessed that this man had died a long time ago, though how long ago he couldn't be sure.

The Austrian policeman arrived the afternoon of September 20. He had no reason to believe there was anything special about the body. He had no idea that this "Iceman" had come from a place no one alive had ever seen.

He had no idea that the Iceman had brought with him strange tools and clothing from that distant place. They were buried along with him in the ice. The Iceman's body and his clothing and tools were like the pieces of a puzzle, waiting to be put back together.

The policeman nearly destroyed everything. He brought a jackhammer to free the body. He drilled right through the Iceman's hip, shattering the bone. He also ripped to shreds what turned out to be remains of the Iceman's cloak. By luck, the jackhammer ran out of power before it could do further harm. The officer contacted his superiors. He made plans to resume his efforts the following week. It was the next time a helicopter would be available to return him to the site.

> The Iceman's body and his clothing and tools were like the pieces of a puzzle, waiting to be put back together.

Before he left, the policeman took some photographs. He also discovered a crude hand ax. It consisted of a small, tongue-shaped blade stuck into the end of an L-shaped branch. The policeman removed the ax as possible evidence of a crime.

Word began to spread about the man in ice. The next day, six mountaineers visited the body. They tried to free it, but failed. Before leaving, they also took some photographs.

On September 22, the chairman of the Austrian mountain rescue team arrived with a friend. Together they freed the body, using a pickaxe, then informed the local police it was ready to be retrieved. The two also carried away from the site the remains of the Iceman's clothing, along with what was probably his backpack frame, part of a bow, and some clumps of grass. They left these objects at a local hotel in the Ötz valley.

The following day Rainer Henn found a note on his desk, informing him of this man in ice. Henn, the director of forensic medicine (medicine related to crimes and accidents) at the University of Innsbruck,[2] had already

---

2 **Innsbruck**: city in Austria

examined six bodies that had emerged from glaciers that year. One of those victims had died in 1934, 57 years ago. Transformed by adipocere and terribly **mutilated**, the victim had resembled a damaged statue. Henn had found railway tickets and a membership card to a mountaineering club in the victim's pockets. But Henn had heard nothing of the condition of this body, the strange ax, or any of the other objects found at the site. Who would this new victim turn out to be?

**mutilated**
cut or torn up; disfigured

Each year the Alps prove too **treacherous** for some skiers or hikers. The weather can change suddenly. Warm sunshine can instantly become a blinding snowstorm. At the altitude, or height, where the body was found, the air is thin. Breathing is difficult. It's easy to become tired and careless, to stumble and fall. Each year about 200 people lose their lives in the Alps from accidents or exposure to the cold.

**treacherous**
dangerous; hazardous

When Henn arrived by helicopter at the site, he was surprised to discover another helicopter already there. It belonged to an Austrian television crew. The man in ice was making the news. There were rumors that he might be over 500 years old.

Though freed from the ice the previous day, the body had refrozen into the surrounding slush overnight. Not having brought any tools along with him, Henn was forced to borrow an ice pick and some ski poles to chip the body free. Like Pirpomer, Henn was immediately struck by the condition of the body. He wondered why it hadn't developed adipocere. He guessed that somehow the body had completely dried out, or mummified, before it was captured within the glacier. Then he discovered a dagger. It was made with a wooden handle and had a small stone blade.

What was this twentieth-century hiking victim doing with a tool from the Stone Age?

Henn immediately ordered his helpers to proceed with caution. This body is old, he told them.

With great effort Henn and his helpers removed the body from the ice, wrapped it in plastic, and forced it into a wooden coffin. It was then transported by helicopter and ambulance to the nearest morgue. The objects that had been found alongside the body were gathered and sent along. Henn's next step, by Austrian law, would be to perform an autopsy on the body to determine its cause of death.

The Iceman was about to be cut open and taken apart like a laboratory frog.

Fortunately archaeologist Konrad Spindler got to the body first. As dean of the Institute for Pre- and Protohistory at the University of Innsbruck, Konrad Spindler is an expert on life in the Alps. Having heard some of the rumors about the man in ice, Spindler contacted Henn and expressed an interest in seeing the body and the objects found alongside it.

"This is one of the most remarkable archaeological discoveries of the century."

Spindler got his wish the following morning. He was astonished. The objects appeared to be the tools someone would carry if he was wandering around the mountains thousands of years ago! And then there was the body. Though his hip was damaged, the Iceman had arrived from the distant past remarkably whole. Scientists would be able to study his body as well as any doctor studying a patient.

Though brown, leathery, dried out, and somewhat hideous to look at, the Iceman was probably the most magnificent sight Konrad Spindler had ever witnessed.

"I felt like Howard Carter[3] when he opened the coffin of Tutankhamen— King Tut—and saw the golden face of the pharaoh," Spindler said. "From that first moment I saw that we would want to spend a lot of time studying this man and his equipment. This is one of the most remarkable archaeological discoveries of the century."

Helmut and Erika Simon had discovered a prehistoric man, possibly on his way to work. Who was this man? How did he live? How did he die? When did he last walk the paths of the Alps, and what could he tell us about his

---

3 **Howard Carter**: British archaeologist who discovered the tomb of the Egyptian pharaoh Tutankhamen in 1922

world? As chief archaeologist at the University of Innsbruck, Spindler would head the team of scientists that would seek to answer those questions.

### Dating the Iceman

The first step was to get the Iceman to reveal his secrets. How could scientists learn when he lived?

What clues did the Iceman offer? Simply looking at his body, scientists couldn't tell if he died 2,000 or 80,000 years ago. True, he was brown and leathery and so dried out that he weighed 29 pounds. The dehydration must have taken some time. And the shape of his face had been changed by the weight of the ice continuously pressing down on him. This too must have taken a long time. But how long?

> What was the man in ice doing with a dagger with a stone blade? Why didn't he have a Swiss Army knife . . . ?

Spindler turned to the Iceman's artifacts for clues. Artifacts are any objects that are made by people. To learn about ancient people, archaeologists study what artifacts are made of, how they are made, and what they were used for. The Iceman's artifacts were particularly fascinating. What was the man in ice doing with a dagger with a stone blade? Why didn't he have a Swiss Army knife with a stainless-steel blade? Daggers with stone blades hadn't been used in Europe for thousands of years!

Then there was that "murder weapon," the ax. Its shaft was made from an L-shaped branch of a yew tree. Like the dagger blade, that shaft also belonged to a period in Europe called the Stone Age. The Stone Age began in Europe about a million years ago and ended about 5,000 years ago. During this period people used stones, such as flint, for their tools. The Iceman had been found with a stone knife blade and two arrows with stone points. Could he have lived during the Stone Age?

The ax found with the Iceman.

No, he couldn't, was Spindler's first guess. The Iceman's ax appeared to be bronze. Stone Age people didn't have the technology to make bronze tools. The Bronze Age followed the Stone Age. It began in Europe about 5,000 years ago and lasted for nearly 2,000 years. During this time people in Europe began to master the technique of melting copper in furnaces that reached 1,981 degrees Fahrenheit and alloying[4] it with tin to make bronze.

If the ax's blade was bronze, its Stone-Age-style handle suggested it was made at the beginning of the Bronze Age.

"The archaeological dating can't be wrong," Spindler said. "So the ax dates from approximately 2,000 b.c. or 2,000 years before the birth of Christ."

If the policeman's suspicions were correct, then the ax would be evidence of a crime committed over 4,000 years ago.

The next step was to test Spindler's hypothesis[5] scientifically. The archaeologists working with Spindler returned to the Iceman's body. They removed tiny fragments of the hipbone damaged by the policeman. About

---

4 **alloying**: combining two or more metals

5 **hypothesis**: a proposed explanation for some thing or event

an ounce, or the weight of a paper clip, was sent to Robert Hedges at his Oxford University laboratory in England. Hedges would count how many atoms of carbon 14 the bones still contained. This would help him tell when the Iceman died.

All living things take in carbon. Plants absorb it as they "breathe" in carbon dioxide. People absorb it by eating plants or by eating animals that eat plants. A small but constant percentage of that carbon is carbon 14, which is radioactive. It is continually decaying, or coming apart.

If we look at the carbon atoms as marbles, then a sample of something that was once alive, such as a piece of bone, can be compared to a jar filled with trillions of marbles. In that jar are just a handful of strange marbles. While all the other marbles remain the same over thousands of years, the strange ones, the carbon-14 marbles, slowly disappear.

After counting the carbon 14 in the sample of bone, Hedges determined that the Iceman died about 5,300 years ago.

When a person dies, he or she stops taking in carbon. The quantity of regular carbon (carbon 12) stays the same, but the quantity of carbon 14 gets smaller and smaller as the carbon 14 atoms decay. The rate of this decay is as precise as the ticking of a clock. A slow clock! It takes 5,730 years for half the carbon 14 in a sample to tick away and disappear.

After counting the carbon 14 in the sample of bone, Hedges determined that the Iceman died about 5,300 years ago. This placed him more than 1,000 years farther back in time than Spindler's estimate. Hedge's carbon-14 dating pushed the Iceman backward out of the Bronze Age into the end of the Stone Age.

Scientists in Zurich, Switzerland, used another sample of the Iceman for radiocarbon dating. They followed the same procedure as Hedges. They arrived at a similar answer. The Iceman was clearly over 5,000 years old.

But what about that ax? How could a man who lived during the Stone

Age carry a bronze tool that wasn't invented for another thousand years or so? That was like finding a computer buried beside a Viking.

Dietrich Ankner, a metallurgist at the Roman-Germanic Museum in Mainz, Germany, analyzed the ax blade. Bronze is an alloy of copper and tin. If Ankner found any tin in the composition of the blade, that would indicate it was bronze. His tests showed no tin. This meant the blade was almost pure copper. Spindler had made a reasonable mistake. Copper and bronze look the same to the naked eye.

> He roamed the Alps at a time when the wheel was a new invention!

The Iceman lived more than 3,000 years before the invention of gunpowder or paper. Carbon-14 dating placed him in Europe over 3,000 years before Julius Caesar ruled the Roman Empire, 2,000 years before the first Olympic Games in Greece, and more than 700 years before Imhotep designed the first pyramid in Egypt. He roamed the Alps at a time when the wheel was a new invention! His **contemporaries** in central Europe lived in wooden houses that were built on stilts above the shorelines of lakes. These villages were often surrounded by a fence. Inside, people raised wheat and barley, kept animals in pens, and probably considered cooked dog a pretty good meal. Cheese was also a new invention. They used deer antler and chipped stone for tools. They buried their dead in rows in huge stone tombs. Men were placed on their right side, females on their left side. People were buried with what they would need in the afterlife: axes, knives, and beads.

**contemporaries** people living at the same time

Since the Iceman died on his way to work, he wasn't buried in a tomb. Even so, the Iceman is the oldest, best-preserved body ever discovered.

A number of chance events made the Iceman's trip to the present possible.

Most creatures disappear shortly after they die, especially if they die and are left out in the open, as the Iceman was. Blood stops flowing in their veins, and the body starts to decay. **Scavengers**, such as vultures, rodents,

**scavengers** hunters; foragers

from *Frozen Man*    417

A reconstruction of the Iceman

and insects, dine on the decaying body. Flies lay eggs in its eyes. Microscopic organisms finish off what the bigger animals started. The weather, wind, and rain scatter what's left.

The Iceman avoided disappearing by chance. He died at the bottom of a gap between two large rock formations in the mountains. This shelter probably hid him from most large scavengers, such as vultures. By luck, it probably began to snow right as he died. Soon he was covered in a white blanket. This further helped hide his body from the animals that would make a meal of it.

Somehow, and scientists are still not exactly sure how, his body was mummified. Many archaeologists believe a steadily blowing wind passed through the loosely packed snow, carrying away the moisture from his body. "He was freeze-dried," said Konrad Spindler. The Iceman was too dry to develop adipocere, or grave wax. Drying is one way to prevent decay. Egyptians mummified their pharaohs' bodies to make sure they would survive into the afterlife. More commonly, everyone from Native Americans to European explorers has dried meats and fish over smoky fires to preserve the food for long periods.

Another method to preserve meat, or a human body, is refrigeration. Extreme cold prevents decay. Think of a refrigerator.

But how did the Iceman survive the forces of the glacier? At times the ice towered 100 to 200 feet above his body, the height of a 20-story building. How was he not crushed? And why wasn't he dragged down over the mountain with the movement of the glacier? How did he remain in one piece?

Luck. The Iceman died in a deep, narrow gap between two rocky ridges. These ridges acted like train tracks. The glacier slid down the mountain over these tracks while the Iceman lay safely beneath them.

At last, why did the Iceman suddenly appear?

In 1991 a dust storm in the Sahara Desert sent huge amounts of dust into the atmosphere. Some of this dust traveled over the Alps, where it fell and darkened the snow. Dark colors absorb more heat than light colors. This dust, along with an unusually warm summer, caused the snow to melt rapidly, exposing the Iceman for the first time in over 5,000 years!

Editor's Note: *The Iceman (nicknamed Öetzi) was approximately 5' 2" tall. Scientists estimate that he was about 46 years old when he died. He had 57 tattoos on his body and wore a woven grass cape, leather vest, and shoes of bear and deer hides. Found with him were an ax, bow and arrows, a knife, and firestarting materials. In 1994, A CAT scan revealed that the apparent cause of his death was a flint arrowhead lodged in his shoulder.*

# Reviewing

## Frozen Man

### Discussing the Selection
1. What did you learn about unintentional mummies from this selection? Fill in your chart with facts, details, and any statistics you found.

2. Why did the Iceman suddenly appear after all the years of being hidden?

3. Explain the concept of archaeological dating. How did the Iceman's artifacts offer important clues to who he was?

4. What new information about the past did the Iceman's discovery provide?

### Writing: Fact into Fiction
Fiction writers often base their stories on reality. Use what you have read to create a story about the Iceman that tells what he was doing in the mountains and how he met his death. Make your writing rich with details about him, his home and family, and his appearance. Use facts and images from the selection for inspiration.

### About David Getz (1957–)
David Getz is an award-winning author of novels (*Thin Air*, *Almost Famous*) and nonfiction books about science discovery for middle-grade readers, such as *Floating Home*, *Frozen Girl*, and *Life on Mars*. *Frozen Man* was named an Outstanding Science Trade Book for Children. Getz is also the principal of an innovative middle school in New York City that emphasizes science learning. An expert on archaeology, history, math, and science, Getz previously worked as a science staff developer in the New York City school system.

# Previewing

## The Monsters Are Due on Maple Street
by Rod Serling

### Reading Connection

The following story was originally written for *The Twilight Zone*, Rod Serling's groundbreaking television series which began in 1959. Serling's approach was to put ordinary characters into bizarre situations, which allowed him to poke at social issues without fear of censorship. He once said, "I found that it was all right to have Martians saying things Democrats and Republicans could never say." Serling wrote nearly two-thirds of the 156 original scripts, an amazing feat for any writer. *The Twilight Zone* can still be seen in reruns.

### Skill Focus: Jargon

Like many other fields, television production has a specialized language known as jargon. This language includes camera directions, usually written by the screenwriter in order to create a specific visual effect. You will find these terms in the following selection:

- *Fade in/out*: a fade-out consists of a two- or three-second transition from a picture to a black screen and silence; a fade-in is the opposite
- *Shot*: a single camera effect without interruption
- *Pan*: to move the camera from left to right or vice versa

### Vocabulary Builder

You probably already know some of the words below. Cross those off your mental "list" and focus on learning those that are new to you. These are all very useful words to add to your reading, writing, and speaking vocabularies.

| | | | |
|---|---|---|---|
| transfixed | persistent | taut | shrill |
| reflective | optimistic | incisive | menace |
| flustered | defiant | intruded | contorted |
| assent | antagonism | incriminate | |
| intense | revelation | legitimate | |

# The **Monsters** Are **Due** on **Maple Street**

Rod Serling

Twilight Glow, David Arsenault

### Cast of Characters

| | |
|---|---|
| NARRATOR | CHARLIE'S WIFE |
| FIGURE ONE | TOMMY |
| FIGURE TWO | SALLY, *Tommy's mother* |
| DON MARTIN | LES GOODMAN |
| STEVE BRAND | ETHEL GOODMAN, *Les's wife* |
| MYRA BRAND, *Steve's wife* | MAN ONE |
| PETE VAN HORN | MAN TWO |
| CHARLIE | WOMAN ONE |

## ACT ONE

*Fade in on shot of the night sky. The various heavenly bodies stand out in sharp, sparkling relief. The camera begins a slow pan across the heavens until it passes the horizon and stops on a sign which reads "Maple Street." It is daytime. Then we see the street below. It is a quiet, tree-lined, small-town American street. The houses have front porches on which people sit and swing on gliders, talking across from house to house. STEVE BRAND is polishing his car, which is parked in front of a house. His neighbor, DON MARTIN, leans against the fender watching him. A Good Humor man riding a bicycle is just in the process of stopping to sell some ice cream to a couple of kids. Two women gossip on the front lawn. Another man is watering his lawn with a garden hose.*

*As we see these various activities, we hear the NARRATOR's voice.*

**NARRATOR**. Maple Street, U.S.A., late summer. A tree-lined little world of front porch gliders, hopscotch, the laughter of children, and the bell of an ice cream vendor.

*(There is a pause and the camera moves over to a shot of the Good Humor man and two small boys who are standing alongside just buying ice cream.)*

**NARRATOR**. At the sound of the roar and the flash of the light, it will be precisely six-forty-three P.M. on Maple Street.

*(At this moment TOMMY, one of the two boys buying ice cream from the vendor, looks up to listen to a tremendous screeching roar from overhead. A flash of light plays on the faces of both boys and then moves down the street and disappears.*

*Various people leave their porches or stop what they are doing to stare up at the sky.)*

*STEVE BRAND, the man who has been polishing his car, stands there* **transfixed**, *staring upwards. He looks at DON MARTIN, his neighbor from across the street.)*

**transfixed**
fascinated;
hypnotized

**STEVE**. What was that? A meteor?

**DON**. That's what it looked like. I didn't hear any crash though, did you?

**STEVE**. Nope. I didn't hear anything except a roar.

**MYRA** *(from her porch)*. What was that?

**STEVE** *(Raising his voice and looking towards the porch)*. Guess it was a meteor, honey. Came awful close, didn't it?

**MYRA**. Too close for my money! Much too close.

*(The camera pans across the various porches to people who stand there watching and talking in low conversing[1] tones.)*

**reflective**
thoughtful;
considerate

**NARRATOR**. Maple Street. Six-forty-four P.M. on a late September evening. *(A pause)* Maple Street in the last calm and **reflective** moment . . . before the monsters came!

*(The camera takes us across the porches again. A man is replacing a light bulb on a front porch. He gets down off his stool to flick the switch and finds that nothing happens.*

*Another man is working on an electric power mower. He plugs in the plug, flicks the switch of the mower off and on, but nothing happens.*

*Through the window we see a woman pushing her finger back and forth on the dial hook of a telephone. Her voice sounds far away.)*

**WOMAN ONE**. Operator, operator something's wrong on the phone, operator!

*(MYRA BRAND is out on the porch and calls to STEVE.)*

**MYRA** *(calling)*. Steve, the power's off. I had soup on the stove and the stove just stopped working.

**WOMAN ONE**. Same thing over here. I can't get anybody on the phone either. The phone seems to be dead.

*(We look down again on the street. Small and mildly disturbed voices creep up from below.)*

---

1 **conversing**: chatty; conversational

**VOICE ONE**. Electricity's off.

**VOICE TWO**. Phone won't work.

**VOICE THREE**. Can't get a thing on the radio.

**VOICE FOUR**. My power mower won't move, won't work at all.

**VOICE FIVE**. Radio's gone dead!

(PETE VAN HORN, *a tall, thin man, is seen standing in front of his house.*)

**PETE**. I'll cut through the backyard . . . see if the power's still on, on Floral Street. I'll be right back!

(*He walks past the side of his house and disappears into the backyard. The camera pans down slowly until we are looking at ten or eleven people standing around the street and overflowing to the curb and sidewalks. In the background is* STEVE BRAND's *car.*)

**STEVE**. Doesn't make sense. Why should the power go off all of a sudden *and* the phone line?

**DON**. Maybe some kind of an electrical storm or something.

**CHARLIE**. That don't seem likely. Sky's just as blue as anything. Not a cloud. No lightning. No thunder. No nothing. How could it be a storm?

**WOMAN ONE**. I can't get a thing on the radio. Not even the portable.

(*The people again murmur softly in wonderment.*)

**CHARLIE**. Well, why don't you go downtown and check with the police, though they'll probably think we're crazy or something. A little power failure and right away we get all **flustered** and everything—

**flustered**
nervous;
disturbed

**STEVE**. It isn't just the power failure, Charlie. If it was, we'd still be able to get a broadcast on the portable.

(*There is a murmur of reaction to this.* STEVE *looks from face to face and then over to his car.*)

**STEVE**. I'll run downtown. We'll get this all straightened out.

*(He walks over to the car, gets in, and turns the key. Looking through the open car door, we see the crowd watching STEVE from the other side. He starts the engine. It turns over sluggishly and then stops dead. He tries it again, and this time he can't get it to turn over. Then very slowly he turns the key back off and gets out of the car.*

*The people stare at STEVE. He stands for a moment by the car and then walks toward them.)*

**STEVE**. I don't understand it. It was working fine before—

**DON**. Out of gas?

**STEVE** *(shakes his head)*. I just had it filled up.

**WOMAN ONE**. What's it mean?

**CHARLIE**. It's just as if . . . as if everything had stopped. *(Then he turns toward STEVE.)* We'd better *walk* downtown.

*(Another murmur of **assent** to this.)*

**STEVE**. The two of us can go, Charlie. *(He turns to look back at the car.)* It couldn't be the meteor. A meteor couldn't do *this.*

*(He and CHARLIE exchange a look. Then they start to walk away from the group.*

*TOMMY comes into view. He is serious-faced young boy in spectacles. He stands halfway between the group and the two men who start to walk down the sidewalk.)*

**TOMMY**. Mr. Brand . . . you'd better not!

**STEVE**. Why not?

**TOMMY**. They don't want you to.

*(STEVE and CHARLIE exchange a grin and STEVE looks back toward the boy.)*

**STEVE**. *Who* doesn't want us to?

**TOMMY** *(jerks his head in the general direction of the distant horizon)*. Them!

**STEVE**. Them?

**CHARLIE**. Who are *them?*

**TOMMY** *(intently)*. Whoever was in that thing that came by overhead.

*(STEVE knits his brow for a moment, cocking[2] his head questioningly. His voice is **intense**.)*

**STEVE**. What?

**TOMMY**. Whoever was in that thing that came over. I don't think they want us to leave here.

*(STEVE leaves CHARLIE, walks over to the boy, and puts his hand on the boy's shoulder. He forces his voice to remain gentle.)*

**STEVE**. What do you mean? What are you talking about?

**TOMMY**. They don't want us to leave. That's why they shut everything off.

**STEVE**. What makes you say that? Whatever gave you *that* idea?

**WOMAN ONE** *(from the crowd)*. Now isn't that the craziest thing you ever heard?

**TOMMY (*persistent** but a little frightened)*. It's always that way, in every story I ever read about a ship landing from outer space.

**WOMAN ONE** *(to the boy's mother, SALLY, who stands on the fringe of the crowd)*. From outer space yet! Sally, you better get that boy of yours up to bed. He's been reading too many comic books or seeing too many movies or something!

**SALLY**. Tommy, come over here and stop that kind of talk.

**STEVE**. Go ahead, Tommy. We'll be right back. And you'll see. That wasn't any ship or anything like it. That was just a . . . a meteor or something. Likely as not— *(He turns to the group, now trying very hard to sound more **optimistic** than he feels.)* No doubt it did have

---

**intense**
forceful;
serious

**persistent**
stubborn;
determined

**optimistic**
hopeful;
confident

---

2 **cocking**: tilting to the side

something to do with all this power failure and the rest of it. Meteors can do some crazy things. Like sunspots.[3]

**DON** *(picking up the cue).* Sure. That's the kind of thing—like sunspots. They raise Cain[4] with radio reception all over the world. And this thing being so close—why there's no telling the sort of stuff it can do. *(He wets his lips, smiles nervously.)* Go ahead, Charlie. You and Steve go into town and see if that isn't what's causing it all.

*(STEVE and CHARLIE walk away from the group down the sidewalk as the people watch silently.*

*TOMMY stares at them, biting his lips, and finally calls out again.)*

**TOMMY**. Mr. Brand!

*(The two men stop. TOMMY takes a step toward them.)*

**TOMMY**. Mr. Brand . . . please don't leave here.

*(STEVE and CHARLIE stop once again and turn toward the boy. In the crowd there is a murmur of irritation and concern, as if the boy's words—even though they don't make sense—were bringing up fears that shouldn't be brought up.*

**defiant**
bold; rebellious

*TOMMY is partly frightened and partly **defiant**.)*

**TOMMY**. You might not even be able to get to town. It was that way in the story. *Nobody* could leave. Nobody except—

**STEVE**. Except who?

**TOMMY**. Except the people they sent down ahead of them. They looked just like humans. And it wasn't until the ship landed that—*(The boy suddenly stops, conscious of the people staring at him and his mother and of the sudden hush of the crowd.)*

**antagonism**
unfriendliness;
aggression

**SALLY** *(in a whisper, sensing the **antagonism** of the crowd).* Tommy, please son . . . honey, don't talk that way—

---

3 **sunspots**: dark spots that appear on the sun's surface and are thought to interrupt electrical currents

4 **raise Cain**: cause trouble. In the Bible, Adam and Eve's son Cain killed his brother Abel.

**MAN ONE**. That kid shouldn't talk that way . . . and we shouldn't stand here listening to him. Why this is the craziest thing I ever heard of. The kid tells us a comic book plot and here we stand listening—

(STEVE *walks toward the camera, and stops beside the boy.*)

**STEVE**. Go ahead, Tommy. What kind of story was this? What about the people they sent out ahead?

**TOMMY**. That was the way they prepared things for the landing. They sent four people. A mother and a father and two kids who looked just like humans . . . but they weren't.

*(There is another silence as* STEVE *looks toward the crowd and then toward* TOMMY. *He wears a tight grin.*)

**STEVE**. Well, I guess what we'd better do then is to run a check on the neighborhood and see which ones of us are really human.

*(There is laughter at this, but it's a laughter that comes from a desperate attempt to lighten the atmosphere. The people look at one another in the middle of their laughter.)*

**CHARLIE** *(rubs his jaw nervously)*. I wonder if Floral Street's got the same deal we got. *(He looks past the houses.)* Where is Pete Van Horn anyway? Didn't he get back yet?

*(Suddenly there is the sound of a car's engine starting to turn over.*
*We look across the street toward the driveway of* LES GOODMAN's *house. He is at the wheel trying to start the car.)*

**SALLY**. Can you get started, Les?

(LES GOODMAN *gets out of the car, shaking his head.*)

**LES**. No dice.

*(He walks toward the group. He stops suddenly as, behind him, the car engine starts up all by itself,* LES *whirls around to stare at it.*
*The car idles roughly, smoke coming from the exhaust, the frame shaking gently.*

LES's *eyes go wide, and he runs over to his car. The people stare at the car.*)

**MAN ONE**. He got the car started somehow. He got *his* car started!

*(The people continue to stare, caught up by this **revelation** and wildly frightened.)*

**WOMAN ONE**. How come his car just up and started like that?

**SALLY**. All by itself. He wasn't anywheres near it. It started all by itself.

*(DON MARTIN approaches the group, stops a few feet away to look toward LES's car and then back toward the group.)*

**DON**. And he never did come out to look at that thing that flew overhead. He wasn't even interested. *(He turns to the group, his face **taut** and serious.)* Why? Why didn't he come out with the rest of us to look?

**CHARLIE**. He always was an oddball. Him and his whole family. Real oddball.

**DON**. What do you say we ask him?

*(The group starts toward the house. In this brief fraction of a moment they take the first step toward a metamorphosis[5] that changes people from a group into a mob. They begin to head purposefully across the street toward the house. STEVE stands in front of them. For a moment their fear almost turns their walk into a wild stampede, but STEVE's voice, loud, **incisive**, and commanding, makes them stop.)*

**STEVE**. Wait a minute . . . wait a minute! Let's not be a mob!

*(The people stop, pause for a moment, and then much more quietly and slowly start to walk across the street.*
   *Les stands alone, facing the people.)*

**LES**. I just don't understand it. I tried to start it and it wouldn't start. You saw me. All of you saw me.

---

5 **metamorphosis**: the process of changing from one thing to another

*(And now, just as suddenly as the engine started, it stops, and there is a long silence that is gradually **intruded** upon by the frightened murmuring of the people.)*

**LES**. I don't understand. I swear . . . I don't understand. What's happening?

**DON**. Maybe you better tell us. Nothing's working on this street. Nothing. No lights, no power, no radio. *(Then meaningfully)* Nothing except one car—*yours!*

*(The people's murmuring becomes a loud chant filling the air with accusations and demands for action. Two of the men pass DON and head toward LES, who backs away from them against his car. He is cornered.)*

**LES**. Wait a minute now. You keep your distance—all of you. So I've got a car that starts by itself—well, that's a freak thing—I admit it. But does that make me some kind of a criminal or something? I don't know why the car works—it just does!

*(This stops the crowd momentarily and LES, still backing away, goes toward his front porch. He goes up the steps and then stops, facing the mob.)*

**LES**. What's it all about, Steve?

**STEVE** *(quickly)*. We're all on a monster kick, Les. Seems that the general impression holds that maybe one family isn't what we think they are. Monsters from outer space or something. Different from us. Fifth columnists[6] from the vast beyond. *(He chuckles.)* You know anybody that might fit that description around here on Maple Street?

**LES**. What's this, a gag? *(He looks around the group again.)* This a practical joke or something?

*(Suddenly the car engine starts all by itself, runs for a moment, and stops. One woman begins to cry. The eyes of the crowd are cold and accusing.)*

---

6 **fifth columnists**: spys

**LES.** Now that's supposed to **incriminate** me, huh? The car engine goes on and off and that really does it, doesn't it? *(He looks around the faces of the people.)* I just don't understand it . . . any more than any of you do! *(He wets his lips, looking from face to face.)* Look, you all know me. We've lived here five years. Right in this house. We're no different from any of the rest of you! We're no different at all . . . Really . . . this whole thing is just . . . just weird—

**WOMAN ONE.** Well, if that's the case, Les Goodman, explain why—*(She stops suddenly clamping her mouth shut.)*

**LES** *(softly).* Explain what?

**STEVE** *(interjecting).*[7] Look, let's forget this—

**CHARLIE** *(overlapping him).* Go ahead, let her talk. What about it? Explain what?

**WOMAN ONE** *(a little reluctantly).* Well . . . sometimes I go to bed late at night. A couple of times . . . a couple of times I'd come out here on the porch and I'd see Mr. Goodman here in the wee hours of the morning standing out in front of his house . . . looking up at the sky. *(She looks around the circle of faces.)* That's right, looking up at the sky as if . . . as if he were waiting for something. *(A pause)* As if he were looking for something.

*(There's a murmur of reaction from the crowd again as LES backs away.)*

**LES.** She's crazy. Look, I can explain that. Please . . . I can really explain that . . . She's making it up anyway. *(Then he shouts.)* I tell you she's making it up!

*(He takes a step toward the crowd and they back away from him. He walks down the steps after them and they continue to back away. Suddenly he is left completely alone, and he looks like a man caught in the middle of a menacing circle as the scene slowly fades to black.)*

---

7 **interjecting**: interrupting

<small>STREET CROSSING, George Segal, 1992</small>

## ACT TWO

### SCENE 1

*Fade in on Maple Street at night. On the sidewalk, little knots of people stand
around talking in low voices. At the end of each conversation they look toward
LES GOODMAN's house. From the various houses we can see candlelight but
no electricity. The quiet which blankets the whole area is disturbed only by the
almost whispered voices of the people standing around. In one group CHARLIE
stands staring across at the GOODMAN's house. Two men stand across the
street from it in almost sentry-like[8] poses.*

**SALLY** *(in a small, hesitant voice)*. It just doesn't seem right, though,
keeping watch on them. Why . . . he was right when he said he was
one of our neighbors. Why, I've known Ethel Goodman ever since
they moved in. We've been good friends—

---

8 **sentry-like**: like guards or security personnel

**ARLIE**. That don't prove a thing. Any guy who'd spend his time lookin' up at the sky early in the morning—well, there's something wrong with that kind of person. There's something that ain't **legitimate**. Maybe under normal circumstances we could let it go by, but these aren't normal circumstances. Why, look at this street! Nothin' but candles. Why, it's like goin' back into the Dark Ages or somethin'!

(STEVE *walks down the steps of his porch, down the street to the* GOODMAN's *house, and then stops at the foot of the steps.* LES *is standing there;* ETHEL GOODMAN *behind him is very frightened.*)

**LES**. Just stay right where you are, Steve. We don't want any trouble, but this time if anybody sets foot on my porch—that's what they're going to get—trouble!

**STEVE**. Look, Les—

**LES**. I've already explained to you people. I don't sleep very well at night sometimes. I get up and I take a walk and I look up at the sky. I look at the stars!

**ETHEL.** That's exactly what he does. Why, this whole thing, it's . . . it's some kind of madness or something.

**STEVE** *(nods grimly)*. That's exactly what it is—some kind of madness.

**shrill**
sharp-
sounding;
high-pitched

**CHARLIE'S VOICE** (**shrill**, *from across the street*). You best watch who you're seen with, Steve! Until we get this all straightened out, you ain't exactly above suspicion yourself.

**STEVE** *(whirling around toward him)*. Or you, Charlie. Or any of us, it seems. From age eight on up!

**WOMAN ONE**. What I'd like to know is—what are we gonna do? Just stand around here all night?

**CHARLIE**. There's nothin' else we *can* do! *(He turns back, looking toward* STEVE *and* LES *again.)* One of 'em'll tip their hand. They *got* to.

**STEVE** (*raising his voice*). There's something you can do, Charlie. You can go home and keep your mouth shut. You can quit strutting around like a self-appointed hanging judge and just climb into bed and forget it.

**CHARLIE**. You sound real anxious to have that happen, Steve. I think we better keep our eye on you, too!

**DON** (*as if he were taking the bit in his teeth, takes a hesitant step to the front*). I think everything might as well come out now. (*He turns toward* STEVE). Your wife's done plenty of talking, Steve, about how odd *you* are!

**CHARLIE** (*picking this up, his eyes widening*). Go ahead, tell us what she's said.

(STEVE *walks toward them from across the street.*)

**STEVE**. Go ahead, what's my wife said? Let's get it *all* out. Let's pick up every idiosyncrasy[9] of every single man, woman, and child on the street. And then we might as well set up some kind of kangaroo court.[10] How about a firing squad at dawn, Charlie, so we can get rid of all the suspects. Narrow them down. Make it easier for you.

**DON**. There's no need getting' so upset, Steve. It's just that. . . well . . . Myra's talked about how there's been plenty of nights you spent hours down in your basement workin' on some kind of radio or something. Well, none of us have ever *seen* that radio—

(*By this time* STEVE *has reached the group. He stands there defiantly.*)

**CHARLIE**. Go ahead, Steve. What kind of "radio set" you workin' on? I never seen it. Neither has anyone else. Who do you talk to on that radio set? And who talks to you?

---

9 **idiosyncrasy**: odd mannerism or behavior

10 **kangaroo court**: a court where the outcome is decided before the trial begins

**E**. I'm surprised at you, Charlie. How come you're so dense all of a sudden? *(A pause)* Who do I talk to? I talk to monsters from outer space. I talk to three-headed green men who fly over here in what looks like meteors.

(MYRA BRAND *steps down from the porch, bites her lip, calls out.*)

**MYRA**. Steve! Steve, please. *(Then looking around, frightened she walks toward the group.)* It's just a ham radio set, that's all. I bought him a book on it myself. It's just a ham radio set. A lot of people have them. I can show it to you. It's right down in the basement.

**STEVE** *(whirls around toward her)*. Show them nothing! If they want to look inside our house—let them get a search warrant.

**CHARLIE**. Look, buddy, you can't afford to—

**STEVE** *(interrupting him)*. Charlie, don't start telling me who's dangerous and who isn't and who's safe and who's a **menace**. *(He turns to the group and shouts.)* And you're with him, too—all of you! You're standing here all set to crucify[11]—all set to find a scapegoat[12]—all desperate to point some kind of a finger at a neighbor! Well now look, friends, the only thing that's gonna happen is that we'll eat each other up alive—

*(He stops abruptly as CHARLIE suddenly grabs his arm.)*

**CHARLIE** *(in a hushed voice)*. That's not the *only* thing that can happen to us.

*(Down the street, a figure has suddenly materialized[13] in the gloom, and in the silence we hear the clickety clack of slow, measured footsteps on concrete as the figure walks slowly toward them. One of the women lets out a stifled cry. SALLY grabs her boy, as do a couple of other mothers.)*

> **menace**
> threat; danger

---

11 **crucify**: to torture or persecute

12 **scapegoat**: someone singled out for blame and ridicule

13 **materialized**: become visible

**TOMMY** (*shouting, frightened*). It's the monster! It's the monster!

(*Another woman lets out a wail and the people fall back in a group staring toward the darkness and the approaching figure.*

*The people stand in the shadows watching,* DON MARTIN *joins them, carrying a shotgun. He holds it up.*)

**DON**. We may need this.

**STEVE**. A shotgun? (*He pulls it out of* DON's *hand.*) No! Will anybody think a thought around here? Will you people wise up? What good would a shotgun do against—

(*The dark figure continues to walk toward them as the people stand there, fearful, mothers clutching children, men standing in front of their wives.*)

**CHARLIE** (*pulling the gun from* STEVE's *hands*). No more talk, Steve. You're going to talk us into a grave! You'd let whatever's out there walk right over us, wouldn't yuh? Well, some of us won't!

(CHARLIE *swings around, raises the gun, and suddenly pulls the trigger. The sound of the shot explodes in the stillness.*

*The figure suddenly lets out a small cry, stumbles forward onto his knees, and then falls forward on his face.* DON, CHARLIE *and* STEVE *race forward to him.* STEVE *is there first and turns the man over. The crowd gathers around them.*)

**STEVE** (*slowly looks up*). It's Pete Van Horn.

**DON** (*in a hushed voice*). Pete Van Horn! He was just gonna go over to the next block to see if the power was on—

**WOMAN ONE**. You killed him, Charlie. You shot him dead!

**CHARLIE** (*looks around at the circle of faces, his eyes frightened, his face **contorted***). But . . . but I didn't know who he was. I certainly didn't know who he was. He comes walkin' out of the darkness—how am I supposed to know who he was? (*He grabs* STEVE.) Steve—you know why I shot! How was I supposed to know he wasn't a monster or

**contorted**
twisted;
distorted

The Monsters Are Due on Maple Street          437

something? *(He grabs* DON*)* We're all scared of the same thing. I was just tryin' to . . . tryin' to protect my home, that's all! Look, all of you, that's all I was tryin' to do. *(He looks down wildly at the body.)* I didn't know it was somebody we knew! I didn't know—

*(There's a sudden hush and then an intake of breath in the group. Across the street all the lights go on in one of the houses.)*

**WOMAN ONE** *(in a hushed voice).* Charlie . . . Charlie . . . the lights just went on in your house. Why did the lights just go on?

**DON**. What about it, Charlie? How come you're the only one with lights now?

**LES**. That's what I'd like to know.

*(A pause as they all stare toward* CHARLIE.*)*

**LES**. You were so quick to kill, Charlie, and you were so quick to tell us who we had to be careful of. Well, maybe you *had* to kill. Maybe Pete there was trying to tell us something. Maybe he'd found out something and came back to tell us who there was amongst us we should watch out for—

*(*CHARLIE *backs away from the group, his eyes wide with fright.)*

**CHARLIE**. No . . . no . . . it's nothing of the sort. I don't know why the lights are on. I swear I don't. Somebody's pulling a gag or something.

*(He bumps against* STEVE *who grabs him and whirls him around.)*

**STEVE.** A gag? A gag? Charlie, there's a dead man on the sidewalk and you killed him! Does this thing look like a gag to you?

*(*CHARLIE *breaks away and screams as he runs toward his house.)*

**CHARLIE**. No! No! Please!

*(A man breaks away from the crowd to chase* CHARLIE.

As the man tackles him and lands on top of him, the other people start to run toward them. CHARLIE gets up, breaks away from the other man's grasp,* *lands a couple of desperate punches that push the man aside. Then he forces his way, fighting, through the crowd and jumps up on his front porch.*

    CHARLIE *is on his porch as a rock thrown from the group smashes a window beside him, the broken glass flying past him. A couple of pieces cut him. He stands there perspiring, rumpled, blood running down from a cut on the cheek. His wife breaks away from the group to throw herself into his arms. He buries his face against her. We can see the crowd converging[14] on the porch.)*

**VOICE ONE**. It must have been him.

**VOICE TWO**. He's the one.

**VOICE THREE**. We got to get Charlie.

*(Another rock lands on the porch.* CHARLIE *pushes his wife behind him facing the group.)*

**CHARLIE.** Look, look I swear to you . . . it isn't me . . . but I do know who it is . . . I swear to you, I do know who it is. I know who the monster is here. I know who it is that doesn't belong. I swear to you I know.

**DON** *(pushing his way to the front of the crowd).* All right, Charlie, let's hear it! (CHARLIE's *eyes dart around wildly.)*

**CHARLIE**. It's . . . it's . . .

**MAN TWO** *(screaming).* Go ahead, Charlie, tell us.

**CHARLIE**. It's . . . it's the kid. It's Tommy. He's the one.

*(There's a gasp from the crowd as we see* SALLY *holding the boy.* TOMMY *at first doesn't understand and then, realizing the eyes are all on him, buries his face against his mother.)*

**SALLY** *(backs away).* That's crazy! He's only a boy.

**WOMAN ONE**. But he knew! He was the only one who knew! He told us all about it. Well, how did he know? How *could* he have known?

---

14 **converging**: gathering; crowding together

*(Various people take this up and repeat the question.)*

**VOICE ONE**. How could he know?

**VOICE TWO**. Who told him?

**VOICE THREE**. Make the kid answer.

*(The crowd starts to converge around the mother, who grabs* TOMMY *and starts to run with him. The crowd starts to follow, at first walking fast, and then running after him.*

    *Suddenly* CHARLIE's *lights go off and the lights in other houses go on, then off.)*

**MAN ONE** *(shouting)*. It isn't the kid . . . it's Bob Weaver's house.

**WOMAN ONE**. It isn't Bob Weaver's house, it's Don Martin's place.

**CHARLIE**. I tell you it's the kid.

**DON**. It's Charlie. He's the one.

*(People shout, accuse, and scream as the lights go on and off. Then, slowly, in the middle of this nightmarish confusion of sight and sound the camera starts to pull away until once again we have reached the opening shot looking at the Maple Street sign from high above.)*

## SCENE 2

*The camera continues to move away while gradually bringing into focus a field. We see the metal side of a spacecraft which sits shrouded[15] in darkness. An open door throws out a beam of light from the illuminated interior. Two figures appear, silhouetted against the bright lights. We get only a vague feeling of form.*

**FIGURE ONE**. Understand the procedure now? Just stop a few of their machines and radios and telephones and lawn mowers . . . throw them into darkness for a few hours, and then just sit back and watch the pattern.

---

15 **shrouded**: covered; cloaked

**FIGURE TWO**. And this pattern is always the same?

**FIGURE ONE**. With few variations. They pick the most dangerous enemy they can find . . . and it's themselves. And all we need do is sit back . . . and watch.

**FIGURE TWO**. Then I take it this place . . . this Maple Street . . . is not unique.

**FIGURE ONE** *(shaking his head)*. By no means. Their world is full of Maple Streets. And we'll go from one to the other and let them destroy themselves. One to the other . . . one to the other . . . one to the other—

## SCENE 3

*The camera pans up for a shot of the starry sky, and over this we hear the NARRATOR's voice.*

**NARRATOR**. The tools of conquest do not necessarily come with bombs and explosions and fallout.[16] There are weapons that are simply thoughts, attitudes, prejudices—to be found only in the minds of men. For the record, prejudices can kill and suspicion can destroy and a thoughtless, frightened search for a scapegoat has a fallout all its own for the children . . . and the children yet unborn. *(A pause)* And the pity of it is . . . that these things cannot be confined to . . . The Twilight Zone!

*(Fade to black.)*

---

16 **fallout**: radioactive particles that land on earth's surface after nuclear explosions

# Reviewing

## The Monsters Are Due on Maple Street

### Discussing the Selection

1. Think about the title of the play. Is there any reason why Serling sets it on Maple Street?

2. As it is defined in this story, a scapegoat is "one who is singled out for blame." How does that term apply to this story? Who is/are the scapegoats?

3. Whom do you think is responsible for the death of Pete Van Horn? Explain your answer.

4. Do you agree with how the aliens judge human beings? Explain why or why not.

### Writing a Screenplay

Using Rod Serling's play as a model for the format, write a short screenplay about the subject of your choice. It can be a realistic drama—serious or humorous—a science fiction or fantasy piece, or a combination of both. Use finely tuned dialogue to move the plot forward, show relationships, and express emotion. Good dialogue makes a scene come alive. Remember that screenplays must include camera directions. Visualize how you want the picture to appear on the screen. Then describe your camera shots using either jargon (find definitions on the Web) or detailed explanations.

### About Rod Serling (1924–1975)

Rod Serling began college as a physical education major, switched to language arts, and ended up becoming one of the finest motion picture dramatists in America. His long-running series *The Twilight Zone* made television history. He won six Emmy awards for excellence for his challenging dramatic teleplays. Serling went on to write film scripts, including the celebrated drama *Requiem for a Heavyweight* and the satire *Planet of the Apes*. His youth in working-class New York and experience with the horrors of World War II contributed to his strong moral and political beliefs. Frustrated with television's commercial pressures, he became a college teacher at the end of his career.

# Previewing

## Where the Sidewalk Ends
by Shel Silverstein

### Reading Connection

If you really want to understand a Shel Silverstein poem, you must pay attention to the author's illustrations. Silverstein's simple line drawings accompany all his poems, often adding the necessary punch-line or making the poem's meaning clearer. As a child, he discovered he wasn't much of an athlete and so he began to devote himself to writing and drawing. In the army during the Korean War, he worked as an artist for the *Pacific Stars and Stripes*, the military newspaper. Long before Silverstein became a celebrated children's writer, he was a regular cartoonist for a major American magazine.

### Skill Focus: Fantasy

Shel Silverstein's poems display a gentle form of fantasy. The settings do not rely on science or technology, as settings tend to do in science fiction. They are more magical—much like the worlds of Dr. Seuss or Harry Potter. Things happen that could not happen in reality, and magic is a primary element in the plot, theme, and/or setting.

# Where the Sidewalk Ends

Shel Silverstein

There is a place where the sidewalk ends
And before the street begins,
And there the grass grows soft and white,
And the sun burns crimson bright,
And there the moon-bird rests from his flight          5
To cool in the peppermint wind.

Let us leave this place where the smoke blows black
And the dark street winds and bends.
Past the pits where the asphalt flowers grow
We shall walk with a walk that is measured and slow,    10
And watch where the chalk-white arrows go
To a place where the sidewalk ends.

Yes we'll walk with a walk that is measured and slow,
And we'll go where the chalk-white arrows go,
For the children, they mark, and the children, they know   15
The place where the sidewalk ends.

# Reviewing

## Where the Sidewalk Ends

### Discussing the Selection

1. How do you know the setting of this poem is a fantasy world? Explain.

2. Notice the repetition of the word "and" at the beginning of many of the poem's lines. What does this add to the poem?

3. Point out some of the sensory details the poet uses. What feeling or mood do they provide?

4. Shel Silverstein is legendary among people of all ages, even those who do not usually care for poetry. What do you think explains the popularity of poems such as "Where the Sidewalk Ends"? Share your own feelings and/or memories about this particular poem.

### Writing a Fantasy Poem

"Where the Sidewalk Ends" is a poem about one of the most common of everyday sights—a sidewalk! And yet it has become a favorite childhood poem for many. Look out the window and try to see something familiar with fresh eyes. Write a poem about it. Throw away the rules of reality and apply some word-magic.

### About Shel Silverstein (1930–1999)

One of the most popular children's writers in the world, Shel Silverstein was also a successful cartoonist, composer, singer, and songwriter. He wrote such hit songs as "The Unicorn Song," "A Boy Named Sue" and "The Cover of the Rollin' Stone." Silverstein composed music and wrote screenplays for several Hollywood movies. He often claimed that his youthful lack of ability to throw balls or attract girls led him to plow his energy into writing. Millions of readers have read his books *The Giving Tree*, *Falling Up*, and *A Light in the Attic*, and in 1984 he won a Grammy for Best Children's Album for *Where the Sidewalk Ends*—"recited, sung and shouted" by the author.

# Acknowledgments

"Abd al-Rahman Ibrahima" by Walter Dean Myers from *Now Is Your Time: The African-American Struggle for Freedom*. Copyright © 1991 by Walter Dean Myers. Reprinted by permission of HarperCollins Publishers.

"All Summer in a Day" by Ray Bradbury from *Magazine of Fantasy and Science Fiction*, March 1, 1954. Copyright © 1954, renewed 1982 by Ray Bradbury. Reprinted by permission of Don Congdon Associates, Inc.

"All-American Slurp" by Lensey Namioka from *Visions*, ed. By Donald R. Gallo. Copyright © 1987 by Lensey Namioka. Reprinted by permission of Lensey Namioka. All rights reserved by the Author.

"Ballad of Birmingham" by Dudley Randall from *Cities Burning*. Copyright © 1968 by Dudley Randall. Reprinted by permission of Broadside Press.

"Change" by Charlotte Zolotow from *River Winding*. Copyright © 1970 by Charlotte Zolotow. Reprinted by permission of Scott Treimel, New York.

"Charles" by Shirley Jackson from *The Lottery, or the Adventures of James Harris*. Copyright © 1943, renewed 1971 by Shirley Jackson. Reprinted by permission of Farrar, Straus & Giroux, Inc.

"The Circuit" by Francisco Jiménez from *The Arizona Quarterly*, Autumn 1973. Copyright © 1973 by Francisco Jiménez. Reprinted by permissions of the author.

"Country Boys" by Bruce Catton from *Reflections on the Civil War*. Copyright © 1981 by Gerald Dickler as the executor of the estate of Bruce Catton and John Leckley. Reprinted by permission of Doubleday Books, a division of Random House, Inc.

"The Curious Treasure of Captain Kidd" by Alvin Schwartz from *Gold and Silver, Silver and Gold*. Copyright © 1988 by Alvin Schwartz. Reprinted by permission of Farrar, Straus & Giroux, Inc.

"Dog of Pompeii" by Louis Untermeyer. Copyright © 1932 by Louis Untermeyer. Permission is granted by arrangement with the Estate of Louis Untermeyer, Norma Anchin Untermeyer c/o Professional Publishing Services. Reprinted by permission of Laurence S. Untermeyer.

"Elephants Cross Under River, Making Hearts Rise" by Michael Kaufman from *The New York Times*, March 24, 1995. Copyright © 1995 by The New York Times Co. Reprinted with permission.

"Eleven" by Sandra Cisneros from *Woman Hollering Creek*. Copyright © 1991 by Sandra Cisneros. Published by Vintage Books, a division of Random House Inc. Reprinted by permission of Susan Bergholz Literary Services, New York. All rights reserved.

"Frozen in Time" by David Getz from *Frozen Man*. Copyright © 1994 by David Getz. Reprinted by permission of Henry Holt and Company, LLC.

"Homeless" by Anna Quindlen from *Living Out Loud*. Copyright © 1987 by Anna Quindlen. Reprinted by permission of Random House, Inc.

"Knoxville, Tennessee" by Nikki Giovanni from *Black Feeling, Black Talk, Black Judgment*. Copyright © 1968, 1970 by Nikki Giovanni. Reprinted by permission of HarperCollins Publishers.

"The Living Kuan-yin" by Carol Kendall and Yao-wen Li from *Sweet and Sour*. Copyright © 1978 by Carol Kendall and Yao-wen Li. Reprinted by permission of Clarion Books, an imprint of Houghton Mifflin Company. All rights reserved.

Excerpt from *Marley and Me: Living with the World's Worst Dog* by John Grogan. Copyright © 2005 by John Grogan. Reprinted by permission of HarperCollins Publishers.

"The Monsters Are Due on Maple Street" by Rod Serling. Reprinted by permission of the Estate of Rod Serling.

"My Father's Hand Held Mine" by Normal H. Russell. Reprinted by permission Norman H. Russell.

# Images

Every reasonable effort has been made to properly acknowledge ownership of all material used. Any omissions or mistakes are unintentional and, if brought to the publisher's attention, will be corrected in future editions.

**Image Credits**  Page 3: © Miles G. Batt. Page 4: (top) Photos.com; (middle) © CORBIS; (bottom) © CORBIS. Page 5: (top) © CORBIS; (middle & bottom) iStockphoto.com. Page 6: (top) © CORBIS; (middle & bottom) Photos.com. Page 7: (top) Photos.com; (middle & bottom) © CORBIS. Pages 8-9: Photos.com. Page 14: © SuperStock, Inc. / SuperStock ; © 2006 Artists Rights Society (ARS), New York / BG Bild-Kunst, Bonn. Page 25: © CORBIS. Page 30: © Bruno Morandi / age fotostock. Page 36: Maura Vazakas, Artist, www.mauravazakas. com. Page 45: © Ellen Harvey, 2000. Page 46: Photos.com. Page 47: © Diana Ong / SuperStock. Page 50: © Erich Lessing / Art Resource, NY. Page 54: © Ellen Harvey, 2000. Page 60: © Melora Kuhn. Pages 66-67: © CORBIS. Page 70: © Daniel DeSiga. Page 74: Michael Melford/The Image Bank/Getty Images. Page 80: © Bildarchiv Preussischer Kulturbesitz / Art Resource, NY. Page 81: Andrew Wyeth Foundation: "Granddaughter, 1956 drybrush watercolor © Andrew Wyeth"; "Wadsworth Atheneum Museum of Art, Hardford, CT. Gift of Mrs. Robert Montgomery";Photographed by Joseph Szaszfai. Page 84: © The Mukashi Collection / SuperStock. Page 91: © Mary Anne Lloyd. Page 98: © Erich Lessing/Art Resource, NY; © 2006 Artists Rights Society (ARS), New York / VG Bild-Kunst, Bonn. Page 104: Adam Crowley / Photographer's Choice / Getty Images. Page 107: Photos.com. Page 116: © age fotostock / SuperStock. Page 122: © Diana Ong / SuperStock. Pages 126-127: iStockphoto.com. Page 130: © Werner Forman / Art Resource, NY. Page 141: The Granger Collection, New York. Page 144: Chris Hondros / Getty Images. Page 150: Art Resource, NY; © 2006 Milton Avery Trust / Artists Rights Society (ARS), New York. Page 158: © Smithsonian American Art Museum, Washington, DC; Art Resource, NY. Page 179: The Granger Collection, New York. Page 182: The Granger Collection, New York. Page 186: M.C. Escher's "Three Worlds" © 2006 The M.C. Escher Company-Holland. All rights reserved. www.mcescher.com; Art Resouce, NY. Page 202: © Penny Tweedie / CORBIS. Page 208: The Granger Collection, New York. Pages 220-221: CORBIS. Page 226: © Lance Richbourg / SuperStock. Page 236: The Granger Collection, New York. Page 242: © 2006 Artists Rights Society (ARS), New York / ADAGP, Paris. Page 250: © 1948, 176 Rosemary A. Thurber. Reprinted by arrangement with Rosemary A. Thurber and The Barbara Hogensen Agency, Inc. Page 256: © Scala/Art Resource, NY. Page 266: © SuperStock, Inc. / SuperStock. Page 274: Art © Estate of John T. Biggers/Licensed by VAGA, New York, NY; Art Resource, NY. Page 278: © age fotostock / SuperStock. Page 284-285: Photos.com. Page 288: © HIP / Art Resource, NY. Page 298: Library of Congress. Page 302: © Erich Lessing / Art Resource, NY. Page 310: The Granger Collection, New York. Page 322: Private Collection / Photography courtesy of the Brandywine River Museum. Page 326: Illustrations copyright © 1991 Michael McCurdy. Page 331: Illustrations copyright © 1991 Michael McCurdy. Page 334: © The New York Public Library; Art Resource, NY. Page 340: Jacob Lawrence, "Strike," © 1949 / © The Jacob and Gwendolyn Lawrence Foundation; Art Resource, NY. Page 346: © age fotostock / SuperStock. Page 358: © Jaime Abecasis / SuperStock. Pages 364-365: CORBIS. Page 370: © M.L. Campbell / SuperStock. Page 376: © Craig Denston, www.craigdenston.com. Page 387: "Magnetically Distorted City", by Robert Kauffmann, © 1994. Page 390: © Robert Vickery/Liscensed by VAGA, New York, NY. Page 400: Illustration © 1986 Ted Harrison / Kids Can Press Ltd. Page 408: (top) Mike Aspengren / Perfection Learning; (bottom) © CORBIS / CORBIS SYGMA. Page 416: © Vienna Report Agency / Sygma/CORBIS. Page 418: © LANDMANN PATRICK / CORBIS SYGMA. Page 422: Twilight Glow oil on canvas © 1997 David Arsenault. Page 433: © The George and Helen Segal Foundation / Liscensed by VAGA, New York, NY.